SNAP MATTERS

SNAP MATTERS

How Food Stamps Affect Health and Well-Being

Edited by Judith Bartfeld, Craig Gundersen,

Timothy M. Smeeding, and James P. Ziliak

STANFORD UNIVERSITY PRESS
STANFORD, CALIFORNIA

Stanford University Press
Stanford, California

Printed in the United States of America on acid-free,
archival-quality paper

Library of Congress Cataloging-in-Publication Data

SNAP matters : how food stamps affect health and well-
being / edited by Judith Bartfeld, Craig Gundersen, Timothy
M. Smeeding, and James P. Ziliak.
    pages cm — (Studies in social inequality)
  Includes bibliographical references and index.
  ISBN 978-0-8047-9446-6 (cloth : alk. paper) —
  ISBN 978-0-8047-9683-5 (pbk. : alk. paper)
  1. Supplemental Nutrition Assistance Program (U.S.)—
Evaluation. 2. Food stamps—United States—Evaluation.
I. Bartfeld, Judi, editor. II. Gundersen, Craig, editor.
III. Smeeding, Timothy M., editor. IV. Ziliak, James Patrick,
editor. V. Series: Studies in social inequality.
  HV696.F6S63 2015
  362.5'830973—dc23
                         2015022871

ISBN 978-0-8047-9687-3 (electronic)

Typeset by Thompson Type in 10/13 Sabon

CONTENTS

ACKNOWLEDGMENTS

We are grateful for financial support from the Annie E. Casey Foundation; the Economic Research Service in the U.S. Department of Agriculture; the Ford Foundation; grant number AE00102 from the U.S. Department of Health and Human Services, Office of the Assistant Secretary for Planning and Evaluation, which was awarded by the Substance Abuse and Mental Health Services Administration; and an anonymous donor. We thank two anonymous referees, Jay Bhattacharya, Gary Burtless, Thomas DeLeire, Alison Jacknowitz, John Pepper, Isabel Sawhill, Kosali Simon, Jonathan Schwabish, Michele Ver Ploeg, and participants at the September 2013 Five Decades of Food Stamps Conference sponsored by the University of Wisconsin-Madison Institute for Research on Poverty and the University of Kentucky Center for Poverty Research and held at the Brookings Institution for insightful comments on earlier versions of the chapters. We are especially grateful to Ron Haskins and Stephanie Cencula at Brookings, and Stephanie Fahs at the University of Kentucky Center for Poverty Research, for all their assistance in organizing the conference. We also thank Deborah Johnson, Dawn Duren, and David Chancellor at the Institute for Research on Poverty for excellent editing services. The views expressed herein are solely those of the authors and do not necessarily reflect the views of the federal government, authors' universities and institutes, or any sponsoring agency.

Judith Bartfeld is Professor in the School of Human Ecology at the University of Wisconsin–Madison, an Affiliate of the Institute for Research on Poverty (IRP), a Specialist with Cooperative Extension, and Director of IRP's RIDGE Center for National Food and Nutrition Assistance Research. Her research interests are in food security, food assistance programs, child support, and the economic well-being of single-parent families. For more, see her home page at http://sohe.wisc.edu/staff/judi-bartfeld/.

Marianne P. Bitler is Professor of Economics at the University of California-Davis and a Faculty Research Associate of the National Bureau of Economic Research Programs on Health Economics and Children. Her research interests include public economics, health economics, and labor economics, and much of her recent research has focused on childhood poverty. For more, see her home page at economics.ucdavis.edu/people/mbitler.

Christian Gregory is an Agricultural Economist at the U.S. Department of Agriculture's Economic Research Service. His recent work focuses on federal food assistance programs, household food security, health, and nutrition outcomes. For more, see his home page at www.ers.usda.gov/ers-staff-directory/christian-gregory.aspx.

Craig Gundersen is the Soybean Industry Endowed Professor of Agricultural Strategy in the Department of Agricultural and Consumer Economics at the University of Illinois. His research is primarily focused on the causes and consequences of food insecurity and on evaluations of food assistance programs, with emphasis on the Supplemental Nutrition Assistance Program (SNAP). For more, see his home page at http://ace.illinois.edu/directory/cggunder.

Hilary Hoynes is Professor of Public Policy and Economics and holds the Haas Distinguished Chair in Economic Disparities at the Goldman School of Public Policy at the University of California, Berkeley. Her research specialties include the study of poverty, inequality, and the impacts of government tax and transfer programs on low-income families. For more, see her home page at https://gspp.berkeley.edu/directories/faculty/hilary-hoynes.

Dean Jolliffe is a Senior Economist in the Development Research Group of the World Bank, a Research Fellow of the Institute for the Study of Labor in Bonn, and a Research Affiliate of the National Poverty Center at the University of Michigan. He has expertise in poverty, food security, development, and transition economics. For more, see his home page at www.deanjolliffe.net.

Leslie McGranahan is a Senior Economist and Research Advisor at the Federal Reserve Bank of Chicago. Her research focuses on the effect of government policies on consumption patterns, government expenditure on low-income populations, and the intergenerational transmission of wealth and inequality. For more, see her home page at www.chicagofed.org/people/mcgranahan-leslie.

Robert A. Moffitt is the Krieger-Eisenhower Professor of Economics at Johns Hopkins University. His research interests include the economic analysis of transfer programs, labor economics, and applied microeconometrics. For more, see his home page at http://econ.jhu.edu/directory/robert-a-moffitt/.

Matthew P. Rabbitt is an Economist with the U.S. Department of Agriculture's Economic Research Service. His current focus is on the measurement and determinants of food insecurity, applied econometrics, and food assistance programs. For more, see his home page at www.ers.usda.gov/ers-staff-directory/matthew-rabbitt.aspx.

David C. Ribar is Professorial Research Fellow at the Melbourne Institute of Applied Economic and Social Research, where he is a member of the Labour Economics and Social Policy Program. His research interests include child care, the consequences of teenage fertility, the economic motivations behind public and private transfers, welfare reform, the administrative burdens of assistance programs, people's time use, and food insecurity. For more, see his home page at https://melbourneinstitute.com/staff/dribar/default.html.

Diane Whitmore Schanzenbach is Associate Professor of Human Development and Social Policy and a Research Associate at the National Bureau of Economic Research. Her research focuses on policies aimed at improving the lives of children in poverty, including their education, health, and income support. Her recent work has focused on tracing the Food Stamp Program and early childhood education on children's long-term outcomes. For more, see her home page at www.ipr.northwestern.edu/faculty-experts/fellows/schanzenbach.html.

Timothy (Tim) M. Smeeding is Arts and Sciences Distinguished Professor of Public Affairs and Economics at the University of Wisconsin–Madison and former director of the Institute for Research on Poverty, from 2008 to 2014. His recent work has been on income security policy, measuring poverty, mobility across generations, and inequality, wealth, and poverty in national and cross-national contexts. For more, see his home page at www.lafollette.wisc.edu/facultystaff/smeeding-timothy.html.

Laura Tiehen is an Economist in the Food Assistance Branch of the U.S. Department of Agriculture's Economic Research Service. Her research examines the outcomes associated with federal food assistance including poverty, food security, and health-related behavior. For more, see her home page at www.ers.usda.gov/ers-staff-directory/laura-tiehen.aspx.

James P. Ziliak is the Carol Martin Gatton Endowed Chair in Economics and Founding Director of the Center for Poverty Research at the University of Kentucky. His recent work has been on the causes and consequences of food insecurity, poverty measurement, trends in income volatility, and the effects of tax and welfare policy on labor-market outcomes and family well-being. For more, see his home page at https://sites.google.com/site/jamesziliak/.

SNAP MATTERS

Judith Bartfeld
Craig Gundersen
Timothy M. Smeeding
James P. Ziliak

During the past year, the Department of Agriculture has been conducting a food stamp program in eight pilot areas. There have been encouraging results from this program. Low income families are receiving better diets—they have been able to obtain meat, poultry, fish, milk, eggs, fruits and vegetables. Retail food store sales in these areas increased 8 percent in dollar volume. There have been savings in distribution costs and benefits to the economy of the food stamp communities.
President John F. Kennedy, August 2, 1962[1]

In 1963, President Kennedy proposed making permanent a small pilot project called the Food Stamp Program (FSP). Fifty years later, more than one in seven Americans received benefits at a cost of nearly $80 billion in FY2013, making it the second largest program in the safety net in terms of recipients and fourth largest in terms of expenditure. Renamed the Supplemental Nutrition Assistance Program (SNAP) in 2008, the program today faces political pressure on many fronts, including cost and eligibility standards for certain food items.

Despite the program's size and scope, the social science research necessary to guide policy is nascent compared to that for many other programs in the safety net. This volume brings together leading scholars to answer a wide-ranging set of questions about SNAP to assess the past effectiveness of the program, identify critical gaps in knowledge, and gauge prospects going forward as a major pillar of social and food assistance in America. Collectively, the chapters explore how and why the program has grown over time, how it affects the well-being of participants, and its interconnections with the broader safety net. Providing both a synthesis of existing research as well as new analyses to help fill in critical gaps, the volume addresses a far-reaching set of questions: How does SNAP participation respond to the economy, to demographic pressures, and to policy reforms? What are the antipoverty effects of SNAP, and how does it compare to other programs in the safety net? How is food spending among SNAP-eligible households related to the amount of SNAP benefits, and does the in-kind nature of SNAP alter household's food choices? Does SNAP contribute to or reduce obesity, and does it improve nutrition and health more broadly? To what extent does SNAP work in tandem with other components of the food safety net for children, such as school breakfast and lunch, and how is it related to participation decisions in other safety net programs?

The volume is intended as a resource for policy makers, researchers, and students. As such, it sheds light both on substantive questions surrounding SNAP's role and impact, as well as on the fundamental challenges in evaluating safety net programs. In the following chapters, the authors highlight what is known about SNAP but are candid in noting where research is ambiguous or lacking. The volume provides strong evidence that SNAP is highly responsive to macroeconomic pressures as well as to policy choices intended to enhance access among low-income households. As a result, it has become one of the most effective antipoverty programs overall and is particularly effective at lifting nonelderly households with children out of deep poverty. SNAP is firmly embedded within the broader safety net: Program rules have broader implications for children's access to school meals, for instance, and it often fills in residual gaps remaining after other forms of assistance. As documented throughout this volume, the program differentially serves the most at-risk households, in terms of low income, preexisting food insecurity, and poor health. Although serving the most at-risk is surely desirable from a policy standpoint, it creates substantial challenges in assessing program impacts, a topic also addressed at length in this volume. In addition to the challenges stemming from nonrandom program participation, evaluating program impact is further complicated by issues such as misreporting of program participation in survey data as well as the frequent reliance on binary measures of participation and the lack of sufficiently long time frames. These challenges notwithstanding, the volume is cautiously optimistic with regard to the broader benefits of the program. Higher SNAP benefits appear to reduce the risk of food insecurity, SNAP does not appear to contribute to obesity, and limited evidence suggests that SNAP has long-term benefits on health. Most recipients spend more on food than their benefit amount over the course of a year, suggesting that benefits are not distorting food choices relative to an equivalent amount of unrestricted income. At the same time, there remain considerable gaps in understanding, especially with respect to impacts on nutrition and health outcomes, for which methodological challenges are particularly salient.

SHARING THE NATION'S ABUNDANCE

The authorizing legislation of the Food Stamp Act of 1964 began with a lofty goal: "In order to promote the general welfare, that the Nation's abundance of food should be utilized . . . . to safeguard the health and well-being of the Nation's population and raise levels of nutrition among low-income households."[2] Initial food stamp participation was sluggish, with only a half million participants signed up in the first full year. Even by 1969 there were still fewer than 3 million persons enrolled, despite a new federal poverty measure, which indicated that there were over 24 million Americans living in poverty. It took nearly a decade for the program to fully roll out across the country, in part because states had the option of continuing commodity distribution programs in lieu of adopting the FSP, there was a lack of funding, and there was wide variation across states in determining program eligibility and benefits.

An airing of CBS Reports "Hunger in America" in 1968 highlighted widespread hunger and malnutrition among many children. In response to this and other evidence of hunger across the United States, Congress amended the Food Stamp Act in 1971 to establish national-level eligibility and benefit standards. This led to rapid growth in participation and cost in the mid-1970s, as seen in Figure I.1. Many antihunger advocates still believed that the program was not reaching those in greatest need because

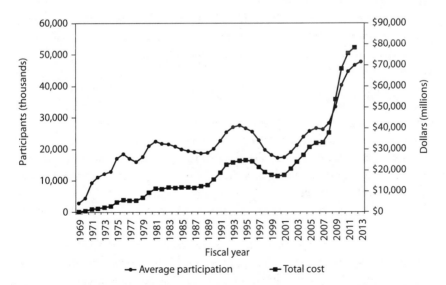

Figure I.1. Trends in Food Stamp Program/SNAP participation and cost.

SOURCE: U.S. Department of Agriculture (USDA), Food and Nutrition Service (FNS), SNAP Program Data.

of the so-called purchase requirement that stipulated that recipients had to purchase the stamps. That is, recipients paid for the stamps (limited to no more than 30 percent of their income with the 1971 amendments) and then received a "bonus" payment to cover the difference between the amount paid and the amount needed to attain a low-cost, nutritionally adequate diet. However, this left behind those families too destitute to buy the stamps and led others to be reluctant to participate, especially if the bonus payment was quite small. The Food Stamp Act of 1977 eliminated the purchase requirement and replaced it with the "net income rule" whereby recipients were expected to spend 30 percent of net income on food and use the stamps as a supplement. Participation in the program jumped by 1.5 million recipients the month following implementation of the new rule in 1979, spawning the modern era of the Food Stamp Program.[3] Subsequent changes went further to reduce barriers to access. By the early 2000s, electronic benefit transfer (EBT) cards replaced vouchers or "stamps" used to make food purchases. This move to EBT was designed to improve program integrity and to reduce the stigma that some potential recipients may feel when using SNAP. Whereas obtaining benefits traditionally involved in-person applications and recertification when income changed, to further reduce hurdles to applying, many states now allow online applications and recertification.

Currently, benefits can be redeemed at nearly 250,000 outlets nationwide for the purchase of food for home consumption, though over 80 percent of benefits are redeemed at big-box supermarkets.

The basic federal structure for eligibility and benefits has remained largely intact since 1979, although states have leeway over some aspects of eligibility, a flexibility that has been more widely used over time (see Ziliak, Chapter One in this volume, for further discussion).[4] To qualify for assistance a household must have gross income below 130 percent of the family-size adjusted poverty guideline and net income below 100 percent of the guideline (the gross income test is waived if the unit contains a disabled person or someone age sixty or older).[5] Moreover, a household must have liquid assets valued at less than $2,000 ($3,250 for seniors and the disabled) and the market value of a vehicle less than $4,650 to qualify—although states have flexibility with regard to both of those restrictions.[6] The vehicle test is typically waived for one vehicle if it is used primarily for work purposes or to transport someone with a disability. Alternatively, households may be deemed categorically eligible if they receive benefits from the Temporary Assistance for Needy Families (TANF) program or from Supplemental Security Income (SSI). Many states have used "broad-based categorical eligibility" to extend eligibility to households with gross income higher than 130 percent of the poverty line and/or assets over the $2,000 limit, consistent with a broader policy trend toward making supports available to low-income working households.

The benefit level varies by the size of the household but is fixed across the lower forty-eight states and District of Columbia (higher in Alaska and Hawaii). Benefits are updated annually by the Consumer Price Index for the twenty-nine food categories that constitute the Thrifty Food Plan, which is a minimal-cost and model-based market basket of foods that serves as the basis for the maximum benefit. The monthly amount received is determined by subtracting 30 percent of net income from the maximum benefit allowed per unit, under the assumption that households are able to spend 30 percent of net income on food. The calculation of net income is intended to provide a more realistic estimate of available income after considering other standard expenses. These expenses are deductible from gross income and include 20 percent of labor market earnings, a standard deduction, dependent care expenses, child support payments, excess shelter costs, and excess out-of-pocket medical expenses for seniors (those over age sixty) and persons with disabilities. Most of the deductions are limited, but, still, over one-third of units report zero net income and thus receive the maximum benefit (see Caswell and Yaktine 2013)—meaning their SNAP benefit is expected to be sufficient to meet all their food needs. The maximum benefit was temporarily increased by an average of 13.6 percent in 2009, with the intent that the increase gradually be phased out. In the face of considerable pressures regarding rising program costs and caseloads, the size of SNAP has been reduced recently. First, the 13.6 percent benefit increase tied to the 2009 American Recovery and Relief Act was ended on November 1, 2013. This was earlier than the scheduled phase-out, which was designed to end in 2015. This resulted in a benefit cut for nearly every SNAP household, reducing benefits back to the inflation-adjusted 2009 levels by about $29 per month for a family of three and reducing benefits by $5.0 billion in 2014 (Dean and Rosenbaum 2013). Second, the Agriculture Act of 2014 contains a $8.55 billion cut over the next ten years, reducing benefits by about $90 a month for 850,000 households in seventeen states. This is due to a change in the calculation of net income for households who receive less than $20 a month in benefits from the Low Income Home Energy Assistance Program (Bolen, Rosenbaum, and Dean 2014).

THE TSUNAMI OF SNAP PARTICIPATION
AND ITS EFFECTS ON POVERTY

For most of the 1980s, nominal spending on food stamps was relatively stable at $11 to $12 billion per year. Participation declined due to decreased need as the macroeconomy improved after the back-to-back recessions of 1980 and 1982. This was followed by a surge in participation and cost from 1990 to 1994 that occurred simultaneously with the growth in the Aid to Families with Dependent Children (AFDC) program. Recipients of AFDC were categorically eligible for food stamps, and at least 90 percent of AFDC families participated in the FSP in a typical year. As policy makers at the state and federal levels set their gaze on reining in the growth of AFDC, attention naturally turned to the FSP at the same time. With passage of the Personal Responsibility and Work Opportunity Reconciliation Act of 1996, also known as "welfare reform," states were granted greater administrative control of food stamps, undoing some of the federalization in the 1971 Food Stamp Act. Moreover, certain classes of recipients were denied access (convicted drug felons and legal noncitizens in the country fewer than five years) or had access limited. Able-bodied adults without dependents between the ages of eighteen and fifty—so-called ABAWDs—had eligibility reduced to three months out of any thirty-six months if they worked fewer than twenty hours per week.[7] By 2000, participation in the FSP was down to its lowest levels since 1979.

The decline in the number of FSP recipients in the late 1990s was followed by a sharp increase in the number of participants starting in the 2000s, with especially large increases starting after the Great Recession. In Chapter One, James Ziliak explores the reasons underlying the growth in the program, focusing on the macroeconomy, SNAP policy, related welfare policy, and demographics. Figure I.1 makes transparent the buoyancy of the caseload with the business cycle from 1979 to 1999, with participation rising during recessions and declining during expansions. The past decade of near uninterrupted growth in participation is unprecedented in the program's history. By most measures the recession of 2001 was mild; with declining unemployment in the aftermath of the recession, past experience would have dictated a tampering down of caseloads. This did not happen, which leads Ziliak to examine the macroeconomic contribution to the caseload of stagnant household incomes and a widening income distribution. SNAP policy at the state level also changed significantly during this period. Take-up rates in the program, that is, the probability a person participates given that he or she is eligible for assistance, fell dramatically after welfare reform, so states used their new authority to expand access and outreach. This included restoring benefits to legal immigrants, expanding categorical eligibility to align more generous income and asset tests in TANF to food stamps and expedited application and recertification processes, among others. Concomitantly there was the push and pull of various demographic forces on the caseload—upward pressure from increasing shares of children being born to low-income single mothers and more reports of disability status and downward pressure from the aging of the population owing to the lower take-up rates of older Americans in the program.

Ziliak assembles over three decades of household data from the Current Population Survey (CPS) to estimate models of SNAP participation. In a series of counterfactual simulations he finds that the macroeconomy accounts for 45 percent of the growth from 2000 to 2011, food stamp policy changes account for 35 percent, nonfood policies such as welfare reform account for 3 percent of the growth, and demographic factors actually reduced growth of the SNAP caseload by 5 percent. Of the macroeconomic factors, the unemployment rate was the most important contributor, but stagnant income and inequality also mattered. This suggests that if growth over the next decade is accompanied by flat wages in the bottom half and increasing incomes at the top, we will not expect SNAP participation to fall as much as predicted based on pre-2000 experience. Although a key argument in favor of adoption of EBT as the mechanism of program delivery was to reduce stigma and thus raise participation among eligible households, Ziliak finds no evidence that the rollout of EBT across states and over time increased participation. On the other hand, liberalized access to the program with broad-based categorical eligibility and the fall in wages for low-income workers will continue to keep participation rates elevated. Demographic shifts, in particular the aging of the population and smaller households, are the seeming allies of policy makers concerned about containing program growth.

With the growing reach of SNAP to more American families, an obvious question is whether it is lifting more families out of poverty. Answering this is not straightforward because the value of food stamps is not counted as income in the official poverty statistics. That is, the official poverty rate counts only cash income in determining whether the family is poor and excludes in-kind transfers such as SNAP, Medicaid, and Medicare, as well as taxes paid and tax credits like the Earned Income Tax Credit (EITC). Another challenge in determining the antipoverty effectiveness of the program is the fact that both the participation rate and the amount of benefits received are grossly underreported in the CPS, which comprises the data for official poverty statistics and for the new Supplemental Poverty Measure, which does count the effects of SNAP. This means measurement error is a serious concern confronting accurate assessment of the program. A related measurement issue is that the standard approach of determining the antipoverty effectiveness of a program like SNAP is to count the number of people lifted above the poverty line. This leads to an understatement of the impact of SNAP insofar as it does not measure those whose level of poverty is diminished, even if the SNAP benefit levels do not raise a family above the poverty line. In fact, the inverse relationship between income and benefits means that SNAP may not raise many participants above the poverty line. Needless to say, even when SNAP benefits are not sufficient to raise someone above the poverty line, the resources available to participants are improved through the receipt of SNAP.

In Chapter Two, Laura Tiehen, Dean Jolliffe, and Timothy Smeeding assemble twenty-four years of data from the CPS to assess the antipoverty effect of SNAP, both the rate and depth. They find in a typical year that SNAP lowers the poverty rate by 5 to 10 percent and that this effect is stronger in recessionary periods. More impressive is the effect of SNAP on deep poverty—the fraction of people living on incomes less than one-half the official poverty line is lowered 10 to 20 percent in any given year by food stamps over the past two decades. In terms of number of persons affected, in 2011 roughly 4 million people were lifted out of poverty and another 3.5 million were lifted out of deep poverty. Children were the greatest beneficiaries of the poverty alleviation benefits of SNAP. The authors also show that if one makes an adjustment for the underreporting of SNAP benefits in the CPS, the antipoverty bite of the program is double that with no adjustment, and the corrected estimates suggest that SNAP lifts more out of poverty than the EITC. This makes it the most effective antipoverty program among the non-elderly. Furthermore, state policy options designed to strengthen program access, such as removal of asset tests and use of longer recertification periods for workers, have increased the antipoverty effectiveness of the program.

SAFEGUARDING THE HEALTH AND WELL-BEING OF THE NATION

The focal goal of SNAP is to alleviate hunger by providing resources to purchase a nutritious diet. Although the United States does not collect data on the physiological condition of hunger, since 1995 the USDA has collected survey data on "food insecurity," which means that there is inadequate or unsure access to enough food for an active, healthy life due to economic reasons. This survey is fielded as a supplement to the CPS in December of each year, where each of the 50,000 to 60,000 households is asked to respond to a series of eighteen questions (ten if no children are present) on the Core Food Security Module regarding worries about having enough food to eat and reductions in food intake. Figure I.2 presents trends in food insecurity and very low food security—where the latter is a more severe measure of hardship as reflected in responses to the food security supplement—from 1995 to 2012. The figure shows that both rates held steady until 2008, when they increased about 30 percent with the onset of the Great Recession, and have remained at these elevated rates in the ensuing years.

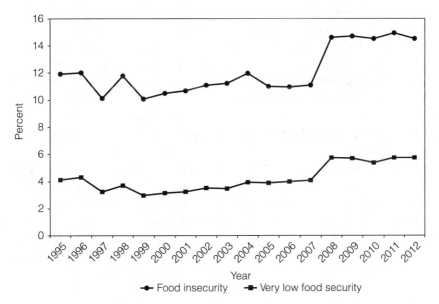

Figure I.2.   Trends in food insecurity in the United States.
SOURCE: USDA, Economic Research Service, Key Statistics and Graphics.

If SNAP participation increased so much after 2000, and really accelerated after 2007, why did food insecurity rise in tandem? Did SNAP fail in its key mission to enhance food security? Or did it ensure that the extent of food insecurity did not rise more than it would have in the absence of SNAP? Answering this question is quite challenging and yet of first-order importance for assessing program effectiveness. The challenge comes from the missing counterfactual: What would food insecurity have been in the absence of SNAP? The problem is that in quantifying how much SNAP reduces food insecurity we have to worry about reverse causation—those who sign up for SNAP are more likely to be food insecure in the first place! An extensive literature has emerged that has primarily used nonexperimental evaluation techniques to ascertain the impact of SNAP on food insecurity.

Christian Gregory, Matthew Rabbitt, and David Ribar in Chapter Three review the evidence on the effect of SNAP on food insecurity and also present new estimates. They highlight that the nonexperimental estimates in the literature have diverged widely—from SNAP having an ameliorative effect on food insecurity to the program having the perverse effect of exacerbating it, where the latter tend to be studies that treat take-up of SNAP as exogenous to food insecurity. There is also a range of estimates that are statistically indistinguishable from zero. In their detailed replication analysis, Gregory and his colleagues find results largely consistent with the literature—estimates showing that participation in SNAP lowers the odds of household food insecurity are relatively uncommon and, when they are obtained, are often statistically insignificant. They identify a more fruitful strategy known as the "dose-response" model that examines how a dollar increase in SNAP affects food insecurity. This approach offers more variation for identification beyond the blunt binary comparisons used in most applications. In these models they tend to find results consistent with theory and generally robust across specifications—higher SNAP benefits lead to lowered probabilities of food insecurity.

One reason it might be difficult to uncover a substantive ameliorative effect of SNAP on food insecurity is that the basic question of how SNAP affects food consumption is not straightforward. Standard economic theory suggests that if you provide income to households then they will increase consumption of so-called normal goods, and over a century of research indicates that food falls into that category. SNAP, of course, is not a cash transfer but instead is a targeted in-kind benefit for use on food purchases only. This has led researchers to question whether households would be better off if we provided cash directly instead of in the form of an in-kind benefit. The answer hinges crucially on whether households are "inframarginal," meaning that they spend more on food than the benefit received. If they are inframarginal, then the household in practice treats the SNAP benefit as if it were just like cash—food spending will go up with SNAP but by less than the full amount of the benefit. Thus, knowing whether SNAP households are inframarginal is critical to understanding the impact of SNAP. The policy implications are especially important here too because, if SNAP benefits are equivalent to cash, then efforts to restrict certain products from the program (see the following discussion) are likely to have little effect because participants will just substitute cash for benefits with those purchases.

In Chapter Four, Hilary Hoynes, Leslie McGranahan, and Diane Schanzenbach provide new evidence regarding whether households are inframarginal using detailed consumption data in the Consumer Expenditure Survey (CEX). They show that, among all households, as well as those with incomes less than twice the federal poverty line, over 70 percent spend more on food than their predicted SNAP benefit. Although this is lower than some earlier estimates in the literature placing the figure in the 80 to 90 percent range, the authors attribute this to the underreporting of food spending in the CEX, which has gotten worse over time. Thus, a substantial majority of households are inframarginal. Hoynes and her colleagues also show that per capita food spending declines more rapidly with family size than assumed by the Thrifty Food Plan, suggesting that the relative importance of SNAP in meeting overall food needs may differ across larger versus smaller households.

Marianne Bitler returns to the issues of identification of causal effects on SNAP in Chapter Five, but her focus is on the wider set of health and nutrition outcomes. Similar to estimating the impact of SNAP on food insecurity, evaluating the effect of SNAP on health and nutrition is difficult in survey data due to the possibility of reverse causation—those in worse health may self-select into SNAP. Bitler begins with a descriptive examination of nutrition and health status among SNAP recipients and nonrecipients using data from both the National Health Interview Survey (NHIS) and the National Health and Nutrition Examination Survey (NHANES). The evidence presented makes clear the negative selection into SNAP: Recipients are much less likely to be in excellent or very good health; much more likely to be disabled or to have a family member who suffers from functional limitations; much more likely to have been diagnosed with attention deficit disorder (ADD), asthma, diabetes, back problems, stroke, heart attack, and ulcer; and much more likely to have contact with the medical system but less likely to be able to afford care. Many of the health differences involve long-term conditions not realistically influenced by SNAP participation; these underlying differences confirm the importance of controlling adequately for possible selection bias in evaluations of the impact of SNAP on health. Moreover, although we might expect relatively short exposure to SNAP (that is, short spells on the program) to have an effect on food insecurity because this condition is based on limitations in access to food, it is much less clear whether short spells on SNAP are likely to affect broader indices of health.

Unfortunately, Bitler's assessment of the literature to date is not encouraging. Most research does not deal with the reverse causation issue, and when it does it is often reliant on low-power instruments. In addition, the literature generally does not address the "duration-response" issue, which is whether long spells have a more lasting effect on health and nutrition than short spells. There have been some positive developments in recent years in the causal literature, one avenue that exploits the time variation in the roll-out of the FSP across counties in the 1960s and 1970s and another avenue that uses more structural identification assumptions to isolate bounds on the effects of SNAP. Both of these more rigorous approaches present evidence that SNAP improves health outcomes for children and for adults. However, the body of literature here is scarce, and much more research is needed to assess whether SNAP is effectively achieving its chief goal of raising the health and well-being of low-income households.

One health-related issue that has received quite a bit of attention is the increase in rates of obesity since the 1980s. (Rates for both children and adults have largely leveled off over the past fifteen years.) Despite differences in the patterns of SNAP participation and obesity changes, some have raised concerns that participation in SNAP could be a contributor to this because of the relatively few restrictions on the types of foods that can be purchased with SNAP. Specifically, with the exceptions of hot-prepared foods and alcohol, most food products available for home consumption at certified outlets can be purchased with SNAP. Amendments were proposed in both the 1964 and 1977 Food Stamp Acts to ban the purchase of "junk food," but in both occasions they were defeated. In recent years attention has focused on banning or limiting SNAP for the purchase of sugar-sweetened beverages (SSBs) because of potential correlations between SSBs and obesity and other negative health outcomes (including dental caries in children; for example, "Mountain Dew mouth"). As shown in Chapter Four, spending on SSBs by households eligible for SNAP amounts to 7.7 percent of total food-at-home spending, only slightly higher than the 6.2 percent of spending for ineligible households; both groups spend similar shares of food budgets on "healthy" and "nonhealthy" foods. It thus appears unlikely that unhealthy foods in general, or SSBs in particular, create a wedge in obesity risk between SNAP recipients and nonrecipients. Moreover, if SNAP households are mostly inframarginal, then banning SSBs or otherwise restricting "unhealthy foods" is unlikely to affect total intake of those items, just the source of funds used to purchase them.

In Chapter Six, Craig Gundersen explores in detail the potential link between SNAP and obesity. He begins with a theoretical discussion of whether we should expect SNAP to lead to an increase in obesity. Because SNAP increases resources to the family, it enables them to increase food purchases and all other goods. The question then is whether this increase in income tilts consumption to more "healthful foods" or "unhealthful foods." Because there are no restrictions on the use of SNAP except for those few mentioned, it is not obvious why the program would distort preferences in either direction, beyond any shift in preferences that would stem from any other income source.

Gundersen turns to the 2001 to 2010 waves of the NHANES to examine associations between income and obesity. Here he finds that obesity rates actually decline in income but not by much: from 36 percent for adults living in poverty to 31 percent for adults with incomes above four times the poverty line (the gradient is sharper, though, for extreme obesity). This inverse relationship is all driven by women, however, for if anything obesity rates are increasing in income for men. The pattern among children, both boys and girls, seems to mimic mothers more than fathers in that obesity declines in income. The most common measure of obesity is the body-mass index (BMI), which is a function of the height and weight of a person, but other measures have been proposed. Gundersen examines other measures such as waist circumference for adults and skinfold thickness for children, again finding an inverse link between obesity and income. This circumstantial evidence—that obesity decreases with income for most groups—points in favor of SNAP lowering the risk of obesity, or at least not increasing the risk.

Formally evaluating the impact of SNAP on obesity is, of course, subject to the same challenges with regard to nonrandom participation as for other outcomes of interest. Gundersen's review of the literature echoes themes in Chapters Four and Five—the causal effect of SNAP on obesity is not easily quantified—but when substantive steps are taken to isolate robust identifying variation in eligibility, the literature tends to find evidence that SNAP participants are no more likely to be obese than eligible nonparticipants and, in some papers, are less likely to be obese. As such, Gundersen argues that policies that would place purchasing restrictions on SNAP in an effort to mandate healthy food choices could have the perverse impact of worse outcomes, insofar as the stigma and transaction costs would likely lower SNAP participation.

PROMOTING THE GENERAL WELFARE

A key feature of SNAP is its status as a near-universal entitlement; that is, except for having low incomes and assets there are few restrictions on eligibility across age, family structure, or employment status. Given the wide reach of the program, its interaction with other programs available to children and families is an important understudied question for policy makers. For example, is SNAP a gateway to other programs or residual claimant to fill in gaps in assistance?

The school meal programs are of particular importance as a related source of food assistance for many SNAP recipients. Figure I.3 depicts trends in the average daily number of children participating in the free and reduced-price breakfast and lunch programs from 1969 to 2013.[8] To qualify for free meals, the child must live in a household with income less than 130 percent of the federal poverty guideline (the same as the SNAP gross income test) and must have income between 130 and 185 percent of poverty to qualify for reduced-price lunch. Like SNAP, the free and reduced-price school meal programs have seen considerable growth in the past decade, though the increase in the wake of the Great Recession was not as pronounced relative to earlier periods as was the case with SNAP.

In Chapter Seven, Judith Bartfeld examines how SNAP interacts with the school breakfast and lunch programs for children, in terms of policy linkages as well as empirical patterns of participation. Bartfeld highlights how SNAP and the school meal programs have become increasingly interconnected over the past decade. SNAP has the potential to increase school meal participation because if a child's family receives SNAP the child is

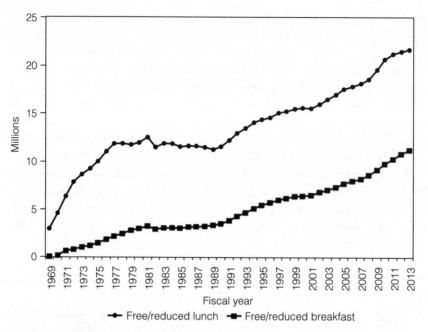

Figure I.3.   Trends in average monthly participation in free and reduced-price school breakfast and lunch programs.
SOURCE: USDA, FNS, Child Nutrition Tables.

adjunctively eligible for free breakfast and lunch,[9] a connection that has become further routinized by obligatory direct certification processes (for example, administrative data matches between schools and SNAP agencies). Moreover, as states implemented reforms to SNAP eligibility such as broad-based categorical eligibility, more children gained simplified access to school meal programs, thus strengthening the ties between SNAP and school meal programs. Further strengthening these cross-program linkages, all schools as of the 2014–2015 school year are able to offer universal free meals if they have a sufficient share of children directly certified via administrative data matching (the new "Community Eligibility Option")—meaning that SNAP participation rates directly affect school-level meal provision options. Overall, these policy linkages imply that changes to SNAP at the state or national level are likely to have spillover effects on access to school meals.

That SNAP works in tandem with the broader food safety net for children is manifest in Bartfeld's analysis of data from the 2008 to 2012 waves of the Survey of Income and Program Participation (SIPP), where 73 percent of SNAP children participate concurrently in school breakfast and 88.5 percent participate in school lunch. Bartfeld finds considerable variation in the ways children gain access to and package programs over time: Some children begin participating in school meals only after receiving SNAP, consistent with direct certification processes; more commonly, children add SNAP later, after already receiving free meals from one or both school meal programs (with those programs, too, often joined sequentially versus simultaneously). Across programs, low-income nonparticipants who are food insecure are substantially more likely to begin participating than are their food-secure counterparts—suggesting strategic use of programs, yet no doubt complicating efforts to link program participation to subsequent food insecurity and other outcomes. Bartfeld concludes by emphasizing the importance of research that examines how food assistance programs work in tandem to affect a range of child outcomes, rather than focusing on SNAP in isolation.

Robert Moffitt expands the discussion of multiple program participation among SNAP households in Chapter Eight to non–school-based programs such as TANF, EITC, Child Tax Credit (CTC), SSI, and Social Security Disability Insurance (DI), Unemployment Insurance, and housing assistance programs (for example, Section 8 housing). Access to SNAP is conferred automatically to recipients of TANF, SSI, DI, and General Assistance, and thus they are exempt from the SNAP eligibility rules. However, cash income from these programs is countable as net income for SNAP, and thus SNAP benefits are reduced as income from these programs increases just as with earnings increases. This means that, in addition to providing a more complete portrait of how SNAP fits into the overall income composition of the household, examining the extent of program bundling is important to our understanding of how cumulative implicit tax rates in the programs may combine to discourage labor market effort. That is, each program has its own set of rules, but one that is common to all means-tested programs is that benefit eligibility and/or generosity declines with labor market earnings, and if the household is using many programs simultaneously this could result in exceptionally high marginal tax rates on earnings.

Moffitt uses data from the same waves of the SIPP as Bartfeld, where he shows that at the onset of the Great Recession 91 percent of SNAP families received assistance from at least one other program or tax credit. This falls, however, to 76 percent of families if he excludes tax credits (about 38 percent of SNAP families receive the EITC). However, over half of these received only one other benefit, and only 10 percent receive assistance from three or more (nontax) programs (the latter jumps to 26 percent if we count the two tax credits). Perhaps surprising, multiple program participation in more than one program beyond SNAP is increasing in income, a result that is heavily driven by the SNAP households containing an elderly person or someone with a disability. Moffitt also examines trends in multiple program receipt from 1993 to 2010, showing declines over time primarily due to the large fall in TANF participation among single-mother families. This decline in TANF participation implies that many fewer SNAP families face large cumulative marginal tax rates on earnings, and indeed many face negative tax rates owing to the refundable EITC and CTC.

SNAP MATTERS: COMPETING PERSPECTIVES

SNAP has evolved over the past five decades from a small-scale program to one at the heart of the nation's safety net. In tandem with this growth has been a concomitant increase in interest and scrutiny from both the research and the policy communities—and in many cases diverging views as to its strengths and limitations. For some, SNAP is to be lauded as a highly responsive countercyclical program that has evolved in strategic fashion to serve not only the destitute but the growing share of households that constitute the working poor and near-poor. Growing caseloads, through this lens, reveal more about structural constraints in the labor market than about flaws in program design. For others, the growth in SNAP is a sign of a bloated safety net and a troublesome reliance on public support—leading to a growing chorus calling for substantive cutbacks to the program. For still others, the increasing prominence of SNAP, coupled with growing public concern over nutrition and obesity, points to thus-far untapped potential to use the program strategically to influence consumption choices among participants. Although some of these differences in perspective are ideological, reflecting fundamental differences with regard to the appropriate role of government programs, others reflect uncertainty about the factors that have contributed to SNAP's growth, as well as lack of clarity about its impacts. The chapters in this volume are intended to add clarity to the discussion while highlighting the unanswered questions that remain and the inherent challenge of conducting high-quality research on public policy when data are often messy or incomplete.

NOTES

1. John F. Kennedy: "Statement by the President on the Food Stamp Program," August 2, 1962. Gerhard Peters and John T. Woolley, *The American Presidency Project*, available online at www.presidency.ucsb.edu/ws/?pid=8801.

2. *The Food Stamp Act of 1964*, Public Law 88-525, 88th Congress, H.R. 1022, August 31, 1964. Available at www.fns.usda.gov/sites/default/files/PL_88-525.pdf.

3. "A Short History of SNAP," USDA Food and Nutrition Service, available at www.fns.usda.gov/snap/short-history-snap, last published November 20, 2014.

4. See "Eligibility" on the USDA Food and Nutrition Service Supplemental Nutrition Assistance Program website for details on income and resource limits, available at www.fns.usda.gov/snap/eligibility, last published October 3, 2014.

5. A SNAP, or food stamp, unit is not the same as a family or household. If the persons in a household share resources, including cooking facilities, then they are deemed to be a single unit. It is therefore possible for a household to contain both SNAP recipients and nonrecipients, or multiple SNAP units. The definition of a food stamp unit has changed over time.

6. Resource limits for automobiles were left to state discretion in 2002, and liquid asset limits were abolished in twenty-eight states during the 2008 to 2009 recession.

7. ABAWDs living in areas with high unemployment and/or limited jobs were eligible for waivers from these requirements.

8. "Child Nutrition Tables," USDA Food and Nutrition Service website, available at www.fns.usda.gov/pd/cnpmain.htm, last published March 6, 2015.

9. Although virtually all schools in the United States have a lunch program that is associated with the National School Lunch Program, that is not the case for the School Breakfast program, which has more limited coverage. The categorical eligibility of children through SNAP for breakfasts is therefore conferred only if they attend a participating school.

REFERENCES

Bolen, E., D. Rosenbaum, and S. Dean. 2014. *Summary of the 2014 Farm Bill Nutrition Title*. Washington, DC: Center on Budget and Policy Priorities. Available at www.cbpp.org/files/1-28-14fa.pdf.

Caswell, J., and A. Yaktine. 2013. *Supplemental Nutrition Assistance Program: Examining the Evidence to Define Benefit Adequacy*. Washington, DC: The National Academies Press.

Dean, S., and D. Rosenbaum. 2013. *SNAP Benefits Will Be Cut for Nearly All Participants in November 2013*. Washington, DC: Center on Budget and Policy Priorities. Available at www.cbpp.org/files/2-8-13fa.pdf.

CHAPTER ONE

Why Are So Many Americans on Food Stamps?

The Role of the Economy, Policy, and Demographics

James P. Ziliak

Since its inception fifty years ago, the Supplemental Nutrition Assistance Program (SNAP) has become a central component of the social safety net in the United States. The program is unique in its status as something akin to a universal entitlement; that is, subject to meeting low-income and asset tests, the program does not impose restrictions on eligibility based on age (Social Security), family structure (Temporary Assistance for Needy Families, or TANF), or work history (Disability Insurance and Unemployment Insurance). Today, one in seven Americans receives assistance from SNAP at a cost approaching $80 billion in FY2013, making it the second largest means-tested transfer in terms of cost after Medicaid. For much of its first three decades, SNAP operated in the shadows of the safety net, in terms of both a policy or research interest, especially in comparison to politically contentious programs like TANF and more expensive programs like Medicaid. What has caught the attention of policy makers and researchers alike in recent years is the rapid growth of the program. Since FY2000, the number participating has increased 171 percent and inflation-adjusted spending by 286 percent.[1] This has led to calls for programmatic reforms, ranging from the 2013 House Bill H.R. 3102 that would cut $39 billion over the next decade to wholesale decentralization in the form of a block grant to states with additional work requirements similar to TANF (Secretaries' Innovation Group 2013).

The aim of this chapter is to document the factors underlying the evolution of program participation since 1980.[2] I emphasize three major points in my analysis: changes in the macroeconomy, both cyclical forces from the labor market and secular trends in income inequality; changes in public policies, both food and nonfood related; and shifting demographics of the American household. I begin by describing the socioeconomic and policy climate in recent decades that have had bearing on SNAP participation, followed by a formal empirical analysis of those determinants and detailed simulations of the relative contributions of the economy, policy, and demographics to changes in SNAP participation over time.[3] The results suggest that SNAP is operating effectively as an automatic fiscal stabilizer—nearly 50 percent of the increase in participation from 2007 to 2011 is due to the weak economy—but policy reforms expanding access and benefit generosity also affected participation, accounting for nearly 30 percent of the increase after the Great Recession. The changing demographics of the American household are helping restrain growth in SNAP.

THE ECONOMY

The rush to cut or reform SNAP may be misplaced if growth in the program is primarily due to the weak labor market and economy over the past decade. There is extensive research evidence that SNAP functions effectively as an automatic fiscal stabilizer, meaning that, as the economy and market incomes fall during recessions, participation in SNAP "automatically" rises to smooth consumption, and as market incomes rise during economic expansions, participation falls (Wallace and Blank 1999; Blundell and Pistaferri 2003; Gundersen and Ziliak 2003; Ziliak, Gundersen, and Figlio 2003; Bitler and Hoynes 2010; Klerman and Danielson 2011; Ganong and Liebman 2013). This suggests that, as the macroeconomy improves in coming years, participation and cost of SNAP will decline. Indeed, assuming no changes in law, the Congressional Budget Office (CBO) (2012) projected that by 2022 spending on SNAP would fall 23 percent because of improving labor market conditions.

That such a countercyclical link exists seems transparent in Figure 1.1, which depicts trends in aggregate SNAP participation and seasonally adjusted unemployment rates.[4] Highlighted in the figure are years that include a macroeconomic recession as defined by the National Bureau of Economic Research. It is clear that peaks in SNAP usage coincide (perhaps with a lag) with peaks in unemployment rates over the past three decades. A simple time-series regression of SNAP participation on the unemployment rate and a linear trend yields:

$$SNAP_t = \underset{(1.03)}{3.47} + \underset{(0.13)}{0.86} * UR_t + \underset{(0.02)}{0.01} * trend, R^2 = 0.57, \tag{1}$$

where standard errors are reported in parentheses. The *r*-squared of 0.57 says that unemployment rates explain nearly 60 percent of the variation in aggregate SNAP participation (the trend adds nothing to the model). The coefficient on the unemployment rates implies that for each percentage point increase in the unemployment rate, SNAP increases by 0.86 points, or almost 10 percent on the average SNAP participation rate of 9.2 percent over the 1980 to 2011 period. Although this time-series model is simply illustrative,

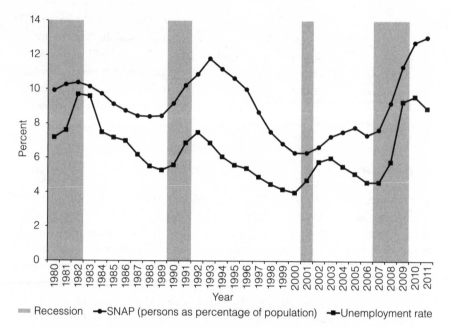

Figure 1.1. Trends in SNAP participation and unemployment rate.
SOURCE: Author's calculations using CPS ASEC and Bureau of Labor Statistics data.

a robust link between the business cycle and SNAP participation remains even in a more fully specified model as estimated in the following discussion.

Concomitant with large swings in unemployment rates, there has also been a sizable secular shift in the distribution of earnings and income that may bear on SNAP participation in recent decades (Piketty and Saez 2003; Autor, Katz, and Kearney 2008; Burkhauser et al. 2012). Figure 1.2 depicts trends in real median household income as well as the ratio of the 90th percentile of real income to the 10th percentile of real income. The median is a robust measure of the center of a skewed distribution, such as income that is used to signify how the typical household is faring, and the 90/10 ratio is a standard measure of inequality. Since 1980, real median income has increased 22 percent to $52,000, whereas 90/10 inequality increased 30 percent. Unlike the expansions of the 1980s and 1990s, however, which each had peaks in income in excess of the prior cycle, median income at the peak of the 2000s cycle was no greater than the 1990s, and in fact by 2011 any gains in median income since 1999 were lost. The flattening out of median income from 2000 to 2007, followed by a sharp decline in the Great Recession, coincides with a sharp increase in income inequality. The latter was driven by continued increases in income at the top coupled with significant declines in income at the bottom of the distribution.

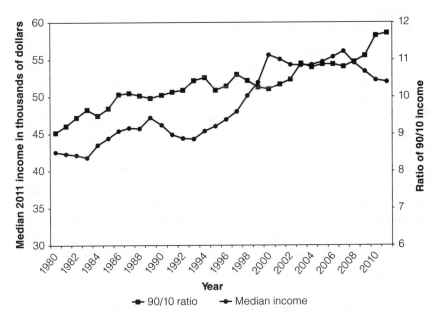

Figure 1.2. Trends in the level and inequality of household income.
SOURCE: Author's calculations using CPS ASEC data.

POLICY REFORMS

There was little change in basic federal eligibility rules in the nearly two decades leading up to the Personal Responsibility and Work Opportunity Reconciliation Act of 1996 (PRWORA, also known as welfare reform). Welfare reform, however, had both a direct and an indirect policy effect on SNAP. Directly, it eliminated eligibility for most legal permanent aliens unless they had at least ten years of work experience or were veterans; it eliminated benefits for convicted drug felons; it limited benefits to three months out of any thirty-six-month period for able-bodied adults without dependents (ABAWDS) between the ages of eighteen and fifty working fewer than twenty hours per week or not meeting other work requirements; it reduced the maximum benefit and froze many deductions used in calculating net income; it allowed states to sanction individuals and households for noncompliance with TANF requirements or child support payments; and it mandated that states adopt the electronic benefit transfer (EBT), replacing paper coupons with debit cards (Gabor and Botsko 1998; Gleason et al. 2001). Indirectly, participation was affected by virtue of the fact that half of the food stamp caseload was categorically eligible for stamps via their receipt of TANF benefits, and as welfare reform pulled people off TANF they also dropped receipt of food stamps, at least temporarily (Ziliak, Gundersen, and Figlio 2003). The other policy change that indirectly affected SNAP, even prior to welfare reform (note that in Figure 1.1 participation started to fall three years before PRWORA), was the 1993 expansion of the Earned Income Tax Credit (EITC) that pulled scores of single mothers into the labor force and off welfare and food stamps (Meyer and Rosenbaum 2001).

As participation in SNAP plummeted over 40 percent from 1993 to 2000, so too did the take-up rate of benefits; that is, the fraction of *eligible* persons participating fell over 25 percent to just over 50 percent (Leftin, Eslami, and Strayer 2011). A decline in participation does not have to be as-sociated with a decline in take-up because the decline in participation could occur only among those no longer eligible. Take-up rates among eligible seniors have always been low (30 to 35 percent depending on the year), and the decline in take-up after 1993 was driven mainly by children and nonelderly adults (Cunnyngham 2002). The fall in take-up, which is likely a spillover effect of former TANF recipients also leaving food stamps even though they remained eligible, was met with alarm (and controversy) in policy circles.

In response, several new initiatives aimed at program outreach and eli-gibility expansion were introduced, and in some cases codified in the Farm Bills of 2002 and 2008, giving much more discretion to the states to improve take-up and program administration.[5] States had always been in charge of day-to-day administration of food stamps, along with employment and training programs, and paid for these duties generally with a 50 percent federal cost share. With the 1996 welfare reform and the ensuing farm bills, states now had greater leeway to tailor the programs to be more consistent with local policy objectives. These included liberalizing vehicle asset tests, such as exempting one or more vehicles from the test, to foster welfare-to-work; expanding (broad-based) categorical eligibility, which allowed states to use more generous TANF asset and gross-income tests to determine eligi-bility; restoring eligibility for legal aliens previously excluded by PRWORA; expanding the option for simplified reporting, which allowed states to relax the frequency and form (that is, phone or online) of benefit recertification; and outreach via advertising campaigns.[6] Not all of the reforms were in-tended to make access easier. Specifically, in the 1990s states responded to financial incentives offered by the USDA to reduce benefit error rates by requiring more frequent certification, especially in households with work-ers, such that by 2000, 36 percent of working households faced three-month or shorter recertification intervals, up from 4.7 percent in 1992 (Kabbani and Wilde 2003). Some of the simplified reporting requirements adopted in recent years were intended to offset the hardship associated with more frequent certification. Another policy that restricted access is fingerprint im-aging and facial recognition software.

TABLE I.I
Number of states implementing SNAP policy reforms

	September 2000	September 2011
Broad-based categorical eligibility	2	41
Broad-based eligibility eliminates asset test	2	38
Call centers (partial state/full state)	4/2	19/14
Combined applications	1	17
Working cases with one- to three-month recertification	41	17
Elderly cases with one- to three-month recertification	27	4
Nonearning cases with one- to three-month recertification	50	26
Compulsory disqualification	15	18
All SNAP dollars redeemed as EBT	32	51
Initial application by phone (partial state/full state)	0/0	41/2
Recertify by phone (partial state/full state)	0/0	44/3
Required fingerprint (partial state/full state)	4/1	2/1
All noncitizen adults SNAP-eligible	9	3
Some noncitizen adults SNAP-eligible	42	48
All noncitizen children SNAP-eligible	10	51
Some noncitizen children SNAP-eligible	41	0
All noncitizen elderly SNAP-eligible	10	5
Some noncitizen elderly SNAP-eligible	41	46
Online application (partial state/full state)	0/0	29/1
Online application digital signature (partial state/ full state)	0	24
Spending on outreach efforts	10	35
Simplified reporting	0	49
All vehicle assets excludable	2	45
Vehicle assets limit higher than federal	0	2
Vehicle assets excludes at least one, not all	2	4

SOURCE: USDA, Economic Research Service, SNAP Policy Database; data were posted on various dates in 2000 and 2011, respectively.

Table 1.1 summarizes changes in the number of states (and the District of Columbia) adopting various SNAP policy options between 2000 and 2011 based on information in the Economic Research Service's SNAP Policy Database.[7] By 2011, forty-one states had implemented broad-based categorical eligibility as a mechanism to join SNAP, compared to only two states in 2000; of those forty-one states, thirty-eight elected to eliminate the SNAP liquid asset test as part of broad-based eligibility. The number of states offering call centers, phone applications, and combined application processes with other transfer programs has exploded, along with the number offering simplified reporting and exempting vehicle assets. As of 2011, forty-nine states used simplified reporting, and forty-five states exempted all vehicle assets from resources in determining eligibility for SNAP. At the same time, states pulled back from imposing short recertification windows of one to three months and restored SNAP eligibility to more noncitizens, especially children.

CHANGING DEMOGRAPHICS

Beyond the macroeconomy and policy changes, there have been important demographic shifts in the U.S. population over the past several decades that could differentially affect the size and composition of the SNAP caseload. On the one hand, the aging of the population suggests that the composition of the caseload should be aging as well. However, because take-up rates among seniors are so much lower than those among adults and children, population aging should put downward pressure on the growth of the caseload; thus it is not clear a priori whether the age distribution of the caseload is likely to change due to population aging. Indeed, because of the decline in marriage the fraction of births to unwed mothers accelerated from 15 percent of live births in 1980 to 40 percent by the mid-2000s (Cancian and Reed 2009; Carlson and England 2011), and, as single-mother families are more likely to be poor, then it is entirely possible that the caseload could be getting larger and younger at the same time.

A similar trend toward a younger, larger caseload could emerge from the growth of the Hispanic population, who, all else being equal, tend to be younger, have lower incomes, and have larger family sizes (Landale, Oropesa, and Bradatan 2006). Another secular trend placing upward pressure on the size of the SNAP caseload is the significant growth of disability, both in the Supplemental Security Income (SSI) and Social Security Disability Income (SSDI) programs (Muller, O'Hara, and Kearney 2006; Autor 2011). Households in which all residents receive SSI automatically qualify for SNAP, but SSDI households and those SSI units where some receive disability and others do not must still meet income and asset restrictions.

Figure 1.3 presents trends in the age composition of households receiving SNAP for children under age eighteen, for adults age eighteen to fifty-nine, and for seniors age sixty and older. The age sixty threshold for seniors is consistent with SNAP policy for eligibility determination. The figure shows that in any given year the participation rate among children is double the rate of adults and triple that of seniors. However, the decline in participation among children and adults during the welfare reform era (1993 to 2000) was substantially higher than among the elderly (46 and 48 percent, respectively, compared to 30 percent), but the subsequent growth from 2000

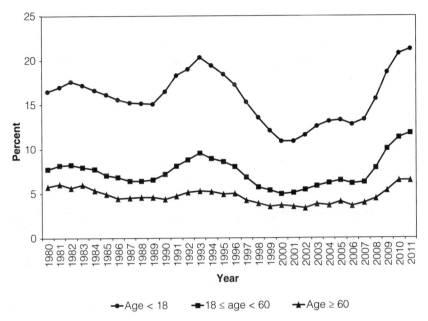

Figure 1.3. SNAP participation rates by age of household member.
SOURCE: Author's calculations using CPS ASEC data.

to 2011 was also higher for those two groups compared to the elderly (95, 138, and 75 percent, respectively). Combined, these changes over the past decade have resulted in a shift in the age composition of households receiving SNAP away from children and elderly and toward adults, as shown in Figure 1.4. In all years prior to the Great Recession about 55 percent of SNAP households consisted of children and the elderly, but by 2009, a slim majority were nonelderly adults.[8]

Coincident with the shift in the age composition of households with SNAP is the shift in the composition toward smaller households and those with multiple generations. Figure 1.5 shows that beginning in the welfare reform era there has been a secular decline in the fraction of SNAP households containing three or more persons and a rise in the fraction of one- and two-person SNAP households. At the same time, households receiving SNAP, like the general population, are increasingly likely to contain multiple generations, as seen in Figure 1.6.[9] A multigeneration household is one that contains two or more adult generations, with or without a grandchild, or a grandparent and grandchild household ("skipped generations"). The upward pressure in multigeneration households stems more from the addition of adults to the household than children, which is consistent with the trend toward more two-person SNAP households.

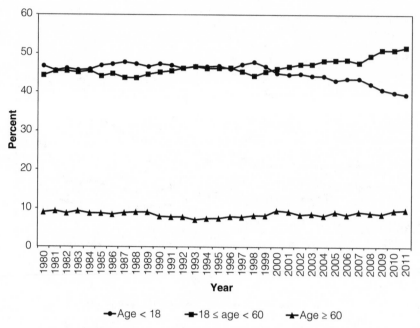

Figure 1.4. Trends in the age composition of SNAP households.

SOURCE: Author's calculations using CPS ASEC data.

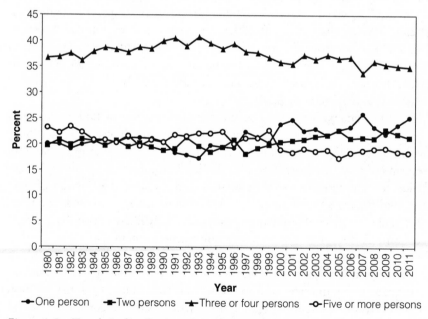

Figure 1.5. Trends in distribution of SNAP households by size.

SOURCE: Author's calculations using CPS ASEC data.

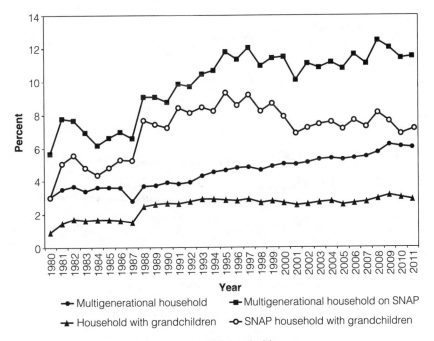

Figure 1.6.   Trends in multigenerational households.
SOURCE: Author's calculations using CPS ASEC data.

A possible concern with the shift toward smaller, prime-age adult households is that it may coincide with an increasing fraction of the SNAP caseload headed by individuals out of the labor force. A more welfare-reliant population could affect public support for SNAP in light of the centrality of work requirements and time limits that fundamentally altered the TANF program during welfare reform (Ziliak 2009). In fact, Figure 1.7 shows that the share of SNAP households headed by a person out of the labor force has been very stable for the past two decades, averaging about 53 percent. The growth has been most rapid among full-time, full-year workers, as well as part-time, full-year workers. In other words, the heads of an increasing share of SNAP households have a very strong attachment to the labor force. Furthermore, Figure 1.8 shows that the fraction of SNAP households headed by a high school dropout has plummeted by more than half to under 30 percent since 1980, and by 2011 more than a third of SNAP households were headed by someone with some college or more.[10] Figure 1.9, which depicts the distribution of SNAP households by household income in relation to the federal poverty guideline given the household size, shows that since the mid-1980s the composition of SNAP households has trended toward those with annual incomes above the poverty line. This suggests that SNAP has evolved into a work supplement for educated, near-poor households.

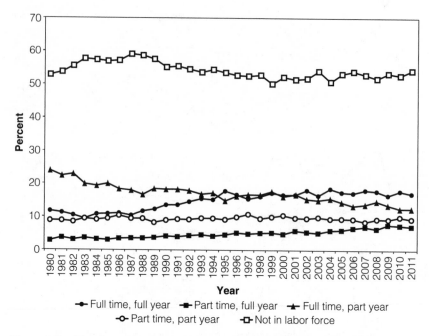

Figure 1.7. Trends in distribution of SNAP households by employment status of head.

SOURCE: Author's calculations using CPS ASEC data.

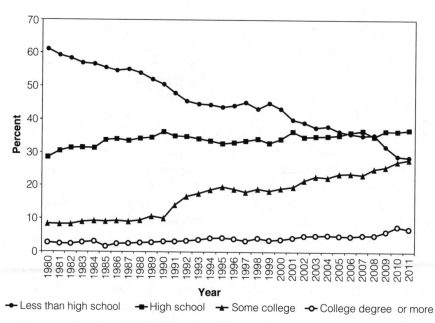

Figure 1.8. Trends in distribution of SNAP households by education attainment of head.

SOURCE: Author's calculations using CPS ASEC data.

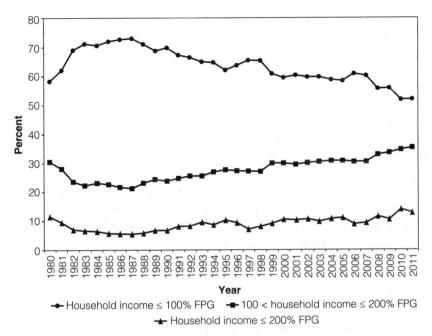

Figure 1.9.   Trends in the distribution of SNAP households by income status.
SOURCE: Author's calculations using CPS ASEC data.

PRIOR LITERATURE

In the aftermath of the 1996 welfare reform there was a flurry of research focused on understanding the relative roles of the macroeconomy and policy on declining food stamp caseloads. Wallace and Blank (1999) attributed about 44 percent of the decline to the strengthening economy and about 6 percent to welfare reform. Figlio, Gundersen, and Ziliak (2000) reached similar conclusions in terms of the role of the economy but ascribed a negligible role to welfare reform. Gleason and colleagues (2001) found that 47 percent of the decline was due to the economy and about 26 percent to welfare reform. And in a recent reevaluation of that period Klerman and Danielson (2011) found that 31 percent of the 1994 to 2000 decline resulted from lower unemployment rates and about 13 percent from welfare reform. In short, the consensus was that the economy mattered by a factor of 2 to 3 more than policy for the decline in food stamps during the second half of the 1990s.

Additionally, several studies have examined various aspects of specific food policy reforms on SNAP caseloads, both for the 1990s and 2000s (Figlio, Gundersen, and Ziliak 2000; Gleason et al. 2001; Kabbani and Wilde 2003; Ziliak, Gundersen, and Figlio 2003; Bartlett, Burstein, and Hamilton 2004; Ratcliffe, McKernan, and Finegold 2007; Burstein et al. 2009; Mabli and Ferrerosa 2010; Dickert-Conlin, Fitzpatrick, and Tiehen 2011; Klerman and Danielson 2011; Ganong and Liebman 2013). There seems to be some consensus that short recertification periods reduced SNAP participation in the 1990s and that broad-based categorical eligibility and simplified reporting led to higher caseloads. There is limited evidence that expanded outreach leads to higher caseloads (Dickert-Conlin, Fitzpatrick, and Tiehen 2011), whereas fingerprinting results in lower caseloads (Burstein et al. 2009; Ratcliffe, McKernan, and Finegold 2007). The evidence is decidedly mixed as to whether the introduction of the EBT, allowing ABAWD waivers, or vehicle asset expansions have affected caseloads.

A few recent studies have updated the 1990s economy-versus-policy debate to identify the relative contributions of each to understanding the post-2000 increase in SNAP participation. Mabli and Ferrerosa (2010), focusing on 2000 to 2008, ascribe 55 percent of the increase in SNAP to economic factors and 20 percent to the food policy reforms. Klerman and Danielson (2011) find a much lower effect of the economy of 27 percent of the caseload increase from 2000 to 2009 and 16 percent to food policy and 6 percent to welfare reform. Ganong and Liebman (2013), zeroing in on the post–Great Recession increase in SNAP from 2007 to 2011, attribute about two-thirds of the growth to the weak economy and about 7.6 percent to food policy changes. Mulligan (2012), on the other hand, argues that just over 20 percent of the increase was due to expanded policy, and Mulligan (2013) finds that two-thirds of the $122 increase in spending per capita from 2007 to 2011 was due to the increased generosity of SNAP benefits and related policies like broad-based categorical eligibility.

Thus, unlike the general agreement over influences of the 1990s decline, there is less consensus on whether the economy or policy drove the increase in participation in the 2000s. The lower estimates of the economy found in Klerman and Danielson compared to Mabli and Ferrerosa most likely stems from their use of a single metric for the macroeconomy— the state unemployment rate—whereas the other study uses a wider set of proxies for the economy in addition to the unemployment rate including the labor force participation rate, the state minimum wage, and the 20th percentile of the wage distribution. Ganong and Liebman differ from both studies in their use of the state and the county unemployment rate, and thus the dual effects of aggregate and local business cycles likely accounts for the difference. Mulligan differs from all the prior studies in his measures of policy reforms and in his empirical methods, using a difference-in-difference approach that does not simultaneously control for both the economy and policy, and thus his larger policy effect likely stems from insufficient controls for the economy.

PUTTING IT ALL TOGETHER: NEW ESTIMATES
FOR THE RISE IN SNAP

I now reexamine in a more formal setting the relative roles of the economy and policy (food and nonfood) in accounting for SNAP participation over time, and in a new twist I also isolate the contribution of changing demographics. The empirical framework is the standard reduced-form setup as

$$SNAP_{ijt} = \alpha + X_{it}\gamma + Z_{jt}\delta + \pi_j + \varphi_t + u_{ijt}, \tag{2}$$

where $SNAP_{ijt}$ is an indicator equal to 1 if anyone in household i residing in state j in time t receives SNAP, X_{it} is a vector of household demographics, Z_{jt} is a vector of state by year economic and policy variables, π_j is a set of indicators for each state, φ_t is a set of indicators for each year, and u_{ijt} is a random error term. For the model I restrict attention to the household head and thus do not include multiple observations from the same family. I estimate equation (2) via least squares, which means the linear probability standard errors must be corrected for heteroskedasticity. In addition, because much of the focus is on the economic and policy variables at the state level, I also cluster the standard errors by state to account for the within-state autocorrelation arising from the fact that multiple households are present in each state.[11]

The demographic controls include indicators for the head's age (over age seventy-five is the omitted group), education attainment (relative to high school dropout), race (relative to white), Hispanic ethnicity, household size, number of related children under age eighteen, and indicators for whether the household is multigenerational, headed by a woman, headed by a married person, or residing in a metro area. Because participation is means tested, I do not include household earnings or non-SNAP income in the demographics to avoid potential endogeneity.

The measures of the macroeconomy that vary by state and year include the unemployment rate, real median household income, and the ratio of 90/10 real income. Given the apparent lag in SNAP participation to changes in unemployment in Figure 1.1, in some of the specifications I allow a two-year lag in state unemployment rates (Figlio, Gundersen, and Ziliak 2000; Klerman and Danielson 2011; Ganong and Liebman 2013).[12]

The nonfood policy variables include the real value of the maximum of the federal or state minimum wage in a given year, the phase-in subsidy rate for the EITC, an indicator variable if the state has a separate EITC program, an indicator if the state ever implemented a federally approved waiver from its AFDC program between 1992 and 1996, and an indicator for when the state implemented its TANF program. Because some states set their minimum wage above the federal wage and others below, I use the maximum of the two as a proxy for wage incentives to work. Thus, a higher minimum wage is expected to lower participation. The EITC subsidy rate, because it makes work relatively more attractive, is expected also to lower participation. The same is true of a state's EITC supplement. Even though it is set nationally, the EITC subsidy rate is identified by the fact that it varies over time and by the number of qualifying children (Hotz and Scholz 2003).[13] Although some of the waiver and TANF policies were designed to make it more attractive to combine welfare and work (for example, higher earnings disregards and asset limits), on net most of the policies made AFDC/TANF participation less attractive, and thus both the AFDC waiver and TANF indicators are expected to lower participation in SNAP.

For the SNAP policy variables I assign the real maximum benefit guarantee for a one-, two-, three-, or four-person household based on family size (the four-person guarantee is assigned to households with four or more persons) to measure the financial generosity of the program. Thus, the higher the guarantee the higher is the expected participation in SNAP. Like the EITC subsidy rate, the SNAP benefit is identified in the model because it varies over time and by household size.[14] For the remaining SNAP variables I use the SNAP Policy Database assembled by the Economic Research Service in the U.S. Department of Agriculture. These variables, which vary across states and time, include the fraction of SNAP dollars redeemed via the EBT, indicators for whether the state allows broad-based categorical eligibility, whether the state operates call centers (either statewide or partial state), whether the state allows combined SSI/SNAP applications, whether it imposes short recertification periods of three months or less for households with a working member, whether noncitizens are eligible for benefits, whether the household must be fingerprinted (either statewide or partial state), whether the household is disqualified for being sanctioned by another program such as TANF, whether the state allows online applications (either statewide or partial state), whether the state adopted simplified reporting, whether it excludes the full value of a vehicle for eligibility, and the real spending on outreach. The expected signs on these variables are all intuitive and reflect the series of carrots and sticks that states have adopted in administering their SNAP programs. Finally, to proxy for state variation in politics, I include an indicator variable as to whether the governor of the state is a Democrat and expect the sign on the coefficient to be positive, suggesting that Democratic governors create policy environments more supportive of SNAP participation.[15]

Table 1.2 presents linear probability estimates of the effect of the economy, policy, and demographics on SNAP household participation weighted by the CPS ASEC (Current Population Survey Annual Social and Economic Supplement) household weight. In column 1 the only measure of the economy is the state unemployment rate, where the estimate of 0.41 says that a one percentage point increase in the unemployment rate leads to a 0.41 point increase in SNAP participation, or about 5.3 percent on the average SNAP household participation rate of 7.6 percent from 1980 to 2011. This effect of unemployment is about one-half the size from the time-series regression reported in equation 1, indicating that the time-series model attributed too much to the economy once one controls for policy and demographics in the pooled cross-sectional models of equation 2.[16] In column 2, when we add controls for state median income and income inequality, the effect of the business cycle is attenuated by about 27 percent, although once we admit a two-year lagged effect of the unemployment rate in column 3 the total effect of the business cycle of 0.38 points nearly returns to the baseline estimate. Columns 2 and 3 show that increases in the real median income lead to modest reductions in SNAP participation, whereas increases in inequality lead to more economically substantive increases. A unit increase in inequality leads to a 0.26 point increase in SNAP participation.

The next panel of Table 1.2 contains the estimates of the nonfood policy variables. Expansions of the EITC subsidy rate over the past thirty years have had an economically and statistically important disincentive effect on SNAP participation—each percentage point increase in the subsidy rate reduces SNAP participation by 0.1 points, or about 1.3 percent at the mean level of SNAP usage. The 20 percentage point increase in the subsidy rate for two qualifying children in the mid-1990s suggests that increased EITC generosity had a substantive effect on reductions in SNAP during that period. SNAP participation, holding other factors constant, is at least a percentage point lower after implementation of TANF, suggesting an important spillover effect of welfare reform onto the SNAP caseload.

The third panel of Table 1.2 presents estimates of the food policy variables. Each $100 increase in the real maximum benefit guarantee leads to a 1.9 point increase. Evaluated at the means of the data, the elasticity of SNAP participation with respect to the benefit guarantee is 0.88, which means that the 13.6 percent increase in benefits as part of ARRA is expected to increase participation 12.2 percent.[17] On the converse, with the expiration of the ARRA benefit increase in October 2013, participation is expected to fall by the same magnitude. Across the various other policy variables, only a few have a consistent economic and statistical effect on participation. Broad-based categorical eligibility and simplified reporting are each associated with increases in SNAP participation. States that have adopted these policies have SNAP participation rates that are 0.6 and 0.8 points higher, respectively. At the same time, if the state requires fingerprinting of its recipients, then participation is about 0.7 points lower (columns 2 and 3).

TABLE I.2
The effects of the economy, policy, and demographics on SNAP participation

	(1)	(2)	(3)
ECONOMY			
Unemployment rate	0.4108***	0.2976***	0.1858***
	(0.0458)	(0.0537)	(0.0679)
Unemployment rate ($t-1$)			0.0225
			(0.0744)
Unemployment rate ($t-2$)			0.1710**
			(0.0664)
Median income ($1000)		−0.0008***	−0.0007***
		(0.0002)	(0.0002)
Household income 90/10 ratio		0.0026***	0.0026***
		(0.0004)	(0.0004)
NONFOOD POLICY			
Minimum wage (maximum federal/state)	−0.0007	−0.0004	−0.0002
	(0.0012)	(0.0012)	(0.0012)
EITC subsidy rate	−0.1027***	−0.1026***	−0.1026***
	(0.0092)	(0.0092)	(0.0091)
State has EITC	0.0031	0.0032	0.0028
	(0.0026)	(0.0024)	(0.0024)
AFDC waiver	−0.0033	−0.0029	−0.0036
	(0.0028)	(0.0025)	(0.0023)
TANF	−0.0138***	−0.0111***	−0.0108***
	(0.0032)	(0.0037)	(0.0032)
FOOD POLICY			
Food Stamp/SNAP ($100)	0.0191***	0.0191***	0.0191***
	(0.0017)	(0.0017)	(0.0017)
EBT issuance	−0.0002	0.0010	0.0008
	(0.0023)	(0.0020)	(0.0020)
Broad-based SNAP eligibility	0.0059**	0.0059**	0.0058**
	(0.0026)	(0.0023)	(0.0023)
Call centers (partial/full)	−0.0011	−0.0020	−0.0018
	(0.0021)	(0.0019)	(0.0018)
Combined applications	0.0010	0.0007	0.0008
	(0.0026)	(0.0026)	(0.0025)
Initiate by phone (partial/full)	−0.0034	−0.0021	−0.0017
	(0.0025)	(0.0022)	(0.0022)
Short certification	0.0012	0.0008	0.0005
	(0.0015)	(0.0016)	(0.0016)
Noncitizens SNAP-eligible	0.0009	0.0021	0.0016
	(0.0029)	(0.0030)	(0.0030)
Required fingerprints (partial/full)	−0.0042*	−0.0065***	−0.0071***
	(0.0021)	(0.0022)	(0.0022)
Compulsory disqualification	0.0021	0.0011	0.0012
	(0.0020)	(0.0020)	(0.0020)
Online application (partial/full)	0.0011	0.0013	0.0011
	(0.0021)	(0.0018)	(0.0018)
Simplified reporting	0.0083**	0.0074**	0.0075**
	(0.0031)	(0.0030)	(0.0028)
Vehicle assets excludable	−0.0007	−0.0013	−0.0009
	(0.0020)	(0.0021)	(0.0021)
Outreach ($100,000)	−0.0017*	−0.0017*	−0.0016*
	(0.0009)	(0.0009)	(0.0009)

TABLE 1.2 (*continued*)
The effects of the economy, policy, and demographics on SNAP participation

	(1)	(2)	(3)
DEMOGRAPHICS			
Age 15–29	0.0712***	0.0712***	0.0712***
	(0.0075)	(0.0074)	(0.0074)
Age 30–44	0.0223***	0.0223***	0.0223***
	(0.0050)	(0.0050)	(0.0050)
Age 45–59	0.0365***	0.0366***	0.0366***
	(0.0045)	(0.0045)	(0.0045)
Age 60–74	0.0337***	0.0337***	0.0337***
	(0.0029)	(0.0029)	(0.0029)
High school diploma	–0.0873***	–0.0873***	–0.0873***
	(0.0041)	(0.0041)	(0.0041)
Some college	–0.1138***	–0.1138***	–0.1138***
	(0.0048)	(0.0048)	(0.0048)
College	–0.1361***	–0.1361***	–0.1360***
	(0.0061)	(0.0061)	(0.0061)
Black	0.0969***	0.0969***	0.0969***
	(0.0056)	(0.0056)	(0.0056)
Other race	0.0238***	0.0238***	0.0238***
	(0.0027)	(0.0027)	(0.0027)
Hispanic	0.0322**	0.0322**	0.0322**
	(0.0150)	(0.0150)	(0.0150)
Household size	–0.0085***	–0.0085***	–0.0085***
	(0.0024)	(0.0024)	(0.0024)
Number children < 18	0.0540***	0.0539***	0.0539***
	(0.0021)	(0.0021)	(0.0021)
Multigenerational household	0.0379***	0.0379***	0.0379***
	(0.0033)	(0.0033)	(0.0033)
Female	0.0422***	0.0421***	0.0421***
	(0.0019)	(0.0019)	(0.0019)
Married	–0.0886***	–0.0886***	–0.0886***
	(0.0034)	(0.0034)	(0.0034)
Metro	–0.0185***	–0.0184***	–0.0184***
	(0.0024)	(0.0024)	(0.0024)
POLITICS			
Governor is a Democrat	0.0032***	0.0034***	0.0032***
	(0.0010)	(0.0009)	(0.0009)
Observations N	2,053,018	2,053,018	2,053,018

SOURCE: Author's calculations using Current Population Survey Annual Social and Economic Supplement (CPS ASEC) data.

Outreach spending has the unexpected sign of reducing participation, though the magnitude is very small.[18]

The next panel of Table 1.2 contains the estimated effects of demographic variables. There is evidence that SNAP participation significantly declines with age and with education attainment. White households are less likely to participate relative to African Americans and members of other races, as are non-Hispanics. Conditional on the number of related children in the household, participation declines in household size. Participation is also about 4 points lower in households that do not contain multiple generations. Finally, participation is higher among female-headed households by about 4 points and lower among married households by almost 9 points and among those in metro areas compared to nonmetro areas.[19]

In Table 1.3 I attempt to summarize the relative influence of the economy, policy, and demographics through a series of counterfactual simulations. Specifically I use the model estimates presented in column 3 of Table 1.2 to examine how much of the increase in SNAP from 2007 to 2011, 2000 to 2011, and 1980 to 2011 can be attributed to economic forces, changes in nonfood policies, changes in food policies, and changes in household demographics if each of the four groupings was held fixed group-by-group at the values at the start of the simulation period. For example, to assess the role of the economy in accounting for the increase in SNAP after the Great Recession from 2007 to 2011, I fix the unemployment rate and its lags, real median income, and real 90/10 income inequality at their 2007 levels and let the remaining variables change over time, including the year effects. I then examine the 2000 to 2011 change by fixing the economic variables at their 2000 level, and finally the 1980 to 2011 change in SNAP by fixing the economy at the 1980 values. This same exercise is conducted for each of the four variable groupings.

From 2007 to 2011, the participation of households in SNAP increased 68.7 percent. If we fixed the economic variables at their 2007 values, we would have predicted that SNAP participation would have increased only 35.8 percent. This implies that changes in the business cycle and income distribution accounted for 47.8 percent (= 100 * (1 − 35.8/68.7)) of the change over the four-year period after the Great Recession began. Although only 1.6 percent of the increase was due to nonfood policies, a substantive 28.5 percent was due to changes in federal and state food policies. Changing demographics explain none of the increase in SNAP participation; in fact, the negative number suggests that changes in demographics after 2007 actually helped dampen SNAP growth because caseloads were predicted to be even higher than actual.

The middle panel of Table 1.3 shows that after 2000 household participation in SNAP more than doubled. If the economic variables were fixed at their 2000 values, then participation was predicted to increase by only 58.4 percent, or the economy accounts for a sizable 45.4 percent of the actual change in participation. We also see that food policies have a more prominent role in the post-2000 period, accounting for 35 percent of the growth. Finally, in the bottom panel we look back over the prior thirty-two years and see that changing unemployment rates along with the income distribution account for 37 percent of the one-third increase in SNAP

TABLE 1.3

Simulations of the effects of the economy, policy, and demographics on changes in household SNAP participation

	Calendar years 2007–2011			
	Economy fixed at 2007 levels	Nonfood policies fixed at 2007 levels	Food policies fixed at 2007 levels	Demographics fixed at 2007 levels
Actual change (percentage)	Share due to economy	Share due to nonfood	Share due to food	Share due to demographics
68.7	47.8	1.6	28.5	–3.7
	Calendar years 2000–2011			
	Economy fixed at 2000 levels	Nonfood policies fixed at 2000 levels	Food policies fixed at 2000 levels	Demographics fixed at 2000 levels
Actual change (percentage)	Share due to economy	Share due to nonfood	Share due to food	Share due to demographics
106.6	45.4	3.1	35.4	–5.0
	Calendar years 1980–2011			
	Economy fixed at 1980 levels	Nonfood policies fixed at 1980 levels	Food policies fixed at 1980 levels	Demographics fixed at 1980 levels
Actual change (percentage)	Share due to economy	Share due to nonfood	Share due to food	Share due to demographics
33.9	37.0	–81.5	76.2	–55.8

SOURCE: Author's calculations based on parameter estimates in Table 1.2, column 3. Simulations hold identified variables fixed and allow others to vary over time. In each case, the year effects are allowed to vary over time. Shares do not sum to 100 percent because some factors are omitted.

participation. However, food policies take center stage with a substantial 76.2 percent of the growth, whereas nonfood policies such as EITC expansions and welfare reform have kept SNAP participation in check, as have changing demographics of the American household.

CONCLUSION

The Supplemental Nutrition Assistance Program continues to be under the policy microscope as Congress debates whether and how to trim funding of the program in the coming decade. The case made to cut the program is based on concerns over the rapid growth in the past decade, both in terms of number of persons served and total cost. However, the evidence presented here suggests that the greatest factor underlying the increase in participation after the Great Recession, and indeed since 2000, is the weak macroeconomy characterized by higher unemployment, lower incomes, and widening inequality. The estimate that the economy accounts for nearly one-half of the increase from 2007 to 2011 is smaller than the two-thirds estimate reported in Ganong and Liebman (2013), most likely due to my inclusion of detailed controls for demographics and the income distribution, which depress the effect of unemployment on SNAP. Even though each study uses different samples and methodologies, however, the common result is that the economy is the most important factor driving short-run changes in participation. That is, the program is operating as intended as an automatic fiscal stabilizer during this extended period of economic distress facing households in the United States. Indeed, descriptive evidence points to growth in participation over the past dozen years among full-time, year-round workers, those with some college education, and those with household incomes between one and two times the federal poverty guideline. In other words, the program is increasingly operating as a work support for higher-educated but low-income households, not unlike the EITC, while still maintaining its universal entitlement to disadvantaged children and seniors and the disabled.

The results also show that policy matters, as do demographics, especially in the long run. To be sure there have been some recent changes in program eligibility such as broad-based categorical eligibility and simplified reporting that have led to significant increases in SNAP participation over the past decade. These programmatic changes were implemented in a bid to stem the tide of declining take-up rates in the late 1990s and to improve program efficiency, and the prime facie evidence suggests they have largely worked. Take-up rates have rebounded to levels at or above those in the early 1990s (Leftin, Eslami, and Strayer 2011), whereas administrative error rates from overissuance and underissuance of benefits have declined by over half since 2000.[20] The CBO (2012) estimates that eliminating broad-based categorical eligibility as proposed in HR Bill 1947 so that all recipients face SNAP income and asset limits will reduce SNAP participation by 4.3 percent from 2013 to 2022. Presumably this will lead to a deterioration of program integrity and to a reduction in the fraction of SNAP recipients who combine work with SNAP, as those persons admitted by these rules tend to be the working near-poor. In addition, the estimates presented suggest that the expiration of the temporary ARRA boost in benefits of 13.6 percent in October 2013 is predicted to reduce participation by just over 12 percent. So, with continued improvements in the economy and return of benefits to pre-ARRA levels, SNAP participation should begin to fall as projected by the CBO.

Over the long run, SNAP policies have loomed larger as a determinant of participation than the economy, and this is not surprising because basic program parameters and eligibility rules can shape the size and composition of the caseload more than in the short run. The estimates here clearly point in the direction of lower participation and program cost because of the aging of the population, fewer children and smaller households, and the ongoing shift to cities from rural areas, among other demographic forces. This suggests that if policy reforms are on the horizon they should be framed within the context of the changing demographics of the U.S. household and be targeted to long-run dimensions of the program and not in response to short-run changes in participation. Terminating eligibility until the recovery has had a chance to fully gain traction is premature and exposes vulnerable families to even greater economic risk.

APPENDIX: DATA

The primary data source used in the analysis comes from the Annual Social and Economic Supplement of the Current Population Survey for calendar years 1980–2011. I do not delete any observations for any reason, including those individuals with imputed responses by the Census Bureau. This results in 5,552,486 individuals residing in 2,053,018 households pooled across all years, or about 173,515 persons in a typical year across the sample period. Figures 1.1, 1.3, and 1.4 of the text rely on individual-level data, while Figures 1.2 and 1.5–1.9, along with Tables 1.2 and 1.3, use household-level information.

Figure 1.1 in the text is the weighted fraction of the noninstitutionalized population that participates in SNAP, where the weight is the individual weight assigned by the Census Bureau that adjusts for the stratified sample design. The Census question for SNAP receipt (HFOODSP) is

"Did anyone in this household get food stamps at any time during [19XX/20XX] (last year)?"

where the yes/no response is assigned to all members of the household whether or not they receive direct assistance from the program. The unemployment rate in Figure 1.1 is the seasonally adjusted average monthly unemployment rate for individuals age sixteen and older constructed by the Bureau of Labor Statistics, Series ID 14000000.

The assumption implicit in this chapter is that if any member of the household receives SNAP, then the entire household unit benefits because of resource pooling, which is consistent with the Bergson-Samuelson formulation of household utility maximization. The Census also asks the following question (HNUMFS for 1980–1986; HFOODNO for 1987–2011) conditional on an affirmative response to SNAP receipt:

"How many of the people now living here were covered by food stamps during [19XX/20XX] (last year)?"

As a check on the trends in SNAP reported in Figure 1.1, in Figure 1.A.1 I show trends in individual-level SNAP participation rates using the ASEC

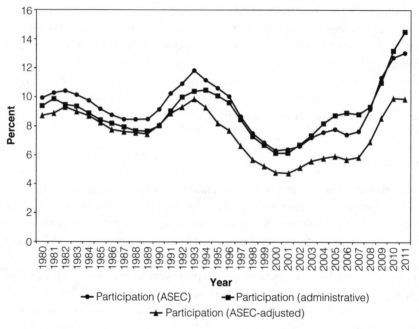

Figure 1.A.1. Comparison of SNAP participation rates in CPS ASEC to administrative data.

SOURCE: Author's calculations using CPS ASEC data, and USDA Food and Nutrition Service administrative data.

alongside an adjusted ASEC series where I multiply each weight by the ratio of the number of SNAP recipients to the number of household members to adjust for the fact that not all members directly receive assistance. I also depict a series constructed using average monthly participation in the fiscal year from FNS administrative data obtained from www.fns.usda.gov/pd/SNAPsummary.htm (the ratio of average monthly participation to the population estimate from the ASEC). Figure 1.A.1 shows that, from 1980 to the mid-1990s, SNAP participation using the definition here results in higher rates relative to both administrative data and the adjusted ASEC series. From 1996–2003, and again in 2008–2010, the definition here coincides with administrative rates, but there is a greater separation in levels of participation in the adjusted ASEC, which seems consistent with increased rates of underreporting (Wheaton 2007; Meyer and Goerge 2011). However, there are no substantive differences in the trends whether assigning all members to SNAP, or using the adjusted series, compared to trends in participation from administrative data.

Figure 1.2 in the text depicts trends in real household median income and inequality. For this series I use total household income (which includes family income plus income, both earned and unearned, of nonfamily members, defined by variables HHINCTOT for 1980–1986 and HTOTVAL for 1987–2011) and deflate it by the personal consumption expenditure deflator using 2011 as the base year obtained from www.whitehouse.gov/sites/default/files/docs/erp2013/ERP2013_Appendix_B.pdf. Because all members of the household are assigned the same total income, I restrict attention to the 2,053,018 household heads across the sample period. For each year I construct median real household income, real income at the 10th percentile, and real income at the 90th percentile, and construct the measure of real inequality using the ratio of the 90th to the 10th percentiles.

Figure 1.3 shows trends in SNAP participation by age category (A-AGE). As in Figure 1.1, SNAP is determined at the household level, and thus Figure 1.3 reflects the participation rates of members of those households by age. Figure 1.4 then conditions on household participation in SNAP and using person-level data computes the age composition of the SNAP caseload.

Figure 1.5 focuses on SNAP households and decomposes the caseload based on household size (NUM-PERS for 1980–1986; H-NUMPER for 1987–2011).

Figure 1.6 depicts trends in the fraction of households containing multiple generations, both across the entire population and conditional on SNAP status. For each year I identify each unique household using the household sequence number (PPSEQNUM for 1980–1987; PH-SEQ for 1988–2011). Within that household I identify that a grandchild is present if RHHDFMS = 13 for years 1980–1987, and if HHDFMX > 22 and < 35 for years 1988–2011. After 1986 I identify that a parent of the head is present if A-EXPRRP = 8 and that HHDFMX > 34 and < 46. Prior to 1987 there is no direct classification of a parent of head, and thus I proxy this if there is an "other relative of head in the family" (REL-HEAD = 5 and RHHDFMS > 20 and RHHDFMS < 25) who is at least fifteen years older than the head. A household is multigenerational if it contains the parent of the adult head or a grandchild of the head.

Figure 1.7 presents trends in the distribution of SNAP households by employment status of the household head during the year prior to the survey and coinciding with the period of SNAP receipt (A-WEWKRS for 1980–1986, WEWKRS for 1987–2011).

Figure 1.8 is trends in the distribution of SNAP households by education attainment of the head. For the years 1980–1990, education attainment is derived by the two variables GRADE-COM and HIGH-GRD, whereas for 1991–2011 it is based on A-HGA.

Figure 1.9 depicts trends in SNAP participation by poverty status of households. A household is poor if total household income (HHINCTOT for 1980–1986; HTOTVAL for 1987–2011) is less than or equal to the

TABLE I.A.I
Weighted summary statistics of households in the CPS ASEC, 1980–2011

	Mean	Standard deviation
SNAP participation	0.076	0.265
ECONOMY		
Unemployment rate	0.064	0.021
Unemployment rate $(t-1)$	0.062	0.021
Unemployment rate $(t-2)$	0.061	0.019
Median income ($1000)	49.612	8.135
Household income 90/10 ratio	8.855	1.498
NONFOOD POLICY		
Minimum wage (maximum federal/state)	6.700	0.709
EITC subsidy rate	0.123	0.129
State has EITC	0.149	0.356
AFDC waiver	0.048	0.201
TANF	0.506	0.496
FOOD POLICY		
Food Stamp/SNAP ($100)	3.493	1.465
EBT issuance	0.446	0.486
Broad-based SNAP eligibility	0.143	0.342
Call centers (partial/full)	0.181	0.385
Combined applications	0.121	0.323
Initiate by phone (partial/full)	0.079	0.269
Short certification	0.547	0.498
Noncitizens SNAP-eligible	0.117	0.319
Required fingerprint (partial/full)	0.138	0.345
Compulsory disqualification	0.16	0.359
Online application (partial/full)	0.13	0.336
Simplified reporting	0.284	0.444
Vehicle assets excludable	0.222	0.41
Outreach ($100,000)	0.363	1.084
DEMOGRAPHICS		
Age 15–29	0.147	0.354
Age 30–44	0.312	0.463
Age 45–59	0.261	0.439
Age 60–74	0.185	0.388
High school diploma	0.321	0.467
Some college	0.237	0.425
College	0.251	0.434
Black	0.118	0.323
Other	0.042	0.201
Hispanic	0.085	0.279
Household size	2.582	1.459
Number children < 18	0.623	1.039
Multigenerational HH	0.047	0.211
Female	0.405	0.491
Married	0.536	0.499
Metro	0.784	0.412
POLITICS		
Governor is a Democrat	0.485	0.500
Observations N	2,053,018	

SOURCE: Author's calculations using CPS ASEC and Food and Nutrition Service administrative data.

poverty guideline for a given household size obtained from www.ssa.gov/policy/docs/statcomps/supplement/2012/3e.html#table3.e8.

Table 1.2 data on SNAP participation and household demographics are obtained from the CPS ASEC. The state-by-year data on the unemployment rate, minimum wage, EITC parameters, AFDC waivers, TANF implementation, household-size specific SNAP benefits, and political party of the governor are obtained from the University of Kentucky Center for Poverty Research (UKCPR) State Welfare Database at www.ukcpr.org/EconomicData/Copy%20of%20UKCPR_National_Data_Set_07_01_13.xlsx. Finally, the SNAP policy variables are obtained from the SNAP Policy Database assembled by the Economic Research Service in the U.S. Department of Agriculture www.ers.usda.gov/data-products/snap-policy-database.aspx#.UhQQ-ZLVC3I. There are missing values in 2010–2011 in the main ERS database for the variables call, cap, compdq, reportsimple, vehexclall, vehexclamt, and vehhexclone. For these I just assumed that the most recent value (0, 1, or 2 depending on variable) continued to the end of the 2011 fiscal year. The variables bbce_asset and oapp_esig each record a –9 as a "no," so I replaced these with 0. As described in the text, for policies that differ based on partial-state or full-state coverage, I combine the two categories into a single indicator of whether the policy is in operation in the state and do not distinguish coverage. Table 1.A.1 contains the sample means of the variables used in the Table 1.2 regression models.

NOTES

I thank Sarah Burns and Robert Paul Hartley for excellent research assistance, and for comments by Jonathan Schwabish, Tim Smeeding, and participants at the UKCPR/UW-Madison IRP Five Decades of Food Stamps Conference on an earlier version. The opinions expressed are solely those of the author and do not necessarily reflect the views of any sponsoring agency.

1. Author's calculations are based on administrative SNAP data in the March 2013 *Economic Report of the President* at www.fns.usda.gov/pd/SNAPsummary .htm and the personal consumption expenditure deflator (Table B-7 of the 2013 Economic Report of the President at www.whitehouse.gov/sites/default/files/docs/erp2013/ERP2013_Appendix_B.pdf).

2. Prior to the Food Stamp Act of 1977, which was implemented in 1979, recipients of assistance faced a so-called purchase requirement, meaning that they were required to spend up to their normal expenditure on food to buy stamps and then would receive a "bonus" amount of stamps based on income level to bring their food spending up to the level of the USDA low-cost diet. Because many low-income families face binding liquidity constraints and were unable to purchase stamps up front, the purchase requirement was believed to have artificially depressed participation (Caswell and Yaktine 2013). Thus I focus on the period after the 1977 Act.

3. I do not cover issues related to process implementation of SNAP reforms, which may have also affected the caseload over the past decade. See, for example, Rowe et al. (2010) and Hulsey et al. (2013).

4. Unless noted otherwise, all data come from the Annual Social and Economic Supplement of the Current Population Survey for calendar years 1980–2011. In the CPS, each person in a household is assigned as a SNAP recipient even if only a subset receives benefits. The assumption is that members of households pool resources; so, even though not all members are direct beneficiaries, indirectly they do benefit from extra resources. This will overstate actual participation, but this is weighed against evidence of underreporting of SNAP receipt in household surveys (Bollinger and David 1997; Wheaton 2007; Meyer and Goerge 2011). It also misses the fact that a household may consist of multiple SNAP units. The appendix describes the data and elaborates on these issues.

5. The American Recovery and Reinvestment Act of 2009 (ARRA) also affected SNAP by raising the maximum benefit guarantee by an average of 13.6 percent, raising the minimum benefit from $14 to $16, and suspending the time limit of receipt among ABAWDs; see the "SNAP Households and ARRA Increase" table on the USDA website at www.ers.usda.gov/topics/food-nutrition-assistance/supplemental-nutrition-assistance-program-(snap)/arra.aspx#.Uh3u6Rtebmc.

6. See the Food and Nutrition Service, USDA, SNAP eligibility guidelines (October 3, 2014), available at www.fns.usda.gov/snap/applicant_recipients/eligibility.htm.

7. SNAP Policy Database (December 5, 2015), Economic Research Service, USDA, available at www.ers.usda.gov/data-products/snap-policy-database.aspx#.Uh3oARtebmc.

8. It is important to recall that the definition of a SNAP household in the CPS differs from the SNAP unit in SNAP Quality Control Data. In the former a household includes recipients and nonrecipients, but in the latter it is only recipients. As a consequence, in QC data a majority of recipients are still children and the elderly (54 percent in 2011 [Strayer, Eslami, and Leftin 2012]).

9. Beginning in 1988, the CPS adopted an improved method of identifying grandchildren and grandparents in households, and thus the jump after 1987 reflects the change in survey design.

10. The CPS changed the measurement of education attainment after calendar year 1990, and thus the jump in some college in the two years after owes in part to the change in the questionnaire.

11. In results not tabulated, I also estimated the standard errors that clustered both by state and year as suggested by Cameron, Gelbach, and Miller (2011). The standard errors were little changed, but there were violations of full column rank in the variance matrix, so I only report results that cluster at the state level.

12. In an earlier version I also examined whether the effect of the economy on SNAP participation differed across decades. There was some evidence that unemployment had a larger effect in the 1990s than the 1980s, but there was no difference from the 2000s. These estimates are available on request.

13. The CPS does not document whether a child in the household qualifies for the EITC, and thus I proxy this by the number of related children under age eighteen.

14. As discussed earlier, the maximum benefit is generally tied to inflation of the food prices in the TFP, but the benefit also deviated from the TFP between

1988 and 1996, and from 2009 to 2011, providing noninflation policy variation for identification.

15. Although the District of Columbia is not a state and has no governor, I set the "governor is a Democrat" variable to 1 for all years for DC residents based on past voting of residents for local government.

16. The average SNAP participation rates differ between equations 1 and 2 because in the former the outcome is persons participating and in the latter it is households.

17. As a comparison, Nord and Prell (2011) estimate that the expanded ARRA benefit lowered food insecurity by 2.2 percentage points among low-income households, or about 8.8 percent on the baseline rate of 25 percent.

18. A detailed examination of the food policy variables was carried out to explore whether the "kitchen sink" approach here was eliminating economic and statistical significance due to collinearity of the policy variables. The short answer is no. Sequentially adding food policy variables or combinations of food policy variables to the baseline set of the maximum benefit, broad-based categorical eligibility, simplified reporting, and fingerprinting did not alter the conclusion that most of the variables are not significant, but they do add to the model in the sense that some of them sharpen the effect of the four consistently significant variables. I also examined whether stopping the analysis in 2006 similar to Ganong and Liebman (2013) made a difference. The argument is that the Great Recession may have changed the relationship between the regressors and SNAP participation. Doing so had no impact on the effect of demographics or the economy on SNAP. The before-TANF welfare variable was slightly stronger, and the effects of broad-based categorical eligibility and simplified reporting were weaker by stopping the analysis in 2006. The only variable that changed direction is outreach spending, which becomes positive and significant. None of these changes had an effect on the counterfactual simulations reported in Table 1.3.

19. I also estimated unweighted versions of equation 2. The qualitative results are unchanged, but there are some differences in the magnitudes of a few of the coefficients. For example, the effects of median income and inequality are stronger in the unweighted models, as are the effects of broad-based categorical eligibility, fingerprinting, and simplified reporting. This has limited effect on the simulation results. Likewise I estimated models restricting attention to those heads with a high school diploma or less in a bid to focus on a population at ex ante greater risk of SNAP use. Again, none of the qualitative results change.

20. This is based on the author's calculations using total errors rates produced by the Food and Nutrition Service from SNAP Quality Control Data on the USDA website at www.fns.usda.gov/snap/qc/pdfs/2011-rates.pdf (June 6, 2012) and www.fns.usda.gov/snap/qc/pdfs/2000-rates.pdf.

REFERENCES

Autor, D. 2011. "The Unsustainable Rise of the Disability Rolls in the United States: Causes, Consequences, and Policy Options." Cambridge, MA: NBER Working Paper 17697.

Autor, D., L. Katz, and M. Kearney. 2008. "Trends in U.S. Wage Inequality: Revising the Revisionists." *Review of Economics and Statistics* 90: 300–323.

Bitler, M., and H. Hoynes. 2010. "The State of the Social Safety Net in the Post-Welfare Reform Era." *Brookings Papers on Economic Activity* 2: 71–127.

Bartlett, S., N. Burstein, and W. Hamilton. 2004. *Food Stamp Program Access Study: Final Report.* Report to the U.S. Department of Agriculture, Economic Research Service. Cambridge, MA: Abt Associates.

Blundell, R., and L. Pistaferri. 2003. "Income Volatility and Household Consumption: The Impact of Food Assistance Programs." *Journal of Human Resources* 38 (Supplement): 1032–1050.

Bollinger, C., and M. David (1997). "Modeling Discrete Choice with Response Error: Food Stamp Participation." *Journal of the American Statistical Association* 92(439): 827–835.

Burkhauser, R. V., S. Feng, S. P. Jenkins, and J. Larrimore. 2012. "Recent Trends in Top Income Shares in the USA: Reconciling Estimates from March CPS and IRS Tax Return Data." *Review of Economics and Statistics* 94(2): 371–388.

Burstein, N., S. Patrabansh, W. Hamilton, and S. Siegel. 2009. "Understanding the Determinants of Supplemental Nutrition Assistance Program Participation." Report submitted to U.S. Department of Agriculture, Food and Nutrition Service. Bethesda, MD: Abt Associates.

Cameron, A. C., J. Gelbach, and D. Miller. 2011. "Robust Inference with Multi-Way Clustering." *Journal of Business and Economic Statistics* 29(2): 238–249.

Cancian, M., and D. Reed. 2009. "Changes in Family Structure, Childbearing, and Employment: Implications for the Level and Trend in Poverty." In M. Cancian and S. Danziger, eds., *Changing Poverty, Changing Policies,* 92–121. New York: Russell Sage Foundation.

Carlson, M., and P. England. 2011. *Social Class and Changing Families in an Unequal America.* Palo Alto, CA: Stanford University Press.

Caswell, J., and A. Yaktine. 2013. *Supplemental Nutrition Assistance Program: Examining Evidence to Define Benefit Adequacy.* Washington, DC: The National Academies Press.

Congressional Budget Office (CBO). 2012. *The Supplemental Nutrition Assistance Program.* Publication 43173. Washington, DC: Author.

Cunnyngham, K. 2002. *Trends in Food Stamp Program Participation Rates: 1994–2000.* Report submitted to U.S. Department of Agriculture, Food and Nutrition Service. Washington, DC: Mathematica Policy Research.

Dickert-Conlin, S., K. Fitzpatrick, and L. Tiehen. 2011. "The Role of Advertising in the Growth of the SNAP Caseload." East Lansing: Michigan State University, Department of Economics Working Paper.

Figlio, D., C. Gundersen, and J. P. Ziliak. 2000. "The Effects of the Macroeconomy and Welfare Reform on Food Stamp Caseloads." *American Journal of Agricultural Economics* 82(3): 635–641.

Gabor, V., and C. Botsko. 1998. "State Food Stamp Policy Choices under Welfare Reform: Findings of 1997 50-State Survey." Report submitted to U.S. Department of Agriculture, Food and Nutrition Service. Washington, DC: Health Systems Research.

Ganong, P., and J. Liebman. 2013. "Explaining Trends in SNAP Enrollment." Mimeo. Cambridge, MA: Harvard University.

Gleason, P., C. Trippe, S. Cody, and J. Anderson. 2001. "The Effects of Welfare Reform on the Characteristics of the Food Stamp Population." Report submitted to U.S. Department of Agriculture, Food and Nutrition Service. Washington, DC: Mathematica Policy Research.

Gundersen, C., and J. P. Ziliak. 2003. "The Role of Food Stamps in Consumption Stabilization." *Journal of Human Resources* 38(Supplement): 1051–1079.

Hanratty, M. J. 2006. "Has the Food Stamp Program Become More Accessible? Impacts of Recent Changes in Reporting Requirements and Asset Eligibility Limits." *Journal of Policy Analysis and Management* 25(3): 603–621.

Hotz, V. J., and J. K. Scholz. 2003. "The Earned Income Tax Credit." In *Means-Tested Transfers in the U.S.*, R. Moffitt, ed., Chicago: University of Chicago Press.

Hulsey, L., K. Conway, A. Gothro, R. Kleinman, M. Reilly, S. Cody, and E. Sama-Miller. 2013. *The Evolution of SNAP Modernization Initiatives in Five States.* Report submitted to U.S. Department of Agriculture, Food and Nutrition Service. Washington, DC: Mathematica Policy Research.

Kabbani, N., and P. Wilde. 2003. "Short Recertification Periods in the U.S. Food Stamp Program." *Journal of Human Resources* 38(Supplement): 1112–1138.

Klerman, J., and C. Danielson. 2011. "The Transformation of the Supplemental Nutrition Assistance Program." *Journal of Policy Analysis and Management* 30(4): 863–888.

Landale, N., R. S. Oropesa, and C. Bradatan. 2006. "Hispanic Families in the United States: Family Structure and Process in an Era of Family Change." In M. Tienda and F. Mitchell, eds., *Hispanics and the Future of America.* Washington, DC: National Research Council.

Leftin, J., E. Eslami, and M. Strayer. 2011. *Trends in Supplemental Nutrition Assistance Program Participation Rates: Fiscal Year 2002 to Fiscal Year 2009.* Report submitted to U.S. Department of Agriculture, Food and Nutrition Service. Washington, DC: Mathematica Policy Research.

Mabli, J., and C. Ferrerosa. 2010. *Supplemental Nutrition Assistance Program Caseload Trends and Changes in Measures of Unemployment, Labor Underutilization, and Program Policy from 2000 to 2008.* Report submitted to U.S. Department of Agriculture, Food and Nutrition Service. Washington, DC: Mathematica Policy Research.

Meyer, B., and R. Goerge. 2011. "Errors in Survey Reporting and Imputation and Their Effects on Estimates of Food Stamp Program Participation." Washington, DC: U.S. Census Bureau, Center for Economic Studies, CES 11–14.

Meyer, B., and D. Rosenbaum. 2001. "Welfare, the Earned Income Tax Credit, and the Labor Supply of Single Mothers." *Quarterly Journal of Economics* 116(3): 1063–1114.

Muller, L. S., B. O'Hara, and J. Kearney. 2006. *Trends in the Social Security and Supplemental Security Income Disability Programs.* Washington, DC: Social Security Administration, Office of Research, Evaluation, and Statistics.

Mulligan, C. 2012. *The Redistribution Recession: How Labor Market Distortions Contracted the Economy.* Oxford, UK: Oxford University Press.

———. 2013. "Behind the Big Increase in Food Stamps." *New York Times Economix Blog,* August 29.

Nord, M., and M. Prell. 2011. *Food Security Improved Following the 2009 ARRA Increase in SNAP Benefits.* Economic Research Report ERR-116. Washington, DC: U.S. Department of Agriculture.

Piketty, T., and E., Saez. 2003. "Income Inequality in the United States, 1913–1998." *Quarterly Journal of Economics* 118: 1–39.

Ratcliffe, C., S-M. McKernan, and K. Finegold. 2007. "The Effect of State Food Stamps and TANF Policies on Food Stamp Program Participation." Washington, DC: The Urban Institute.

Rowe, G., S. Hall, C. O'Brien, N. Pindus, and R. Koralek. 2010. *Enhancing Supplemental Nutrition Assistance Program (SNAP) Certification: SNAP Modernization Efforts.* Report submitted to U.S. Department of Agriculture, Food and Nutrition Service. Washington, DC: The Urban Institute.

Secretaries' Innovation Group. 2013. *Reforming Food Stamps (SNAP).* Available at http://secretariesinnovationgroup.org/images/Reforming%20Food%20 Stamps%20SNAP.pdf.

Strayer, M., E. Eslami, and J. Leftin. 2012. *Characteristics of Supplemental Nutrition Assistance Program Households: Fiscal Year 2011.* Report submitted to U.S. Department of Agriculture, Food and Nutrition Service, SNAP-12-CHAR. Washington, DC: Mathematica Policy Research.

Wallace, G., and R. Blank. 1999. "What Goes Up Must Come Down? Explaining Recent Changes in Public Assistance Caseloads." In S. Danziger, ed., *Economic Conditions and Welfare Reform,* 48–89. Kalamazoo, MI: Upjohn Institute.

Wheaton, L. 2007. "Underreporting of Means-Tested Transfer Programs in the CPS and SIPP." *Proceedings of the American Statistical Association,* Social Statistics Section [CD-ROM], 3622–3629. Alexandria, VA: American Statistical Association.

Ziliak, J. P. 2009. *Welfare Reform and Its Long-Term Consequences for America's Poor.* Cambridge, UK: Cambridge University Press.

Ziliak, J. P., C. Gundersen, and D. Figlio. 2003. "Food Stamp Caseloads over the Business Cycle." *Southern Economic Journal* 69(4): 903–919.

CHAPTER TWO

The Effect of SNAP on Poverty

Laura Tiehen
Dean Jolliffe
Timothy M. Smeeding

On signing the Food Stamp Act of 1964, President Johnson noted that "as a permanent program, the food stamp plan will be one of our most valuable weapons for the war on poverty" (Johnson 1964). In the late 1960s and early 1970s, when the average monthly benefit was under $20, we did not record the effects of the Food Stamp Program on poverty. But the program was already having major positive impacts on mothers' health and then birth outcomes for poor people, especially for blacks, and then longer-run gains in health and school achievement (Almond, Hoynes, and Schanzenbach 2011; Hoynes, Schanzenbach, and Almond 2012).

Poverty is an important dimension of well-being, often accompanied by food insecurity, poor health, and reduced earnings potential. Growing up in poverty is especially detrimental, increasing children's chances of cognitive and behavioral problems and leading to adverse outcomes when they reach adulthood (Duncan and Brooks-Gunn 1997; Duncan et al. 1998; Duncan, Morris, and Rodrigues 2011). Society also bears a significant cost of childhood poverty, as a result of the diminished productivity of adults who grew up in poverty and the higher levels of public spending due to a greater likelihood of poor health and incarceration (Holzer et al. 2007).

The annual effects of SNAP on poverty itself were first estimated in the late 1970s and then regularly after the Census Bureau began to record recipients and amounts of food stamps in 1979 (for example, see U.S. Bureau of Census 1982). This chapter follows in that tradition and examines SNAP's effectiveness as an antipoverty weapon. We begin with a brief overview of the program. We then estimate the extent to which SNAP reduces the prevalence of poverty and also its depth and severity. Measures of the depth and severity of poverty capture how SNAP benefits increase income among the poor even if they do not lift them out of poverty, providing a more complete picture of how SNAP improves the well-being of poor families. Finally, we discuss the primary challenge to getting an accurate measure of SNAP's antipoverty effect and how the design of the program influences that effect.

IS SNAP TARGETED TO THE POOR?

As Ziliak notes in the previous chapter, SNAP eligibility is not limited to specific demographic groups based on family structure, age, or disability status, so benefits reach a broad range of disadvantaged households. For a three-person household in 2012, the maximum benefit is $526 per month. The SNAP benefit reduction rate is 30 percent, reflecting the expectation that a household can contribute 30 percent of its own income to its food budget. Under this progressive benefit structure, the poorest SNAP households receive the largest benefits.

Indeed, monthly administrative data from USDA show that SNAP benefits are targeted to the poorest of poor households. As shown in Table 2.1, households in deep poverty (with gross income below 50 percent of the poverty guidelines) received over half of SNAP benefits in 2011. SNAP eligi-

TABLE 2.1

Distribution of household and individual SNAP participation benefits across income and demographic groups, 2011

	Percent of SNAP households	Percent of SNAP benefits
HOUSEHOLD INCOME AS A PERCENT OF POVERTY GUIDELINES		
Below 50%	42.6	55.1
50–100%	40.7	36.3
101–130%	11.9	7.2
Above 130%	4.7	1.4
HOUSEHOLD STRUCTURE		
Children in household	47.1	69.2
Single-parent	26.3	37.1
Married head	9.0	15.5
Multiple adults or children only	11.7	16.6
No children in household	52.9	30.8
Elderly in household	16.5	8.5
Disabled nonelderly in household	20.2	15.8
HOUSEHOLD EMPLOYMENT AND PROGRAM PARTICIPATION		
Employed person in household	30.5	35.9
Receives TANF	7.6	—
Receives SSI	20.2	—
Receives Social Security	22.4	—
INDIVIDUAL CITIZENSHIP/ABAWD STATUS		
Legal noncitizen	4.0	4.0
Nondisabled adult in childless household	10.2	13.3

SOURCE: USDA, Food and Nutrition Service, SNAP Quality Control Data.

NOTE: ABAWD = Able-bodied adult without dependents. The poverty guidelines are a simplification of the official poverty thresholds used to determine eligibility for SNAP and other federal assistance programs.

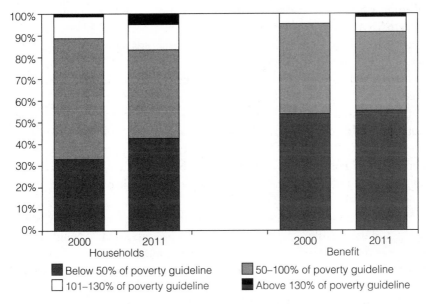

Figure 2.1. The distribution of SNAP benefits across the income distribution, 2000 and 2011.

NOTES: Income is defined as gross monthly income. The poverty guidelines are a simplification of the official poverty thresholds used to determine eligibility for SNAP and other federal assistance programs.

SOURCE: USDA, FNS, Quality Control Data.

bility extends to households with monthly gross income above the poverty line, but their benefit levels tend to be relatively low. Table 2.1 indicates that 16.6 percent of SNAP households had monthly gross income above the poverty guidelines, and these households received less than 9 percent of SNAP benefits.

Recently, concerns have been raised that changes in SNAP administration have resulted in the program being less targeted to the poor (Armor and Sousa 2012; Rector and Bradley 2012). We do find some evidence that a higher percentage of SNAP benefits were received by households above the poverty line in 2011 (8.6 percent) than in 2000 (4.3 percent), as shown in Figure 2.1. However, only a small percentage of total SNAP benefits (1.4 percent) in 2011 were received by households with monthly gross incomes above 130 percent of the poverty line.

It is important to note there are a number of measurement issues that must be considered when assessing the targeting efficiency of a program, such as the appropriate definitions of income and household. For example, the USDA Quality Control data records monthly, rather than annual, income, because monthly income is the basis for SNAP eligibility, which seems appropriate for a program designed to address the immediate needs of hunger and food insecurity. And because households are more likely to turn to SNAP during months of low income, we would expect to see a higher percentage of SNAP benefits received by households above the poverty line when income is measured on an annual basis.

Table 2.1 also illustrates the wide range of demographic groups that receive SNAP. Almost half of SNAP households contain children. Single-adult households make up about half of SNAP households with children, but households with a married head also participate. Married-head households make up 9 percent of all SNAP households and receive 15.5 percent of benefits. SNAP also serves elderly and disabled individuals. Roughly one in six SNAP households contains an elderly person, while one in five contains a nonelderly disabled person.

Although SNAP provides an important safety net for children, the elderly, and the disabled, the program has also become an increasingly important support to the working poor. In 2011, almost one-third of all SNAP households contained an adult who was working during the month of SNAP receipt, up from one-fifth of SNAP households in 1994 (Cody and Castner 1999). Rosenbaum (2013) uses the same USDA administrative data to focus on households with children that contain a nondisabled working-age adult and finds that the percentage who were working during the month of SNAP receipt increased from less than 30 percent in 1990 to over 50 percent in 2011. Using household survey data, Rosenbaum (2013) shows that over 80 percent of SNAP households with children that contain a nondisabled working-age adult have earnings during the year before or after SNAP receipt. In contrast, the percentage of SNAP households receiving cash benefits from the Temporary Assistance for Needy Families (TANF) program has declined dramatically since the 1996 welfare reform legislation, and in 2011 only 7.6 percent of SNAP households received income from TANF.

DOES SNAP REDUCE POVERTY?

In Chapter One, Ziliak finds that economic conditions are an important factor in explaining changes in SNAP participation, particularly after the Great Recession, when weak economic conditions accounted for almost half of the increase in SNAP participation from 2007 to 2011. The program functions as an automatic fiscal stabilizer, which contributes to its responsiveness in alleviating poverty during economic downturns. As shown in Figure 2.2, the SNAP caseload has been very responsive to changes in the number of poor Americans, consistent with the well-established countercyclical nature of the program (Ziliak, Gundersen, and Figlio 2003; Mabli, Martin, and Castner 2009). The extent to which SNAP reduces poverty is an important indica-

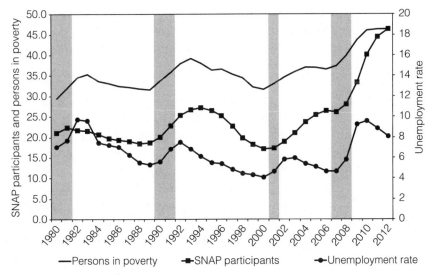

Figure 2.2.   SNAP participants, people in poverty, and the unemployment rate, 1980–2012.
SOURCES: USDA, FNS; U.S. Census Bureau; and U.S. Bureau of Labor Statistics.

tor of the program's effectiveness. In this section, we focus on SNAP's effect on the poverty rate. We build on previous research that has examined the effect of SNAP benefits, as well as other near-cash government benefits, on the poverty rate (Citro and Michael 1995; Iceland et al. 2001; Blank 2008; Garner and Short 2010; Ziliak 2011; Tiehen, Jolliffe, and Gundersen 2012). We first estimate SNAP's effect on the official poverty rate, which allows us to examine the program's antipoverty effect over a twenty-four-year period. Although one can argue that adding refundable tax credits and other types of benefits to family income is not consistent with the official poverty measure threshold, adding SNAP benefits gets right to the heart of the official threshold, which is based on income multiples of a food budget.

We then estimate SNAP's effect on the research Supplemental Poverty Measure (SPM). The SPM, which serves as a complement to the official poverty measure, was developed to provide a more comprehensive view of family well-being. It adjusts family income for taxes paid, in-kind benefits received, and refundable tax credits and constructs a poverty line based on actual consumption of food, clothing, and shelter, adjusted for regional differences in the cost of living (Short 2011). The Census Bureau released the first report on the SPM in November 2011, covering the 2010 calendar year, and provides data to calculate the SPM from 2009 to 2011. We provide more details on the official and SPM poverty measures in the following sections.

Current Population Survey Data

To measure the effect of SNAP on poverty, we use data from the Annual Social and Economic Supplement (ASEC) to the Current Population Survey (CPS). In our primary analysis, we use twenty-four years of CPS-ASEC data, which provide us with estimates of poverty and SNAP benefit levels from 1988 to 2011. The CPS is administered monthly by the Census Bureau for the Bureau of Labor Statistics and collects data from a nationally representative sample of households on employment, unemployment, earnings, occupation, and hours of work. Respondents to the CPS provide information on several different sources of income, including noncash income sources such as SNAP.

We use the CPS because it is the data source for official U.S. poverty estimation and for the Research Supplemental Poverty Measure (SPM). A shortcoming of the CPS is that, as documented by Meyer, Mok, and Sullivan (2009), it underestimates the number of SNAP recipients and the value of SNAP benefits. We find that, in 2011, the reported average monthly individual participation in the CPS is 69.7 percent of the average monthly individual participation in SNAP administrative data, and the reported total benefits in the CPS are 53.4 percent of administrative totals. We consider the implications of correcting for this measurement issue in our discussion of the results.

Official Poverty

The official U.S. poverty measure is based on a comparison of a family's income relative to its estimated needs. The income measure includes all pretax income, such as earnings, unemployment compensation, and Social Security payments. It also includes cash benefits from means-tested transfer programs such as Supplemental Security Income (SSI) and TANF. The measure does not include unrealized capital gains, and because it is a pretax measure it does not include payroll taxes or income taxes paid or Child Tax Credit (CTC) or Earned Income Tax Credit (EITC) payments. The family income measure also does not include any noncash benefits such as SNAP benefits, housing assistance, or Medicaid. The family income measure includes income of all family members in a household but excludes income of nonrelatives, such as unmarried cohabitors. The poverty threshold defines a family's needs and is estimated following a cost-of-basic-needs methodology. The U.S federal poverty thresholds vary for persons of different ages and families of different sizes. In 2012, for example, the poverty threshold was set at $11,945 for an individual under sixty-five years of age, $15,825 for a two-person family with one child and one adult, and $23,283 for a family with two adults and two children.[1] If family income is less than the poverty threshold, then all members of the family are considered poor.

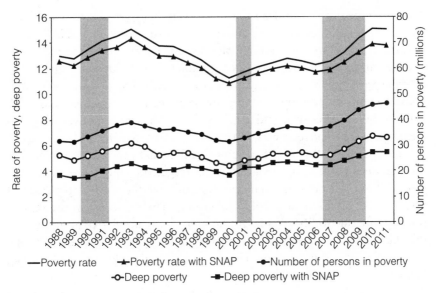

Figure 2.3. The effect of SNAP benefits on official U.S. Poverty, 1988–2011.
SOURCE: Authors' calculations using Current Population Survey (CPS) data.

Because SNAP benefits are not included in the family income measure for official U.S. poverty estimation, the program's role in reducing poverty is not reflected in official poverty statistics. To understand the effect of SNAP on poverty, we examine how supplementing income with SNAP benefits affects the official poverty rate. Figure 2.3 displays the official poverty rate from 1988 through 2011, as well as the poverty rate if SNAP benefits are included in family income.

It is clear from Figure 2.3 that the antipoverty effect of SNAP is stronger when poverty rates increase during difficult economic conditions (shaded gray), consistent with the countercyclical nature of the program. Figure 2.3 also shows an increase in the antipoverty effect of SNAP after the onset of the Great Recession and particularly during the period since 2009, when the American Recovery and Reinvestment Act (ARRA) had increased SNAP benefits and removed eligibility restrictions on jobless adults. For example, in 2011, the official poverty rate was 15.0 percent, whereas accounting for SNAP benefits in family income reduced the poverty rate to 13.8 percent. This 8 percent reduction in the poverty rate means that SNAP lifted approximately 3.9 million people out of poverty in 2011.

SNAP benefits have an even stronger effect on those in deep poverty, whose family incomes are below 50 percent of the poverty line. In 2011, 20.4 million Americans (6.6 percent of the population) lived in deep poverty. SNAP reduced the rate of deep poverty in 2011 by 16.6 percent, lifting

3.4 million people out of deep poverty. Given that over half of SNAP benefits go to households in deep poverty, it is not surprising that SNAP's antipoverty effect is stronger among this group. Recent research finds even stronger antipoverty effects of SNAP among households with children in extreme poverty, whose cash income does not exceed $2 per person per day. SNAP benefits reduced the rate of extreme poverty among households with children by 48 percent in mid-2011, helping to curtail otherwise large increases in extreme poverty between 1996 and 2011 (Shaefer and Edin 2013).

Although SNAP's benefit structure ensures that benefits are targeted to those in deep poverty, the program is not targeted to specific demographic groups. Table 2.2 provides some evidence on how the antipoverty effect of SNAP varies across demographic subgroups. The reduction in the official poverty rate due to SNAP is largest among children, relative to adults and the elderly. SNAP benefits reduce poverty more among blacks than among other racial and ethnic groups. The poverty reduction due to SNAP among Hispanics (7.0 percent) was somewhat lower than the national average in 2011, although the official poverty rate among Hispanics is similar to the

TABLE 2.2

The antipoverty effect of SNAP on individuals, by demographic groups, 2011

	Official poverty rate	Rate if SNAP included as income	Percent difference
AGE			
Under 18	21.9	19.7	9.9
18–64	13.7	12.8	6.7
65 and older	8.7	8.0	8.8
RACE/ETHNICITY			
Non-Hispanic white	9.8	9.1	7.9
Black	27.6	25.2	8.8
Hispanic	25.3	23.6	7.0
Asian	12.3	11.5	6.3
Other	21.8	19.5	10.6
CITIZENSHIP STATUS			
Citizen	14.3	13.1	8.5
Noncitizen	24.3	23.3	4.3
EMPLOYMENT STATUS			
Employed	6.7	6.1	7.8
Unemployed	26.8	25.0	6.7
HOUSEHOLD STRUCTURE			
Two-parent family	7.4	6.7	10.2
Single-parent family	26.9	25.0	7.0

SOURCE: Authors' calculations using CPS data.

rate among blacks. This may be partially a result of the legal noncitizen eligibility restrictions in SNAP, as Table 2.2 also shows that SNAP has a much smaller effect on the poverty rate of noncitizens than of citizens. Interestingly, SNAP has a stronger effect on the poverty rate of employed adults than on unemployed adults. Although we saw in Table 2.1 that employed adults make up a relatively small proportion of SNAP participants, they are more likely to have income close to the poverty line than other participants and therefore are more likely to be lifted over the poverty line by their SNAP benefits. Thus, the program is operating as an important support to the working poor. SNAP also has a strong effect on the poverty rate of individuals in two-parent families, relative to those in single-parent families. Although there is variation in the antipoverty effect of SNAP across demographic subgroups, the overall finding from Table 2.2 is that the program reduces poverty among a broad range of disadvantaged populations.

The Supplemental Poverty Measure

Official U.S. poverty estimates do not account for SNAP and other in-kind benefits in family income. In 1995, Congress asked the National Academies to address this and other shortcomings of the official poverty measure. The National Academies panel recommended that the poverty thresholds be based on a typical low-income family with children's expenditures for food, clothing, shelter, and a "small amount for other needs" for things like personal items and household supplies (Citro and Michael 1995). It also recommended using a disposable income concept to measure family resources. Such a measure would more accurately reflect the income available to a family by adding the value of in-kind benefits and any tax credits to cash income and subtracting taxes owed and other necessary expenses, such as work-related child care and transportation and medical out-of-pocket expenses. The SPM is largely based on recommendations of the 1995 National Academies panel, with some modifications based on research and data developed since then.

The earliest available Census Bureau data allow for the calculation of the SPM beginning in 2009. We estimate the effect of SNAP on poverty from 2009 to 2011 using the SPM, and the results are shown in Figure 2.4. Under the SPM, 16.1 percent of Americans were considered to be poor in 2011, compared with the official poverty rate of 15.2 percent. If SNAP benefits were excluded from income, the SPM poverty rate would have been 17.6 percent. The difference in SPM poverty rates due to SNAP alone is almost 10 percent or 4.6 million fewer poor people (Short 2012). Only two other government transfers—Social Security benefits and refundable tax credits (the EITC and the refundable portion of the CTC) had larger antipoverty effects

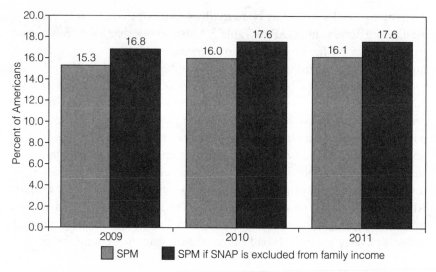

Figure 2.4. Effect of SNAP on the Research Supplemental Poverty Measure, 2009–2011.

SOURCE: Authors' calculations using CPS data.

than SNAP in 2011 (Short 2012). TANF benefits made little difference in overall SPM poverty in 2011 (Short 2012), which is not surprising given the long-term declines in program expenditures since welfare reform. However, other research has shown significant poverty-reducing effects among single-parent families of combined SNAP, EITC, and TANF benefits, along with housing assistance (Ben-Shalom, Moffitt, and Scholz 2012). The antipoverty effect of SNAP using the improved SPM measure is somewhat larger than the effect of SNAP using the official poverty measure and further validates the importance of accounting for SNAP's role in reducing poverty.

IS SNAP MORE EFFECTIVE AT REDUCING THE DEPTH AND SEVERITY OF POVERTY THAN THE PREVALENCE OF POVERTY?

The SPM represents a major advance in the measurement of U.S. poverty and the role of government assistance in reducing poverty. However, even when in-kind benefits are included as income in poverty estimates, a simple poverty rate—how many people are living below the poverty threshold—may not show how hardship is reduced by government programs with progressive benefit structures, such as SNAP. Recent studies have paid greater attention to how government transfers have decreased the aggregate poverty gap, or the sum of the differences between the poverty line and the incomes of the poor (Ziliak 2005, 2008; Scholz, Moffitt, and Cowan 2009), and others have examined trends in the distribution of government transfers to different income classes and demographic groups among the poor (Ziliak 2008; Moffitt and Scholz 2010; Ben-Shalom, Moffitt, and Scholz 2012).

To get a broader understanding of the effect of SNAP on poverty, we examine how supplementing income with SNAP benefits affects the poverty gap and squared poverty gap indices. These measures are from the Foster-Greer-Thorbecke (1984, hereafter referred to as FGT) family of poverty indices. The poverty gap index measures the depth of poverty and is defined by the mean distance below the poverty threshold, where the mean is formed over the entire population (the nonpoor are counted as having zero poverty gap). The second measure is the squared poverty gap index, which provides a measure of the severity of poverty, and is defined as the mean of the squared proportionate poverty gaps.

The FGT class of poverty indices also referred to as P_α, can be represented as:

$$P_\alpha = 1/n \sum_i I(y_i < z) \ [(z - y_i)/z]^\alpha \tag{1}$$

where n is the population, i subscripts the individual or family, y is income, z is the poverty threshold, and I is an indicator function, which takes the value of one if the statement is true and zero otherwise. When $\alpha = 0$, the resulting measure is the proportion of people in poverty, or P_0. When $\alpha = 1$, the FGT index results in the poverty gap index, or P_1 and the squared poverty gap index (P_2) results when $\alpha = 2$.

The usefulness of these measures can be illustrated by considering a transfer of money from a rich person to a poor person that is not large enough to move the poor person above the poverty threshold. This transfer has no effect on the poverty rate, but the poor person is better off, and this welfare improvement is reflected in a reduction of both the poverty gap and squared poverty gap indices. As another example, a transfer of income from a poor person to a poorer person will not alter either the headcount or the poverty gap index, but it improves the distribution of income of the poor, and this change is reflected by a reduction of the squared poverty gap index.[2]

The difference between the poverty-gap index and the squared-poverty-gap index can be illustrated by considering two possible transfers of equal amounts from a nonpoor person. The first is a transfer to a poor person whose income is equal to 50 percent of the poverty threshold, and the second is a transfer to a poor person with higher income, equal to 75 percent of the poverty threshold. Again, the transfers are not enough to lift either person above the poverty threshold, and therefore neither transfer will reduce the poverty rate. Because the transfers are of equal amounts, they will each reduce the poverty-gap index by the same amount. However, the squared poverty gap will be reduced more by the first transfer, which is received by a relatively poorer person, than by the second transfer. In general, the lower the income of the poor person who receives a transfer from a nonpoor person, the greater will be the effect on the squared-poverty-gap index.

These examples point to an important reason to consider the poverty gap and squared poverty gap indices in addition to the commonly reported poverty rate. As discussed in the preceding paragraphs, SNAP benefits are inversely related to net income; as a consequence, adding benefits to income will raise only a small subset of recipients above the poverty threshold. However, the progressive benefit delivery design will be relatively more effective at reducing the depth and severity of poverty than at reducing the prevalence of poverty.

To examine the efficacy of SNAP benefits in reducing poverty one needs both measures of poverty and measures of their sampling variance to know if changes in poverty are statistically significant or simply an artifact of the sampling procedure. We estimate the variance of P_α using an estimation technique that accounts for the fact that the CPS data are not derived from a simple random sample.[3]

Our next step is to examine the impact of SNAP on poverty, by adding SNAP benefits to family income, as in:

$$P'_\alpha = 1/n \sum_i I(\{y_i + fsb_i\} < z) \ [(z - \{y_i + fsb_i\})/z]^\alpha \qquad (2)$$

where fsb_i is the value of SNAP benefits for family i and all other terms are defined as in equation 1.

For this analysis, we again focus on the official poverty measure, which allows us to examine a longer time period than is feasible with the SPM. The percentage declines in the rate, depth, and severity of official poverty from including SNAP benefits are calculated as $[(P_\alpha - P'_\alpha) / P_\alpha] * 100$. The percentage declines from 1988 to 2011 are displayed in Figure 2.5. The figure shows that the reduction in the poverty rate fails to capture much of the poverty alleviation properties of SNAP benefits. The reductions to both the depth and severity indices due to SNAP benefits were much larger than the reductions to the poverty rate. For example, from 2000 to 2011, supplementing income by the value of SNAP benefits had the effect of reducing the poverty gap index by an average of 11.0 percent and reducing the squared poverty gap index by an average of 14.0 percent. These poverty reductions are much greater than when just considering the change in the poverty rate, which was reduced by the inclusion of SNAP benefits by an average of 4.9 percent during the 2000 to 2011 period.

Although there are not comparable estimates of the effect of other safety-net programs on the poverty gap and squared poverty gap indices, our results are consistent with other research that finds that the recent

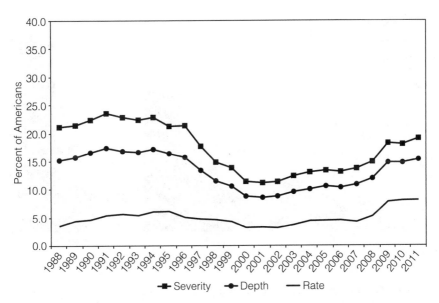

Figure 2.5.   Percent reduction in official poverty due to SNAP, 1988–2011.
SOURCE: Authors' calculations using CPS data.

expansions of SNAP and Unemployment Insurance (UI) during the Great Recession benefited those at the bottom of the income distribution, while EITC benefits are more targeted to households just below and just above the poverty line (for an in-depth discussion of the EITC and other program participation, see Chapter Eight, by Robert Moffitt).

Although SNAP's effect on the depth and severity of poverty is much stronger than its effect on the poverty rate, the changes over time are similar, showing the protective effect of the program during economic downturns. It is somewhat surprising to see, however, that the percentage declines in the depth and severity of poverty are somewhat lower in 2011 than in 1994, even though the 2011 SNAP caseload is nearly double the caseload in 1994. One explanation for this is the decline in the reporting rates of SNAP benefits over time, as documented by Meyer, Mok, and Sullivan (2009), which finds that the reporting rate of SNAP benefits in the CPS declined from 72.1 percent of administrative totals in 1988 to 53.9 percent in 2007.

SNAP's effect on children is especially important, given that children experience higher rates of poverty than the overall population; the poverty depth and severity indices are also higher for children than for the overall population (Tiehen, Jolliffe, and Gundersen 2012). Figure 2.6 compares the average annual reductions in poverty due to SNAP among children, adults, and the elderly from 2000 to 2011. The evidence that SNAP is more effective

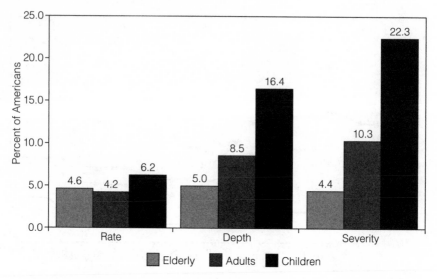

Figure 2.6. Average annual percent decline in official poverty due to SNAP, by age, 2000–2011.

 SOURCE: Authors' calculations using CPS data.

at reducing the depth and severity of poverty than the prevalence of poverty is even stronger when we consider poor children. From 2000 to 2011, for example, SNAP reduced the child poverty rate by an average of 6.2 percent while reducing the depth index by 16.4 percent and the severity index by 22.3 percent. The percent declines in poverty are the smallest among the elderly, and the annual declines are not statistically significant in most years. In contrast with the results for the overall population, SNAP's effect on the depth and severity of elderly poverty are not greater than its effect on the rate of elderly poverty. This likely reflects the fact that SNAP take-up is lower among the elderly than among children and that the severity of poverty, before accounting for SNAP benefits, is lower among the elderly than among children.

HOW DOES THE DESIGN OF SNAP INFLUENCE ITS ANTIPOVERTY EFFECT?

We consider two features of the design of SNAP that have been subject to policy debate and that would be expected to influence the antipoverty effect of the program. The first feature is that the SNAP maximum benefit level is uniform across the continental United States (although it is higher in Alaska and Hawaii). The SNAP maximum benefit level is intended to cover the cost of a nutritionally adequate diet for a given household size. It is difficult to justify a uniform maximum SNAP allotment, given the growing body of evidence of substantial variation in food prices across regions and between urban and rural areas (Leibtag 2007; Leibtag and Kumcu 2011; Todd, Leibtag, and Penberthy 2011; Gregory and Coleman-Jensen 2011). A recent Institute of Medicine (IOM) panel examined the adequacy of SNAP benefits and recommended that the USDA examine possible approaches to account for food price variation (Caswell and Yaktine 2013). If maximum benefit levels were increased in areas with higher than average food costs, the antipoverty effect of SNAP would be expected to increase in those areas. However, the IOM report notes the difficulty in implementing such an adjustment to the maximum benefit level, given the lack of regional price variation indices (Caswell and Yaktine 2013).

A second feature likely to influence SNAP's antipoverty effect is the increased flexibility given to states in how they administer the program. As noted previously, many states have removed the federal liquid asset test and increased the gross income limit, through a policy option referred to as broad-based categorical eligibility. In another effort to increase program access, states have increased recertification periods—the number of months that could elapse before a SNAP household had to recertify eligibility. Increasing certification periods reduces the transaction costs of participation, particularly for working households who may need to take off from work to complete the recertification process.[4] The increase in certification periods began in the early 2000s, after a decade in which many states decreased certification periods to avoid federally administered penalties for benefit calculation errors (Rosenbaum 2000).

The changes that states have adopted in their administration of SNAP may contribute to state-level differences in the program's antipoverty effect. Recent research documents substantial variation in the antipoverty effect of SNAP across states (Tiehen, Jolliffe, and Gundersen 2013) and even within states (Wimer et al. 2013). As shown in Maps 2.1 and 2.2, adding SNAP benefits to family income reduced the poverty rate by an annual average of 4.4 percent from 2000 to 2009 and reduced the squared poverty gap index by 13.2 percent. In that time period, the average annual reductions in the state-level poverty rate due to SNAP benefits ranged from 2.5 percent in Florida to 9.3 percent in Hawaii. Likewise, the average annual reductions in the squared poverty gap index due to SNAP varied at the state-level from an annual average of 7.1 percent in Nevada to 19.5 percent in Kentucky.

There are a number of other factors that are likely to influence the antipoverty effect of SNAP, including state economic conditions and other state policies affecting low-income populations. Tiehen, Jolliffe, and Gundersen (2013) find that the following three state policies led to significant increases in the program's efficacy in reducing the poverty rate: (1) exempting vehicles

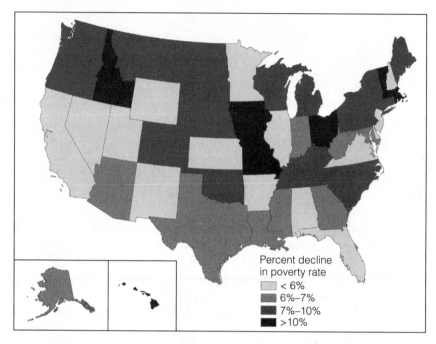

Map 2.1.   Percent decline in official state poverty rate due to SNAP, annual
average, 2000–2009.

N O T E : State poverty rates are calculated as three-year averages.

S O U R C E : Authors' calculations using CPS data.

from the asset test, (2) applying broad-based categorical eligibility to remove
the asset test and/or increase the gross income limits, and (3) extending
recertification periods for earners. These findings provide some evidence
on how the increased access to SNAP in many states has increased the program's ability to reduce poverty. However, the study found little evidence
that recent SNAP policies to increase program access have influenced the
program's efficacy in reducing the severity of poverty. This is perhaps not
surprising, given that most of the recent state policy options were aimed
at increasing participation among the working poor. The poverty severity
index is most sensitive to changes in income among the poorest of the poor,
who are less likely to have their SNAP participation constrained by the asset
test or short recertification periods.

CHALLENGES TO ESTIMATING AN ACCURATE MEASURE OF SNAP'S ANTIPOVERTY EFFECT

In this section, we consider three primary challenges to estimating an accurate measure of SNAP's antipoverty effect. The first challenge is in as-

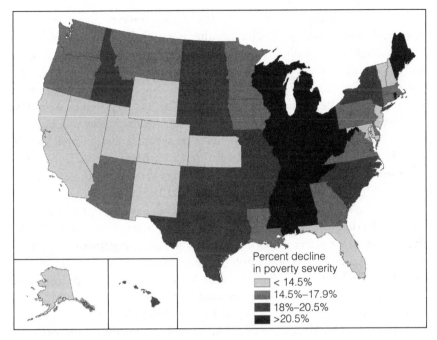

Map 2.2. Percent decline in official state poverty severity due to SNAP, annual average, 2000–2009.

NOTE: State poverty rates are calculated as three-year averages.

SOURCE: Authors' calculations using CPS data.

sessing the value of an in-kind transfer. By supplementing family income with the dollar value of SNAP benefits, our analysis assumes that a household's SNAP benefits are equivalent to cash. Economic theory implies that the value of the in-kind SNAP benefit may be less than its cash value for households whose preferred monthly food budget is less than their SNAP benefit. The consumption of these households is constrained by their receipt of an in-kind benefit, which distorts their spending toward more than the preferred amount of food and less than their preferred amount of other goods. For example, a person living alone with no income would be entitled to a SNAP benefit of $200 per month in 2014. If that person's optimal food budget is $150 per month, she might prefer to have a cash benefit that would allow her to spend $150 on food and $50 on other necessities, and therefore the $200 SNAP benefit would be worth less than $200 to her. However, the predominant judgment of those who have researched this question is that benefits should be equivalent to cash because most SNAP households spend more on food than their SNAP benefit (Smeeding 1977; U.S. Bureau of the Census 1982; Moffitt 1989; Levedahl 1995; Breunig and Dasgupta 2005; Hoynes and Schanzenbach 2009).

The second challenge to measuring SNAP's antipoverty effect is accounting for the work disincentive effects of the program. If the receipt of SNAP benefits leads an individual to work fewer hours, then her earned income will be lower than it would have been in the absence of SNAP, and we would overstate the effect of SNAP on total family income. The benefit reduction rate in SNAP can be considered an implicit tax on earnings, which would be expected to reduce labor supply. Most research suggests, however, that the labor supply response to SNAP benefits is quite small (Fraker and Moffitt 1988; Hagstrom 1996; Keane and Moffitt 1998; Moffitt 2013), though a recent study does find larger effects on single mothers during the early years of the program (Hoynes and Schanzenbach 2012).

However, the labor supply effect also depends on other programs with benefit reduction rates that also reduce work and other programs with benefit structures that increase work effort. For instance, negative work incentive effects could well be offset in more recent years by the joint receipt of the EITC, which encourages work effort for low-wage single parents to a much greater extent than it is discouraged by SNAP.

Finally, the most serious challenge to measuring SNAP's antipoverty effect may be the underreporting of SNAP benefits in household surveys such as the CPS, which results in an underestimate of SNAP's antipoverty effect. A household may fail to report its SNAP participation for a variety of reasons, including a feeling of stigma about program receipt or an inability to recall participation in the past twelve months (the time frame for reporting in the CPS), especially if participation is sporadic. The decline over time in SNAP benefit reporting rates in the CPS means that the underestimate of SNAP's antipoverty effect has also become more severe over time. As we noted previously, almost half of aggregate SNAP benefits are not reported in the CPS. To illustrate the extent to which underreporting influences our estimates of the antipoverty effect of SNAP, we employ a correction that uses 2011 aggregate USDA administrative data on recipients and benefits. We use a weighting procedure to match the number of poor SNAP recipients in the CPS to the number in the administrative data. We then scale up SNAP benefits in the CPS households to match the aggregate benefits to poor recipients reported in the administrative data. In scaling up benefits, we split poor SNAP recipients into those in deep poverty and those whose incomes are between 51 and 100 percent of the poverty line and match each category to administrative totals. The results of this correction approach applied to the 2011 data, displayed in Figure 2.7, are quite striking. The antipoverty effect of SNAP is at least doubled for each of the three poverty measures. These effects are similar to the ones found in other data that adjust for underreporting, nationally (Wheaton et al. 2012), and in the state of Wisconsin (Chung et al. 2013), and in the state of California (Wimer et al. 2013). Underreporting of ben-

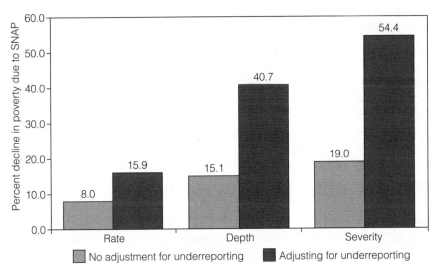

Figure 2.7. Percent decline in official poverty due to SNAP with correction for underreporting, 2011.

SOURCE: Authors' calculations using CPS and USDA SNAP Quality Control data.

efits has the greatest effect on the severity index, where SNAP's antipoverty effect is almost three times larger when we correct for underreporting. This is consistent with evidence that the proportion of total benefits received by participants in deep poverty was much greater in SNAP administrative data than in the CPS (Tiehen, Jolliffe, and Gundersen 2012). Moreover, although recent reports from the Census Bureau (Short 2012; DeNavas-Walt, Proctor, and Smith 2013) suggest that the EITC has a larger antipoverty effect than SNAP, with these adjustments, SNAP surpasses the EITC as the nation's most effective antipoverty program for the nonelderly.[5]

SUMMARY AND CONCLUSION

This chapter has systematically reviewed the work on the antipoverty effect of SNAP using administrative and survey data. SNAP is designed to meet one of our most important needs, ensuring that all eligible people have enough to eat. People who use SNAP to feed their families—on a benefit of about $30 per person per week—work hard to stretch their food budgets and avoid hunger, and, even if close to cash in terms of recipient value, SNAP helps meet these needs.

The program also has an important effect on poverty, even if our national statistics do not always capture all of SNAP's antipoverty effects. The antipoverty effects are even larger than those found in Census Bureau estimates if one adjusts for underreporting. Using reweighting methods to benchmark the CPS to administrative data, the antipoverty effects are then almost again as large as without them. With underreporting adjustments, and depending on the poverty measure being considered, SNAP reduces poverty by 14 to 16 percent. And we conclude that SNAP is our nation's most effective antipoverty program for the nonelderly when adjusted for underreporting, one that is especially good at reducing extreme poverty—by over 50 percent—and also especially effective for poor families with children.

In summary, the SNAP program currently costs one half of one percent (0.5 percent) of GDP (Moffitt 2013). For that amount we get a 16 percent reduction in poverty (8 million fewer poor people) after an adjustment for underreporting based on USDA administrative data. Moreover, we get a 41 percent cut in the poverty gap, which measures the depth of poverty, and a 54 percent decline in the severity of poverty, when we add SNAP benefits to Census money incomes and recalculate the official poverty rate. No other program for the nonelderly does such a great job preventing poverty or alleviating poverty's weight on those who remain poor. We should be heralding and celebrating this success, not trying to reduce the program on the assertion that it goes to those who don't need it.

Does the program go to those who need it? In terms of monthly program rules, USDA administrative data suggest that either by counting beneficiaries or benefits, the program does an excellent job in targeting the poor (below 100 percent poverty) and the near-poor (up to 130 percent poverty). Using annual data, benefits might spill over by about 30 percent beyond the target (Chung et al. 2013), but the program is not administered annually and cannot be judged by the arbitrary time period of one year alone. In our view, SNAP is highly target effective according to its own rules and regulations.

There is much more one can learn about SNAP to make it work even better. For instance, why do we find such large state and regional differences in benefit receipt and antipoverty effect? Can it be explained by administrative discretion, where in some states online applications and telephone interviews help ease the burden of application, whereas in others, fingerprinting of applicants and time-consuming verification processes are required? And these issues extend to within-state consideration. In California alone, Wimer and colleagues (2013, p. 9 and Figure 6) use a Program Access Index (PAI), calculated by the California Food Policy Advocates, to approximate the percentage of eligible SNAP participants who actually participate in the program in their county. They find that the antipoverty effects of SNAP are almost three times higher in high-PAI counties than in low-PAI counties. Hence program delivery and approach to eligibility also matter at the county level. Other differences in values of benefits received, seasonality, and temporality might also be explored. Further analysis of spells of receipt of SNAP using longitudinal data can tell us if participation and changes in participation are concentrated on the cyclically (temporarily) poor or on the chronic (longer-term) poor.

But, at the end of the day, one is left with the impression that SNAP is a well-administered important part of our antipoverty armor that needs protecting, not rebuking. Realistically, SNAP conforms to many of the key demands conservatives and liberals have for safety net programs, such as engaging the private sector by authorizing over 230,000 retailers in which to redeem benefits and allowing participants a high degree of choice in the food they buy. In addition, the program is available to most poor persons without categorical eligibility restrictions and is increasingly accessible to the working poor. And in the end the Agricultural Act of 2014 exempted SNAP from congressional proposals discussed at the time of the September 2013 Five Decades of Food Stamps Conference that would have cut almost 4 million people from the program. We agree that this is good public policy for a true universal safety net program.

NOTES

The views and opinions expressed here are those of the authors and do not necessarily reflect the views of the Economic Research Service, USDA, the World Bank, or the Institute for Research on Poverty. We thank Jim Ziliak, Craig Gundersen, Judi Bartfeld, and especially Isabel Sawhill for comments on an earlier draft of this paper, as well as an anonymous reviewer. We thank them all; the authors, however, retain all ownership of errors of commission or omission.

1. For a complete listing of the poverty thresholds for individuals and families of various sizes, see the U.S. Census Bureau's web page on poverty at www.census .gov/hhes/www/poverty.html/.

2. Unlike the Sen (1976) or Kakwani (1980) poverty indices, the squared poverty gap index also satisfies "subgroup consistency," which means that if poverty increases in any subgroup, and does not decrease elsewhere, then aggregate poverty must increase (Foster and Shorrocks 1991).

3. See Tiehen, Jolliffe, and Gundersen (2012) for details.

4. The federal government requires that states recertify the eligibility status of participants at least once a year, except for households in which all members are elderly or disabled, which can be certified for more than one year.

5. The EITC benefit is also simulated to have a 100 percent take-up rate and therefore may slightly overestimate its effects (DeNavas-Walt, Proctor, and Smith 2013).

REFERENCES

Almond, D., H. Hoynes, and D. Schanzenbach. 2011. "Inside the War on Poverty: The Impact of Food Stamps on Birth Outcomes." *Review of Economics and Statistics May* 93(2): 387–403.

Armor, D. J., and S. Sousa. 2012. "Restoring a True Safety Net." *National Affairs* 13(Fall): 3–28.

Ben-Shalom, Y., R. Moffitt, and J. K. Scholz. 2012. "An Assessment of the Effectiveness of Anti-Poverty Programs in the United States." In P. N. Jefferson, ed., *The Oxford Handbook of the Economics of Poverty*, 709–749. New York: Oxford University Press.

Blank, R. 2008. "How to Improve Poverty Measurement in the United States." *Journal of Policy Analysis and Management* 27(2): 233–254.

Breunig, R., and I. Dasgupta. 2005. "Do Intra-Household Effects Generate the Food Stamp Cash-Out Puzzle?" *American Journal of Agricultural Economics* 87(3): 552–568.

Caswell, J. A., and A. L. Yaktine, eds. 2013. *Supplemental Nutrition Assistance Program: Examining the Evidence to Define Benefit Adequacy*. Washington, DC: National Academies Press.

Chung, Y., J. B. Isaacs, T. M. Smeeding, and K. A. Thornton. 2013 (June). *Wisconsin Poverty Report: Is the Safety Net Still Protecting Families from Poverty in 2011?* Madison: Institute for Research on Poverty, University of Wisconsin.

Citro, C. F., and R. T. Michael (eds.). 1995. *Measuring Poverty: A New Approach.* Washington, DC: National Academies Press.

Cody, S., and L. Castner. 1999. "Characteristics of Food Stamp Households: Fiscal Year 1997." Alexandria, VA: U.S. Department of Agriculture, Food and Nutrition Service.

DeNavas-Walt, C., B. D. Proctor, and C. J. Smith. 2013. *Income, Poverty, and Health Insurance Coverage in the United States: 2012.* U.S. Census Bureau, Current Population Reports, P60-245. Washington, DC: U.S. Government Printing Office.

Duncan, G. J., and J. Brooks-Gunn (eds.). 1997. *Consequences of Growing Up Poor.* New York: Russell Sage.

Duncan G. J., P. A. Morris, and C. Rodrigues. 2011. "Does Money Really Matter? Estimating Impacts of Family Income on Young Children's Achievement with Data from Random-Assignment Experiments." *Developmental Psychology* 47(5): 1263–1279.

Duncan, G. J., W. J. Yeung, J. Brooks-Gunn, and J. Smith. 1998. "How Much Does Childhood Poverty Affect the Life Chances of Children?" *American Sociological Review* 63(3): 406–423.

Foster, J., J. Greer, and E. Thorbecke. 1984. "A Class of Decomposable Poverty Measures." *Econometrica* 52: 761–765.

Foster, J., and A. Shorrocks. 1991. "Subgroup Consistent Poverty Indices." *Econometrica* 59: 687–709.

Fraker, T., and R. Moffitt. 1988. "The Effect of Food Stamps on Labor Supply: A Bivariate Selection Model," *Journal of Public Economics* 35(l): 25–56.

Garner, T. I., and K. Short. 2010. "Identifying the Poor: Poverty Measurement for the U.S. from 1996 to 2005." *Review of Income and Wealth* 56(2): 237–258.

Gregory, C., and A. Coleman-Jensen. 2011. "Do Food Prices Affect Food Security? Evidence form the CPS 2002–2006." Presented at the 2011 Agricultural and Applied Economics Association Annual Meeting, Pittsburgh, PA.

Hagstrom, Paul. 1996. "The Food Stamp Participation and Labor Supply of Married Couples: An Empirical Analysis of Joint Decisions." *Journal of Human Resources* 31(2): 383–403.

Holzer, H. J., D. Whitmore Schanzenbach, G. J. Duncan, and J. Ludwig. 2007. *The Economic Costs of Poverty in the United States: Subsequent Effects of Children Growing Up Poor.* Washington, DC: Center for American Progress.

Hoynes, H. W., and D. W. Schanzenbach. 2009. "Consumption Responses to In-Kind Transfers: Evidence from the Introduction of the Food Stamp Program." *American Economic Journal: Applied Economics* 1(4): 109–139.

———. 2012. "Work Incentives and the Food Stamp Program." *Journal of Public Economics* 96 (February): 151–162.

Hoynes, H. W., D. W. Schanzenbach, and D. Almond. 2012. "Long Run Impacts of Childhood Access to the Safety Net." NBER Working Paper 18535. Cambridge, MA: National Bureau of Economic Research.

Iceland, J., K. Short, T. Garner, and D. Johnson. 2001. "Are Children Worse Off? Evaluating Well-Being Using the New (and Improved) Measure of Poverty." *Journal of Human Resources* 36(2): 398–412.

Johnson, L. B. 1964. "Remarks upon Signing the Food Stamp Act, August 31, 1964." Available at www.presidency.ucsb.edu/ws/?pid=26472.

Kakwani, N. 1980. "On a Class of Poverty Measures." *Econometrica* 48: 437–446.

Keane, M., and R. Moffitt. 1998. "A Structural Model of Multiple Welfare Program Participation and Labor Supply." *International Economic Review* 39(3): 553–589.

Leibtag, E. 2007. "Stretching the Food Stamp Dollar: Regional Price Differences Affect Affordability of Food." *Economic Information Bulletin* 29-2. Washington, DC: U.S. Department of Agriculture Economic Research Service.

Leibtag, E., and A. Kumcu. 2011. "The WIC Fruit and Vegetable Cash Voucher: Does Regional Price Variation Affect Buying Power?" *Economic Information Bulletin* 75. Washington, DC: U.S. Department of Agriculture Economic Research Service.

Levedahl, J. 1995. "A Theoretical and Empirical Evaluation of the Functional Forms Used to Estimate the Food Expenditure Equation of Food Stamp Recipients." *American Journal of Agricultural Economics* 77: 960–968.

Mabli, J., E. Sama Martin, and L. Castner. 2009. "Effects of Economic Conditions and Program Policy on State Food Stamp Program Caseloads: 2000 to 2006." CCR-56, Economic Research Service, USDA.

Meyer, B. D., W. K. C. Mok, and J. X. Sullivan. 2009. "The Under-Reporting of Transfers in Household Surveys: Its Nature and Consequences." NBER Working Paper 15181.Cambridge, MA: National Bureau of Economic Research.

Moffitt, R. A. 1989. "Estimating the Value of an In-Kind Transfer: The Case of Food Stamps." *Econometrica* 57(2): 385–410.

————. 2013. "The Great Recession and the Social Safety Net." *The Annals of the American Academy of Political and Social Science* 650: 143–166.

Moffitt, R. A., and J. K. Scholz. 2010. "Trends in the Level and Distribution of Income Support." In J. R. Brown, ed., *Tax Policy and the Economy, Volume 24,* 111–152. Chicago: University of Chicago Press.

Rector, R., and K. Bradley. 2012. "Reforming the Food Stamp Program." *Welfare and Welfare Spending Backgrounder* 2708. Washington, DC: Heritage Foundation.

Rosenbaum, D. 2000 (September). "Improving Access to Food Stamps: New Reporting Options Can Reduce Administrative Burdens and Error Rates." Washington, DC: Center on Budget and Policy Priorities.

————. 2013 (January). "The Relationship between SNAP and Work among Low-Income Households." Washington, DC: Center on Budget and Policy Priorities.

Scholz, J. K., R. A. Moffitt, and B. Cowan. 2009. "Trends in Income Support." In M. Cancian and S. Danziger (eds.), *Changing Poverty, Changing Policies,* 203–241. New York: Russell Sage Foundation.

Sen, A. 1976. "Poverty: An Ordinal Approach to Measurement." *Econometrica* 44: 219–231.

Shaefer, H. L., and K. Edin. 2013. "Rising Extreme Poverty in the United States and the Response of Means-Tested Transfers." *Social Service Review* 87(2): 250–268.

Short, K. 2011. *The Research Supplemental Poverty Measure: 2010.* Current Population Report No. P60-241. Washington, DC: U.S. Census Bureau.

————. 2012. *The Research Supplemental Poverty Measure: 2011.* Current Population Report No. P60-244. Washington, DC: U.S. Census Bureau.

Smeeding, T. M. 1977. "The Anti-Poverty Effectiveness of In-Kind Transfers." *Journal of Human Resources* XII(3): 360–378.

Tiehen, L., D. Jolliffe, and C. Gundersen. 2012. "Alleviating Poverty in the United States: The Critical Role of SNAP Benefits." Washington, DC: U.S. Department of Agriculture Economic Research Service, Economic Research Report 132.

————. 2013 (January). "How State Policies Influence the Efficacy of SNAP in Reducing Poverty." Presentation at American Economic Association Annual Meeting, San Diego, CA.

Todd, J., E. Leibtag, and C. Penberthy. 2011. "Geographic Differences in the Relative Prices of Healthy Foods." *Economic Information Bulletin* 78. Washington, DC: U.S. Department of Agriculture Economic Research Service.

U.S. Bureau of the Census. 1982 (March). *Alternative Methods for Valuing Selected In-Kind Transfer Benefits and Measuring Their Effect on Poverty.* Technical Paper No. 50. Washington, DC: U.S. Government Printing Office.

U.S. Department of Agriculture. 2013. "Supplemental Nutrition Assistance Program Participation and Costs." USDA Food and Nutrition Service. Available at www.fns.usda.gov/pd/SNAPsummary.htm.

Wheaton, L., M. Martinez-Schiferl, L. Giannarelli, and S. Zedlewski. 2012 (November). "The Effect of Food Assistance Programs on Poverty: 2007 to 2009." Presented to the APPAM Fall Conference, Baltimore, MD.

Wimer, C., M. Mattingly, C. Danielson, and S. Bohn. 2013 (October). *The California Poverty Measure: A Portrait of Poverty within California Counties and Demographic Groups*, Figure 6. Stanford Center on Poverty and Inequality. Available at www.stanford.edu/group/scspi/poverty/cpm/CPMBrief_CPI.pdf

Ziliak, J. P. 2005. "Understanding Poverty Rates and Gaps: Concepts, Trends, and Challenges." *Foundations and Trends in Microeconomics* 1(3): 127–199.

———. 2008. "Filling the Poverty Gap, Then and Now." In Peter Rupert, ed., *Frontiers in Family Economics, Volume 1*, 39–114. Bingley, UK: Emerald Group Publishing.

———. 2011 (August). "Recent Developments in Antipoverty Policies in the United States." Presentation at the East-West Center and Korea Development Institute Conference on Social Welfare Issues in Honolulu, HI.

Ziliak, J. P., C. Gundersen, and D. Figlio. 2003. "Food Stamp Caseloads over the Business Cycle." *Southern Economic Journal* 69(4): 903–919.

The Supplemental Nutrition Assistance Program and Food Insecurity

Christian Gregory
Matthew P. Rabbitt
David C. Ribar

The Supplemental Nutrition Assistance Program is intended to help low-income households obtain more nutritious food than they could otherwise afford. In so doing, SNAP should—in both a normative and a positive sense—reduce households' food hardships; however, only recently has research begun to confirm this commonsense association.

Since 1995, the United States has regularly measured food hardships nationally, using the Food Security Scale, a ten- to eighteen-item index that is intended to capture households' "access at all times to enough food for an active, healthy life" (Coleman-Jensen et al. 2012). The latest data indicate that 85 percent of U.S. households were food secure in 2011, while 15 percent (17.9 million households with 50.1 million people) were not. More often than not, researchers find that SNAP participation is associated with more, rather than fewer, food hardships. For example, Coleman-Jensen and colleagues (2012) report that, among households with incomes below 130 percent of the poverty line (households that meet the gross income test for SNAP receipt), 52 percent of SNAP participants reported being food insecure compared to 28 percent of nonparticipants.

Obviously, this example demonstrates simple association, rather than causation. But it hasn't been until quite recently that any methods have begun to get results consistent with the expectation that SNAP would reduce food insecurity. Are our commonsense predictions wrong, or are there statistical problems that confound the estimates? What are the methodological implications of the results? This chapter reviews and synthesizes previous research on these questions and conducts new analyses using several years of data from the Food Security Supplement of the Current Population Survey (CPS-FSS).

Our conceptual analyses provide ample support for the commonsense predictions of negative associations between SNAP and food insecurity; however, those same analyses also point to numerous characteristics that could confound the empirical findings. Our review of the empirical literature uncovers many studies that report counterintuitive findings but also some studies—usually using one of a few selected statistical techniques—that generate the expected findings. In our own analyses of the data we are mostly able to replicate the range and pattern of findings from previous studies. As with the existing literature, expected findings consistent with SNAP reducing food insecurity are confined to a narrow set of statistical methods and those using dose-response designs. Although these latter methods are more econometrically defensible than those that do not address the endogeneity of SNAP participation, they have not, in general, been tested for their robustness to alternatives that also address this issue. Nonetheless, methods that focus on the dollar value of SNAP benefits on food insecurity tend to be quite robust to a range of methods and perhaps offer one promising avenue of further research.

MEASURING FOOD INSECURITY AND OTHER FOOD HARDSHIPS

The principal instrument for measuring food security in the United States is the Food Security Module of the CPS-FSS. The module is administered to households with income less than 185 percent of the federal poverty line, that report food insufficiency on a preliminary screener question, or that indicate they stretched their food budget. The module asks ten questions of all these households and an additional eight questions of households with children, regarding progressively more severe hardships that range from anxiety over food running out to shortages of amounts and kinds of food to episodes of adults and children going without food for an entire day. All of the questions refer to the previous twelve months and are framed in terms of either shortages of money or affordability. The CPS-FSS also asks thirty-day questions based on the same items. The items in the twelve-month module are listed in the appendix to this chapter.

The Food Security Module was developed after extensive research that began with a conceptualization of food security and insecurity and proceeded to qualitative fieldwork to elicit themes for potential items, the development of candidate items, statistical and qualitative analyses of the items' validity and reliability, a selection of items, and a final scaling (see Hamilton et al. 1997). The testing included formal Item Response Theory modeling (specifically Rasch modeling) and indicated that the items were consistent with a unidimensional underlying, or latent, measure.

Household food security status is determined by summing the affirmed responses from the module, as shown in Table 3.A.1. Households that affirm two or fewer items are classified as being "food secure," meaning that they have "consistent, dependable access to enough food for active, healthy living" (Coleman-Jensen et al. 2012, p. v). Households without children that affirm three to five items and households with children that affirm three to seven items are classified as experiencing "low food security," meaning that they "reported multiple indications of food access problems, but typically . . . reported few, if any, indications of reduced food intake" (Ibid., p. 4). Households that affirm more items (six or more for households without children and eight or more for households with children) are classified as experiencing "very low food security," meaning that the "food intake of one or more members was reduced and eating patterns (were) disrupted because of insufficient money and other resources for food" (Ibid., p. 4). The low and very low food security categories together constitute food insecurity.

The CPS-FSS Food Security Module has some limitations that should be kept in mind. In a careful review of the food security scale, the National Academy of Sciences (Wunderlich and Norwood 2006) identified several problems, including that the module captures other relevant food hardships, such as problems with the supply, safety, or quality of food; that the unidimensional model for developing the scale might not be appropriate; and that the CPS-FSS is based on a household sampling frame that omits institutionalized and homeless people.[1] Also, to lower the response burden on CPS subjects and to reduce the risks of false positive indications, the module is not asked of all households in the CPS-FSS but rather only of households that are at risk of insecurity because they have incomes below 185 percent of the poverty line, indicated that they are food insufficient, or indicated that they undertook actions to stretch their food budget. Although the food security measure is strongly associated with households' income-to-needs ratios (see, for example, Coleman-Jensen et al. 2012), researchers have found that it has weak external validity in terms of some nutrition outcomes (Bhattacharya, Currie, and Haider 2004) and food expenditures (Gundersen and Ribar 2011) and that items may have low reliability among parents and children (Fram et al. 2011).

In addition to using the twelve-month, eighteen-item food security scale, research on SNAP has used other measures of food hardships. One of these, the food insufficiency measure, has already been mentioned. The food insufficiency question asks households if they have "enough of the kinds of food (they) want to eat, enough but not always the kinds of food (they) want to eat, sometimes not enough to eat, or often not enough to eat?" The CPS-FSS also follows up affirmative responses to the twelve-month food security questions with questions about whether the hardships were experienced in the last thirty days; the responses from these questions are used to construct a thirty-day measure of food insecurity.

The eighteen-item food security module has been included in other U.S. surveys, such as the Panel Study of Income Dynamics and the National

Health and Nutrition Examination Survey. Due to time and budget constraints, however, some other surveys either ask the single-item food sufficiency question or a subset of the food security questions. For example, recent panels of the Survey of Income and Program Participation (SIPP) have asked six food security questions covering the previous four months; a food security scale has been developed from responses to five of these questions. The National Health Interview Survey currently fields the ten-item questionnaire. In general, measures derived from the full eighteen-item module, the food sufficiency question, and shorter modules are highly correlated.

Conceptual Analysis

To consider the ways in which SNAP might affect food hardships, we rely on Barrett's 2002 theoretical rational-choice model of how household food security is determined.[2] Barrett extended the household production framework of Becker (1965) and Gronau (1977) and the health production framework of Grossman (1972) to include household nutrition and food security. In Barrett's model, households choose purchases, savings or borrowing, and allocations of time to further the objective of maximizing their members' physical well-being and general consumption in the present, where they have full information about their circumstances, and in the future, where they have expectations about circumstances. Households pursue these objectives subject to production, health, budget, and time constraints. Specifically, each period's physical well-being depends on the level of well-being from the previous period; inputs of nutrition, other goods or services, and activities; and arbitrary shocks from illnesses and injuries. The nutritional inputs to physical well-being, in turn, are produced using inputs of food and other goods and of members' time. Each of these production functions is also conditioned by the household members' human capital. Also, households face subsistence constraints in the form of minimum amounts of nutrition to avoid hunger and minimum amounts of physical well-being to avoid impairment. With respect to the budget constraint, households' total per-period expenditures on food, other goods, and services must not exceed the sum of the members' earnings plus the return on their savings and other assets plus any borrowing and less any savings. The household members also have limits on the time available each period to work or participate in other activities.

From Barrett's framework, we can identify structural characteristics of households that increase the risk of food hardships. First, hardships are more likely to occur if household members have low labor productivity (through circumstances such as disability, a lack of education, or very young or old age) that reduce their ability to work in the home and the labor market.

Second, households are at greater risk for hardships if they confront adverse terms of trade in the form of either low wages for the work they perform or high prices for the goods they purchase. Third, households are also at increased risk of hardships if they lack access to labor markets or goods markets; access to markets is generally lower in rural areas but also in inner-city neighborhoods that are spatially mismatched from jobs and services. Fourth, risks are higher for households with low levels of savings and assets and for households with limited abilities to borrow and save. Fifth, risks increase if households have weak social or public support systems; these include social networks through friends and relatives and also cash and in-kind public assistance programs. Sixth, households face higher risks of food insecurity if their circumstances frequently leave them near the subsistence or food security thresholds, as this increases the chances that a given shock will knock them below the thresholds. Seventh, a general susceptibility to negative shocks, perhaps because of marginal health, residence in an area with a volatile economy, or work in a vulnerable industry or occupation increases the risks of becoming food insecure.

Empirical studies seldom characterize households' risk factors so comprehensively; however, they do typically control for many of the factors that Barrett considered. For example, controls for health, disability, education, and job market experience account for the productivity risk factors. Controls for wages and possibly local area prices account for adverse terms of trade. Geographic controls account for market access. Controls for assets, net savings, and homeownership account for wealth and borrowing ability. Controls for social networks and public assistance account for support systems.

We can also use Barrett's model to consider how SNAP should affect households' food security. In principle, the program's EBT assistance should expand participating households' budget sets and relax their resource constraints. This should allow households to purchase more food and reduce the incidence of food hardships, including food insecurity. We would also anticipate complementary effects from the educational component of SNAP, which should increase household members' shopping, planning, and food preparation skills and thereby make them more effective at transforming budgetary and other resources into nutritional inputs and physical well-being outcomes.

At the same time, other elements of SNAP participation might work against these effects. First, means testing of SNAP eligibility and benefits imposes an extra tax on market work, reducing poor people's incentives to work and earn (or possibly incentivizing them to work "off-the-books" in less stable informal jobs). These effects might be especially strong for households with children, where the receipt of SNAP confers categorical eligibility for free meals under the National School Lunch Program (NSLP) and School Breakfast Program (SBP) and adjunctive financial eligibility for the Special Supplemental Nutrition Program for Women, Infants and Children (WIC). Second, program participants are vulnerable to losses of benefits if they fail to comply with program rules regarding recertification and mandated work activities (Ribar, Edelhoch, and Liu 2008, 2010). Ribar and Edelhoch (2008) found that recertification had especially detrimental participation effects for recipients who were marginally eligible financially and for recipients in very unstable circumstances. More generally, income volatility could both increase the risks of food insecurity (Gundersen and Gruber 2001) and affect eligibility for food assistance (see, for example, Jolliffe and Ziliak 2008). Third, monthly cycles associated with SNAP issuance, spending, and benefit exhaustion could give rise to periodic shortages of food (Wilde and Ranney 2000). Fourth, the increased time and preparation associated with SNAP-eligible food purchases as compared to other types of food purchases might negatively affect families. Although each of these issues might reduce the effectiveness of SNAP, we would still expect the program's net effects to be positive.

Although theory predicts a positive effect of SNAP on food security, there are many reasons why empirical analysis might differ. First and foremost, participation in SNAP is endogenous. That is, SNAP participation is a behavioral outcome. Food security and SNAP participation are each influenced by a host of characteristics, and failure to measure or account for these characteristics in an empirical analysis can give rise to spurious associations. For example, Joyce and colleagues (2012) document a host of hardships, including health problems, housing insecurity, and losses of utilities, that often accompany food hardships. If these hardships also prompt people to enroll in SNAP, they could lead to SNAP recipients being more disadvantaged and less food secure than nonrecipients and to a negative empirical association between SNAP and food security.

There is also a possibility that food hardships may prompt SNAP participation and that the empirical association may be affected by simultaneity bias. Again, this could lead to a negative association between SNAP receipt and food security. Nord and Golla (2009) examined trajectories of food hardships prior to and after entering SNAP; they found that food hardships rose in the months leading up to SNAP entry, suggesting that increased hardships motivated entry. As we discuss in the next section, the endogeneity of SNAP participation has been a predominant methodological concern in empirical research. Finally, mismeasurement and misreporting of food hardships and of SNAP participation may alter the observed relationships.

PREVIOUS RESEARCH

A vast number of studies have investigated the impacts of SNAP on Americans' food outcomes. Comprehensive reviews by Barrett (2002), Currie (2003), and Fox, Hamilton, and Lin (2004) summarize the research as consistently indicating that SNAP is associated with higher expenditures on food and greater food and nutrient availability within households. However, Currie (2003), Fox and coauthors (2004), and Wilde and Nord (2005) reach much different conclusions regarding the impact of SNAP on food insecurity and insufficiency and report that the results across studies are mixed and inconsistent. A more recent review by Caswell and Yaktine (2013) is more sanguine about the studies of SNAP and food hardships, although it also acknowledges many inconclusive and counterintuitive results. Our review will focus on the statistical methodologies that studies have employed, summarize findings associated with those methodologies, and draw interpretations regarding potential biases.[3]

Comparisons of SNAP Participants and Nonparticipants

Most of the research on the potential effects of SNAP on food hardships has been based on comparisons of outcomes for program participants and nonparticipants. The studies generally restrict their analyses to people with incomes that are below or near the gross-income eligibility limit for SNAP.[4] The restrictions are intended to make the samples of participants and nonparticipants more comparable. For studies that use the CPS-FSS, the restrictions also ensure that everyone in the samples was asked the questions in the food security module and thus avoid an artificial sample selection issue that arises from the screening conditions for the module.

Descriptive results (comparisons of means) from each year's CPS-FSS are reported by the Economic Research Service in its *Household Food Security in the United States* series (for example, Coleman-Jensen et al. 2012). Descriptive methods were also used in early research, such as Cohen and coauthors (1999). The descriptive comparisons indicate that food insecurity is substantially higher in SNAP households than in other households. However, these comparisons do not account for observed and unobserved characteristics that could lead to spurious associations.

Multivariate statistical models include other observed measures, such as household size, race, and education of the household head, that are likely to be associated with both food hardships and SNAP participation and that may be sources of such associations. Several researchers, including Alaimo and coauthors (1998) and Bhattacharya and Currie (2001) estimated standard binary or continuous regression models of food hardships, and Ribar and Hamrick (2003) estimated binary event-history models of entry into and exit from these conditions. Although the use of observed controls reduced the associations of SNAP participation and food hardships in these studies, substantial positive conditional associations remained, raising the possibility that unobserved characteristics were still contributing to the associations.

A few standard-regression studies have generated different findings using narrower analysis samples and alternative participation comparisons in attempts to mitigate selection issues. Kabbani and Kmeid (2005) found that SNAP participation was negatively associated with thirty-day food insecurity among a low-income sample of CPS-FSS households that were food insecure according to the twelve-month measure. Rather than considering general comparisons of SNAP participants and nonparticipants, Gundersen and Gruber (2001) and Mykerezi and Mills (2010) focused on households that had lost benefits and found that such losses raised households' risks of food insufficiency and insecurity. Mabli and coauthors (2013) compared food security outcomes for SNAP households at the beginning of their participation spells and six months into those spells and found that food hardships decreased with households' SNAP tenures.

Matching techniques offer a more general and robust approach to addressing selection based on observable characteristics. Gibson-Davis and Foster (2006) employed propensity-score matching (PSM) (Rosenbaum and Rubin 1983) to compare SNAP participants and nonparticipants. They found that matching led to lower associations between SNAP and the incidence of food insecurity than standard logistic binary regressions but that many of the associations remained significantly positive. In a few specifications, that jointly (a) considered the food insecurity Rasch score, (b) were restricted to households that affirmed at least one food security item, and (c) were limited to a narrow range of propensity scores, Gibson-Davis and Foster found the expected negative associations.

Standard regression models and matching techniques address selection based on observable variables—at least on the observable characteristics they can control for. If we assume that the theoretical model is indeed correct, the preponderance of counterintuitive findings from the regression and matching studies indicates that selection must be coming from unobservable characteristics or simultaneity. When longitudinal data are available, multivariate fixed-effects methods can be used to account for time-invariant unobserved characteristics that might be confounded with both SNAP participation and food hardships. Wilde and Nord (2005) estimated household-level fixed effects models using the two-year panels that can be constructed from the CPS-FSS, and Greenhalgh-Stanley and Fitzpatrick (2013) estimated fixed effects models using data on households with elderly people from the Health and Retirement Survey. Both studies found that SNAP participation continued to be positively associated with food insecurity, even after fixed-effects controls were applied. The findings suggest that time-varying unobserved influences or simultaneity is a source of bias.

Instrumental variables methods, including two-stage least squares (2SLS), endogenous latent variable models, and dummy endogenous variable models, can address these other sources of bias. 2SLS and endogenous latent variable models effectively substitute a predicted value or index of SNAP participation based entirely on observed measures for actual SNAP participation and omit the potentially biasing unobserved characteristics. These methods rely on variable exclusions for identification, that is, on variables that are used in the predictions but that do not appear elsewhere in the model for food insecurity. For these exclusions to be valid, the excluded variables—the instruments—must be strongly predictive of SNAP participation and must only affect food hardships through their effects on SNAP participation (that is, must not independently predict food hardships). Dummy endogenous variable models, such as bivariate probit, are an alternative approach and can be formally identified through the functional forms in the model if there is sufficient variation in the explanatory variables (Wilde 2000). In practice, however, this source of identification can be weak, and researchers typically bolster identification of dummy endogenous variable models through variable exclusions. A challenge for endogenous variable studies has been to uncover appropriate instruments.

Results based on two-stage and latent endogenous variable methods have been inconclusive. Borjas (2004) examined the effects of public assistance (including but not limited to SNAP receipt) on food insecurity, using citizenship and years since migration as instruments. Borjas found the anticipated negative associations, but most of his estimates were only marginally significant and thus could not convincingly reject positive associations. Gundersen and Oliveira (2001) and Huffman and Jensen (2003) applied endogenous latent variable methods but obtained imprecise and statistically insignificant results that were consistent with both positive and negative effects. Greenhalgh-Stanley and Fitzpatrick (2013) estimated 2SLS models for elderly households from the Health and Retirement Survey in specifications that also included household-specific fixed effects. They generated estimates that were imprecise and statistically insignificant. Shaefer and Gutierrez (2012) also estimated 2SLS models using data from three panels of the SIPP and obtained statistically insignificant results.

In contrast, researchers who have applied dummy endogenous variable models have estimated strong negative associations. Yen and colleagues (2008) found that SNAP participation was negatively associated with households' thirty-day food insecurity Rasch scores; however, the researchers used a choice-based sample (the 1996–1997 National Food Stamp Program Survey) with an overrepresentation of SNAP participants.[5] Mykerezi and Mills

(2010) estimated a negative association between households' SNAP participation and food insecurity using data from the Panel Study of Income Dynamics. Ratcliffe, McKernan, and Zhang (2011) and Shaefer and Gutierrez (2012) obtained similar findings with data from the Survey of Income and Program Participation. Shaefer and Gutierrez estimated dummy endogenous variable models with and without variable exclusion restrictions with little change in their results, which suggested that identification for this entire group of studies may have been obtained mainly from functional form.

The preceding statistical approaches all make strong assumptions in order to identify an effect of SNAP on food hardships. Additionally, these methods differ in what they measure. For example, propensity score matching models identify the average treatment effect on the treated (ATET), whereas 2SLS methods isolate the local average treatment effect (LATE)—that is, the effect of SNAP participation for those whose decision to participate is altered by the value of instruments or excluded variables. The dummy endogenous variables models mentioned here are aimed at identifying the average treatment effect (ATE) of SNAP—that is, the expected outcome if SNAP were given to a randomly assigned person in the population of interest. Although the ATE might also be identified by longitudinal models, such models rely on the additional assumption that endogenous unobservables are time invariant; as noted, this assumption seems to be at odds with current evidence.[6]

An alternative approach to introducing model assumptions a priori is to bound the possible impacts first using logical probability restrictions and then to introduce relatively weak assumptions (see Manski 1995 as a general reference). Although this approach reduces the reliance on strong assumptions, it tends to produce a wide range of plausible effects. Gundersen and Kreider (2008) have used the bounds approach to show that the same data that generate counterintuitive differences in participants' and nonparticipants' food hardships are also consistent with underlying negative impacts when the possible influence of measurement error is accounted for.

Dose-Response Relationships

Another branch of the research literature has considered how food hardships change with more generous SNAP benefits or more intense participation (that is, with a higher "dose" of the SNAP "treatment"). For example, in the most recent *Household Food Security in the United States* report, Coleman-Jensen and coauthors (2012) estimate that the rate of food insecurity was 56.0 percent among households that received SNAP benefits for one to eleven months during the preceding year but only 49.1 percent among households that receive SNAP benefits for all twelve months. Similarly,

Mabli and coauthors (2013) found that food security prevalence decreased significantly for households that participated in SNAP for six months.

Studies with multivariate designs find similar evidence. Rose, Gundersen, and Oliveira (1998) estimated logit models of food insufficiency and found that higher levels of SNAP benefits were significantly negatively associated with food insufficiency. DePolt, Moffitt, and Ribar (2009) obtained similar results, estimating longitudinal multiple indicator, multiple cause models of food insecurity. Van Hook and Balistreri (2006) used predicted measures of unmet program need in the form of reduced probabilities of SNAP participation and reduced SNAP allotments and found that these were positively associated with hardships. Watson, Shore Sheppard, and Schmidt (2012) found a strong dose-response effect of SNAP in reducing children's food insecurity.

Indirect Analyses

All of the preceding studies examined how an individual household's receipt or use of SNAP benefits was associated with its own food hardships. Several studies have investigated how measures of characteristics that are associated with the general availability of SNAP are associated with hardships. For example, Borjas (2004) showed how food insecurity for noncitizen immigrants jumped relative to food insecurity for native and naturalized citizens following the enactment of the Personal Responsibility and Work Opportunity Reconciliation Act of 1996. Nord and Prell (2011) compared thirty-day food insecurity before and after SNAP benefits were increased as part of the American Recovery and Reinvestment Act of 2009; they found that food insecurity fell for households that were income-eligible for SNAP but not for near-eligible households, suggesting that the higher benefits reduced hardships. Other studies, however, have found weaker associations or no associations. Using data from the CPS-FSS, Bartfeld and Dunifon (2006) found that state-level SNAP participation was associated with food security for above-poverty, low-income households but not for below-poverty households. Using data from Oregon, Bernell, Weber, and Edwards (2006) found that county-level SNAP participation was not associated with food insecurity.

REPLICATION ANALYSIS

Although there are many consistent results and patterns across the empirical studies of SNAP and food hardships, there are also considerable differences. Besides differing in their statistical methodologies, previous studies have differed in their measures of food hardships, measures of SNAP receipt, choice of surveys and time periods, and selection of analysis samples within those surveys. In this section, we attempt to replicate previous findings by employing most of the statistical methodologies to a single data set—the 2009 to 2011 waves of the CPS-FSS.[7]

For each of these years of the CPS-FSS, we select households with annual incomes at or below 130 percent of the federal poverty line. Besides being the income cutoff used to examine SNAP in the annual *Household Food Security in the United States* reports, this threshold also leads to a sample that meets the gross income test for SNAP and that satisfies the screen for answering the Food Security Module. We additionally restrict our analysis sample to households that responded to the FSS, that provided sufficient information to determine their food security status, and that provided information for other FSS measures that we use as explanatory variables.

For our analyses, we consider a sample that combines all households that meet the preceding criteria, but we also consider four mutually exclusive subsets of households: unmarried parent households with children under age eighteen, married parent households with children under age eighteen, households consisting entirely of members who are age sixty or older, and other adult-only households. These types of low-income households differ in their susceptibility to food hardships, are subject to different rules under SNAP, and are differently eligible for other types of public assistance. Disaggregating this way increases the comparability of households within groups; it also helps us to ascertain the robustness of our findings and the findings of previous studies that have adopted different analysis groups.

The outcome variable in most of our analyses is a binary indicator for the household being food insecure, which is constructed from the twelve-month eighteen-item Food Security Module. Our principal explanatory variables are indicators for the receipt of any SNAP benefits and a continuous measure of SNAP benefits. In some of our analyses, we use an indicator for the receipt of SNAP benefits any time during the preceding year. This is the first SNAP question that is asked in the CPS-FSS, and its reference period corresponds with the reference period for the Food Security Module items. In other analyses, we use an indicator for the receipt of SNAP benefits in the month preceding the interview. Although this question is asked conditional on the annual measure, it may be more reliably reported. We also consider this measure because of its use in previous research and because preliminary analyses showed that it led to a distinct result pattern. For our final analyses, we use a continuous measure of annual SNAP benefits, which allows us to examine the dose-response of households to SNAP.

For our multivariate analyses, we incorporate numerous additional controls that are available in the CPS-FSS; most of these are standard and have been used in previous research. The controls include the household head's gender, age, race, ethnicity, nativity, marital status, education, and employment status; numbers of adults, children, and disabled members in the household; age of youngest member (households with children); an indicator for elderly members; residence in urban area; the state unemployment rate; household income; homeownership; food needs; receipt of SBP, NSLP, and WIC benefits (households with children); the use of food banks and soup kitchens; and state and year fixed effects. Means and standard deviations for our explanatory variables, calculated separately for SNAP participants and nonparticipants, in each of our four analysis subsamples are in Table 3.A.2 in the appendix to this chapter.

We start our replication analysis by estimating linear probability models (LPMs) of households' food insecurity status. Estimated coefficients and standard errors for the SNAP receipt explanatory variable from alternative specifications and analysis samples are listed in Table 3.1. All the regressions in Table 3.1 incorporate sampling weights provided with the CPS-FSS that adjust for the CPS sampling design and for differential response in the FSS. Estimates for the entire combined sample of households are reported in the first column of the table. The subsequent columns report estimates separately for the mutually exclusive subsamples of unmarried parent households, married parent households, households composed entirely of elderly members, and other adult-only households. The top panel lists estimates from models that include measures of any SNAP receipt in the previous year, whereas the bottom panel lists results from models of SNAP receipt in the previous month.

The first row in each panel of Table 3.1 reports coefficients from simple univariate LPMs of food insecurity regressed on SNAP receipt. The estimates, which represent unconditional differences in average food insecurity between SNAP participants and nonparticipants, are all strongly positive and consistent with estimates from previous descriptive analyses, such as Coleman-Jensen and coauthors (2012). The differences are largest for the two groups of adult-only households and smallest for single-parent households. Also consistent with previous analyses, the differences in food insecurity are appreciably larger when SNAP receipt is measured on a previous-year basis rather than a previous-month basis.

The second rows in the panels list coefficients from LPMs that add controls for demographic characteristics of the households and their heads, geographic attributes, and state and time fixed effects. Adding these controls substantially reduces the estimated associations between SNAP receipt and food insecurity for the two groups of adult-only households but only slightly reduces the associations for the two groups of households with children.

The third rows report coefficients from specifications that also add controls for employment status, household income, homeownership, and

TABLE 3.1

Coefficients on SNAP receipt from linear probability models (LPM)

	All households	Households with children and unmarried parents	Households with children and married parents	Households with all elderly members	Other adult-only households
RECEIVED SNAP IN LAST YEAR					
LPM with no other controls	0.288*** (0.007)	0.188*** (0.015)	0.237*** (0.017)	0.290*** (0.018)	0.314*** (0.012)
LPM with standard controls[a]	0.226*** (0.008)	0.184*** (0.016)	0.231*** (0.018)	0.229*** (0.019)	0.256*** (0.014)
LPM with standard and economic controls[b]	0.207*** (0.008)	0.164*** (0.016)	0.209*** (0.019)	0.215*** (0.019)	0.234*** (0.014)
LPM with standard, economic, and other assistance controls[c]	0.136*** (0.008)	0.088*** (0.017)	0.116*** (0.019)	0.174*** (0.020)	0.161*** (0.014)
RECEIVED SNAP IN LAST MONTH					
LPM with no other controls	0.256*** (0.007)	0.140*** (0.015)	0.198*** (0.018)	0.272*** (0.019)	0.293*** (0.013)
LPM with standard controls[a]	0.187*** (0.008)	0.131*** (0.016)	0.188*** (0.019)	0.206*** (0.020)	0.227*** (0.014)
LPM with standard and economic controls[b]	0.166*** (0.008)	0.108*** (0.016)	0.162*** (0.019)	0.192*** (0.020)	0.204*** (0.015)
LPM with standard, economic, and other assistance controls[c]	0.095*** (0.009)	0.032* (0.016)	0.066*** (0.020)	0.152*** (0.020)	0.132*** (0.014)

SOURCE: Authors' estimates using weighted data from the 2009–2011 Current Population Survey Food Security Supplement (CPS-FSS).

NOTE: Robust standard errors appear in parentheses.

[a] Control for household head's gender, age, age squared, race, ethnicity, nativity, marital status, and education; numbers of adults, children, and disabled members in household; age of youngest member (households with children); elderly members; residence in urban area; state unemployment rate; and state and year fixed effects. Linear probability models (LPMs) for all households also control for household type.

[b] Control for head's employment status, log of household income, homeownership, log of food needs, and indicator for missing food needs.

[c] Control for participation in School Breakfast Program, National School Lunch Program, and Special Supplemental Nutrition Program for Women, Infants and Children (households with children) and use of food pantries or soup kitchens.

* Significant at 0.10 level.
** Significant at 0.05 level.
*** Significant at 0.01 level.

subjectively assessed food needs; the use of these controls attenuates the associations between SNAP receipt and food insecurity more. Finally, the last rows in the panels add controls for SBP, NSLP, and WIC program participation for the households with children and food bank and soup kitchen use for all households. Although these controls further reduce the estimated coefficients, the conditional associations between SNAP receipt and food insecurity remain positive and statistically distinguishable from zero. The

TABLE 3.2

Coefficients on SNAP receipt from simple, linear probability module (LPM),
and propensity-score matching (PSM) comparisons

	All households	Households with children and unmarried parents	Households with children and married parents	Households with all elderly members	Other adult-only households
RECEIVED SNAP IN LAST YEAR					
Bivariate comparison	0.281***	0.186***	0.234***	0.274***	0.300***
	(0.006)	(0.013)	(0.015)	(0.013)	(0.010)
LPM	0.197***	0.165***	0.208***	0.218***	0.227***
	(0.007)	(0.014)	(0.016)	(0.013)	(0.011)
PSM comparison	0.184***	0.174***	0.207***	0.229***	0.230***
	(0.011)	(0.022)	(0.023)	(0.022)	(0.018)
RECEIVED SNAP IN LAST MONTH					
Bivariate comparison	0.252***	0.144***	0.199***	0.258***	0.278***
	(0.006)	(0.013)	(0.016)	(0.013)	(0.011)
LPM	0.159***	0.114***	0.166***	0.200***	0.197***
	(0.007)	(0.014)	(0.017)	(0.014)	(0.012)
PSM comparison	0.135***	0.111***	0.156***	0.165***	0.220***
	(0.011)	(0.021)	(0.024)	(0.023)	(0.019)

SOURCE: Authors' estimates using unweighted data from the 2009–2011 CPS-FSS.

NOTES: LPM and PSM models control for household head's gender, age, age squared, race, ethnicity, nativity, marital status, education, and employment status; numbers of adults, children, and disabled members in household; age of youngest member (households with children); elderly members; residence in urban area; state unemployment rate; log of household income; homeownership; log of food needs; missing food needs; and state and year fixed effects. Models for all households also control for household type. PSM comparisons use nearest-neighbor matching with replacement. Robust standard errors appear in parentheses.

* Significant at 0.10 level.
** Significant at 0.05 level.
*** Significant at 0.01 level.

patterns of results are consistent with previous research findings that observed controls attenuate but do not eliminate the counterintuitive positive associations between SNAP participation and food insecurity.

We next consider matching estimates as a more general way to mitigate confounding influences from observable characteristics. Results from this analysis are reported in Table 3.2, which follows the organization from Table 3.1 with estimates arranged by analysis groups in columns, by the periodicity of SNAP receipt in top and bottom panels, and by the type or specification of the estimator in rows within panels. Because of questions regarding the interpretation of sample weights in matching analyses, we report results computed with unweighted data. For purposes of comparison with our previous estimates, we report unconditional differences in food insecurity between SNAP participants and nonparticipants in the first rows of the panels and report coefficients from LPMs with our standard and economic controls (the same parameterizations as the third rows from Table 3.1) in the second rows. The estimates in the first two rows indicate that weighting has no substantive impact on the estimates for households with children but modest impacts for the two groups of adult-only households.

The third rows of the panels in Table 3.2 list the differences between the average rates of food insecurity between our participant samples and matched nonparticipant samples. The samples were matched using predicted probabilities from logit models of SNAP participation that included our standard and economic controls. For the matching itself, we selected nearest-match neighbors with replacement and restricted the matches to the common support of the predicted probabilities (virtually the entire range of probabilities). Analyses (not shown) confirm that the matched samples were balanced in terms of the observed control variables. Turning to the results in the table, differences in food insecurity in the matched samples are mostly smaller than the unconditional differences and the regression-based conditional differences. Despite the general attenuation in the estimated differences, all of them remain significantly and substantively positive, mirroring the results reported by Gibson-Davis and Foster (2006) for the incidence of food insecurity.

We next consider longitudinal estimators. The design of the CPS, in which rotation groups of households are interviewed for four consecutive months, left alone for eight months, and then reinterviewed for four more consecutive months, allows the construction of short, two-year panels from adjoining years of the CPS-FSS. As with Wilde and Nord (2005), we take advantage of this feature to produce longitudinal analysis data sets and to estimate panel data models. The longitudinal data from the CPS-FSS have some limitations beyond their short lengths. Most important, the units that the CPS follows are physical addresses, not individuals or households. Thus, people who move between surveys cannot be longitudinally linked and effectively attrit from the panels. Also, the CPS does not produce sampling weights for longitudinally linked CPS-FSS households, so we conduct our statistical analyses using unweighted data.

Results from our longitudinal analyses are reported in Table 3.3. For purposes of comparison, we estimate LPMs with our standard and economic controls but using the unweighted longitudinal sample. Estimates from these specifications in the first rows of the panels are all very similar to the LPMs for the full sample. The results reassure us that there is little, if any, selection bias associated with CPS-FSS longitudinal sample attrition.

Estimates from panel-data random- and fixed-effect LPMs are reported in the second and third rows of the top and bottom panels of Table 3.3. Comparisons of these estimates reveal that accounting for unobserved

TABLE 3.3

Coefficients and marginal effects for SNAP receipt from longitudinal models

	All households	Households with children and unmarried parents	Households with children and married parents	Households with all elderly members	Other adult-only households
RECEIVED SNAP IN LAST YEAR					
LPM	0.188***	0.149***	0.184***	0.193***	0.214***
	(0.011)	(0.024)	(0.025)	(0.023)	(0.019)
Random effects LPM	0.176***	0.135***	0.178***	0.190***	0.193***
	(0.010)	(0.024)	(0.023)	(0.018)	(0.018)
Breusch-Pagan test	[0.000]	[0.000]	[0.000]	[0.000]	[0.000]
Fixed effects LPM	0.114***	0.090***	0.126***	0.168***	0.098***
	(0.016)	(0.034)	(0.039)	(0.031)	(0.029)
Hausman-Wu test	[0.000]	[0.175]	[0.150]	[0.000]	[0.000]
Logit	0.169***	0.147***	0.175***	0.163***	0.197***
	(0.011)	(0.024)	(0.024)	(0.022)	(0.019)
Fixed effects logit	0.085	0.049	0.196	0.045	0.102
	(0.073)	(0.090)	(0.136)	(0.119)	(0.078)
RECEIVED SNAP IN LAST MONTH					
LPM	0.159***	0.098***	0.166***	0.183***	0.182***
	(0.011)	(0.024)	(0.026)	(0.024)	(0.020)
Random effects LPM	0.146***	0.085***	0.154***	0.179***	0.163***
	(0.010)	(0.023)	(0.024)	(0.019)	(0.019)
Breusch-Pagan test	[0.000]	[0.000]	[0.000]	[0.000]	[0.000]
Fixed effects LPM	0.082***	0.046	0.085**	0.155***	0.072**
	(0.016)	(0.033)	(0.038)	(0.031)	(0.029)
Hausman-Wu test	[0.000]	[0.197]	[0.044]	[0.000]	[0.000]
Logit	0.140***	0.095***	0.155***	0.156***	0.165***
	(0.011)	(0.023)	(0.025)	(0.021)	(0.020)
Fixed effects logit	0.051	0.024	0.091	0.025	0.078
	(0.048)	(0.048)	(0.151)	(0.076)	(0.066)

SOURCE: Authors' estimates using unweighted data from the 2009–2011 CPS-FSS.

NOTES: Models use longitudinally linked household data and control for household head's gender, age, age squared, race, ethnicity, nativity, marital status, education, and employment status; numbers of adults, children, and disabled members in household; age of youngest member (households with children); elderly members; residence in urban area; state unemployment rate; log of household income; homeownership; log of food needs; missing food needs; and state and year fixed effects. Models for all households also control for household type. Robust standard errors appear in parentheses. *P* values are in brackets.

* Significant at 0.10 level.
** Significant at 0.05 level.
*** Significant at 0.01 level.

time-invariant characteristics through the use of fixed effects reduces the estimated associations between SNAP receipt and food insecurity. However, large and statistically significant associations remain for all groups except for unmarried parent households when SNAP is measured on the basis of the previous month. Formal specification tests are reported below the random-effect (Breusch-Pagan) and fixed-effect (Hausman-Wu) LPM estimates in the top and bottom panels of Table 3.3. The LPMs are strongly rejected by the Breusch-Pagan test in favor of the random effect LPMs for all household types, regardless of how SNAP is measured. Hausman-Wu tests fail to reject the null that the random-effect LPMs are consistent for unmarried parent households. For all other groups, the random-effect LPM is rejected in favor of the fixed-effect LPM. This result strengthens when SNAP is measured on the basis of the previous month.

To investigate the possible sensitivity of these findings to the use of LPMs rather than more specialized binary outcome models, we reestimated the standard and fixed-effects models using standard and conditional fixed-effect logit specifications, respectively. Average marginal effects were calculated for these models to facilitate comparison with the LPMs. Marginal effects from the logit models are qualitatively similar to the coefficients from the LPMs in most cases, though the marginal effects from the fixed-effect logit models are all statistically insignificant.

Next, we investigate evidence from 2SLS and dummy endogenous variable models. Asymptotic standard errors for the average marginal effects generated by the dummy endogenous variable models are estimated using the delta method.[8] For each type of model, we consider two potential instruments, an indicator for the household head being a noncitizen and an estimate derived from the SNAP Quality Control files of the median certification interval from SNAP cases in the household's state of residence. Noncitizen status is a consistently significant explanatory variable in models of SNAP participation for our samples. However, its use as an instrument is controversial because cultural and assimilation differences between noncitizens and other U.S. residents could contribute directly to experiences and reporting of food hardships. Certification intervals have a stronger theoretical basis for serving as instruments, but they are only modestly predictive in our samples.[9] To test the sensitivity of our 2SLS and dummy endogenous variable results, we estimate models first using both instruments and then using just the certification interval instrument. Estimates from our specifications are reported in Table 3.4.

For convenience, we reproduce the LPM estimates from our specifications with standard and economic explanatory variables in the first rows of the panels of Table 3.4. The second rows list estimates and a Hausman-Wu test from 2SLS models that are identified from exclusions on noncitizenship status and certification intervals. The coefficient estimates for all households and for households with children are large and negative, whereas the coefficient estimates for households with all elderly members are large and positive. However, all of the coefficients are imprecise and unable to discriminate

TABLE 3.4

Coefficients and marginal effects for SNAP receipt from LPM, 2SLS, probit, and bivariate probit models

	All households	Households with children and unmarried parents	Households with children and married parents	Households with all elderly members	Other adult-only households
RECEIVED SNAP IN LAST YEAR					
LPM (exogenous)	0.207***	0.164***	0.209***	0.215***	0.234***
	(0.008)	(0.016)	(0.019)	(0.019)	(0.014)
2SLS—citizenship and certification interval instrument	−0.162	−0.123	−0.362	0.549	−0.087
	(0.193)	(0.568)	(0.809)	(0.373)	(0.218)
Hausman-Wu test	[0.044]	[0.603]	[0.442]	[0.372]	[0.603]
2SLS—certification interval instrument	−0.086	−0.100	−0.585	−0.063	0.286
	(0.437)	(0.682)	(0.906)	(5.128)	(0.611)
Hausman-Wu test	[0.490]	[0.694]	[0.299]	[0.956]	[0.933]
Probit (exogenous)	0.199***	0.164***	0.207***	0.194***	0.227***
	(0.008)	(0.016)	(0.018)	(0.019)	(0.014)
Biprobit—citizenship and certification interval instrument	−0.141***	0.366	−0.109	−0.032	−0.174**
	(0.055)	(0.259)	(0.210)	(0.071)	(0.074)
Biprobit—certification interval instrument	−0.165***	0.382*	−0.127	−0.069	−0.212***
	(0.061)	(0.233)	(0.197)	(0.072)	(0.080)
Biprobit—no instruments	−0.178***	0.423**	−0.142	−0.066	−0.225***
	(0.061)	(0.182)	(0.224)	(0.071)	(0.074)
RECEIVED SNAP IN LAST MONTH					
LPM (exogenous)	0.166***	0.108***	0.162***	0.192***	0.204***
	(0.008)	(0.016)	(0.019)	(0.020)	(0.015)
2SLS—citizenship and certification interval instrument	−0.166	−0.087	−0.321	0.772	−0.098
	(0.198)	(0.395)	(0.761)	(0.572)	(0.242)

between large positive or large negative effects. The Hausman-Wu test for all households provides evidence that SNAP is endogenous at the 5 percent level; however, this result weakens when SNAP is measured on the basis of the previous month. For the groups separately, we find no evidence of SNAP being endogenous. In the third row, we list results from 2SLS models that rely entirely on certification intervals for identification. These estimates are even less precise than the preceding estimates. In contrast to the previous 2SLS model, the Hausman-Wu tests do not indicate that SNAP is endogenous for any specifications.

In the next four rows, we list results from probit specifications. The first row lists average marginal effects from standard probit specifications,

TABLE 3.4 *(continued)*

Coefficients and marginal effects for SNAP receipt from LPM, 2SLS, probit, and bivariate probit models

	All households	*Households with children and unmarried parents*	*Households with children and married parents*	*Households with all elderly members*	*Other adult-only households*
RECEIVED SNAP IN LAST MONTH *(continued)*					
Hausman test	[0.081]	[0.619]	[0.510]	[0.280]	[0.201]
2SLS—certification	−0.081	−0.075	−0.578	−0.034	0.320
interval instrument	(0.411)	(0.506)	(0.856)	(2.776)	(0.690)
Hausman-Wu test	[0.538]	[0.716]	[0.333]	[0.933]	[0.866]
Probit (exogenous)	0.158***	0.108***	0.160***	0.172***	0.196***
	(0.008)	(0.016)	(0.019)	(0.019)	(0.015)
Biprobit—citizenship	−0.206***	0.135	−0.207	−0.019	−0.151**
and certification	(0.040)	(0.306)	(0.164)	(0.070)	(0.070)
interval instrument					
Biprobit—certification	−0.228***	0.175	−0.227	−0.034	−0.166**
interval instrument	(0.039)	(0.297)	(0.145)	(0.070)	(0.077)
Biprobit—no	−0.239***	0.253	−0.239	−0.031	−0.176**
instruments	(0.037)	(0.264)	(0.156)	(0.070)	(0.074)

SOURCE: Authors' estimates using weighted data from the 2009–2011 CPS-FSS.

NOTES: 2SLS = two-stage least squares. Models control for household head's gender, age, age squared, race, ethnicity, nativity, marital status, education, and employment status; numbers of adults, children, and disabled members in household; age of youngest member (households with children); elderly members; residence in urban area; state unemployment rate; log of household income; homeownership; log of food needs; missing food needs; and state and year fixed effects. Models for all households also control for household type. Robust standard errors appear in parentheses. *P* values are in brackets.

* Significant at 0.10 level.
** Significant at 0.05 level.
*** Significant at 0.01 level.

and these generate estimates that are qualitatively and quantitatively similar to the LPM estimates. The next row lists estimates from a bivariate probit model that imposes exclusion restrictions on noncitizenship status and certification intervals. The marginal effects for the combined and married-parent samples are significantly negative. Although these particular results are potentially encouraging for the theoretical model, they appear to stem entirely from functional form restrictions in the bivariate probit model. In the final rows of Table 3.4, where we report results from bivariate probit models without any variable exclusion restrictions, the marginal effect estimates are nearly identical in sign, magnitude, and precision to the preceding estimates. Thus, the results from the bottom four rows of Table 3.4 seem to bear out the findings of Greenhalgh-Stanley and Fitzpatrick (2013) and Shaefer and Gutierrez (2012).

Finally, we investigate the dose response of SNAP on food insecurity using cross-sectional and longitudinal models. For each model, we consider two measures of SNAP, an indicator for receipt of SNAP benefits within the past twelve months and the inflation-adjusted annual SNAP benefit amount. Including an indicator for the receipt of SNAP benefits allows us to assess the extent of selection bias in the dose-response literature, whereas the annual measure of SNAP benefits facilitates replication of the existing literature. We begin our dose-response analysis by estimating LPMs, followed by random- and fixed-effect LPMs. Estimated coefficients and standard errors for the SNAP receipt and annual SNAP benefit variables from alternative specifications are listed in Table 3.5. The SNAP receipt coefficients are generally consistent with the discussion presented in the preceding paragraphs, so we will limit our discussion here to the annual SNAP benefit coefficients. Although including observable controls and household fixed-effects reduces the association between SNAP receipt and food insecurity, a strong and highly significant relationship remains. The top panel lists estimates from cross-sectional models, whereas the bottom panel lists results from longitudinal models.

The first rows of the top panel list coefficients from simple univariate LPMs of food insecurity, SNAP receipt, and the annual benefit amount estimated with the cross-sectional sample. The coefficient on annual SNAP benefits is negative and significant for all groups of households. These patterns continue in the second, third, and fourth rows when increasing sets of observed controls are added.

The bottom panel of Table 3.5 considers longitudinal models. For the purposes of comparison, we estimate LPMs with standard and economic controls. The first rows report coefficients for LPMs. The associations between food insecurity and annual SNAP benefits are smaller for all groups with the exception of married parent households when compared to LPMs estimated using the cross-sectional sample.

Estimates from panel-data random- and fixed-effect LPMs are reported in the second and third rows of the bottom panel of Table 3.5. Comparisons of these estimates reveal that accounting for unobserved time-invariant household characteristics through the use of fixed effects reduces the estimated associations between annual SNAP benefits and food insecurity. The coefficients on annual SNAP benefits are negative and insignificant for all household groups except households with all elderly members. Breusch-Pagan and Hausman-Wu tests are reported below the random- and fixed-effect LPMs, respectively. The LPMs are strongly rejected for all household groups by the Breusch-Pagan test in favor of the random-effect LPMs models. In

TABLE 3-5
Coefficients on SNAP receipt and annual benefit amount from cross-sectional and longitudinal models

	All households		Households with children and unmarried parents		Households with children and married parents		Households with all elderly members		Other adult-only households	
	SNAP indicator	Annual SNAP benefit	SNAP indicator	Annual SNAP benefit	SNAP indicator	Annual SNAP benefit	SNAP indicator	Annual SNAP benefit	SNAP indicator	Annual SNAP benefit
CROSS-SECTIONAL MODELS										
LPM with no other controls	0.351*** (0.011)	−0.024*** (0.004)	0.283*** (0.023)	−0.029*** (0.006)	0.331*** (0.029)	−0.029*** (0.008)	0.345*** (0.029)	−0.045** (0.020)	0.391*** (0.019)	−0.043*** (0.009)
LPM with standard controls[a]	0.299*** (0.011)	−0.031*** (0.004)	0.276*** (0.023)	−0.030*** (0.006)	0.319*** (0.030)	−0.027*** (0.008)	0.292*** (0.029)	−0.056*** (0.021)	0.327*** (0.020)	−0.041*** (0.009)
LPM with standard and economic controls[b]	0.286*** (0.011)	−0.035*** (0.004)	0.264*** (0.023)	−0.035*** (0.006)	0.309*** (0.030)	−0.032*** (0.008)	0.283*** (0.029)	−0.061*** (0.021)	0.312*** (0.020)	−0.045*** (0.009)
LPM with standard, economic, and other assistance controls[c]	0.222*** (0.011)	−0.041*** (0.004)	0.194*** (0.023)	−0.039*** (0.006)	0.227*** (0.030)	−0.038*** (0.008)	0.235*** (0.029)	−0.052*** (0.020)	0.234*** (0.020)	−0.044*** (0.009)
LONGITUDINAL MODELS										
LPM	0.261*** (0.016)	−0.031*** (0.005)	0.245*** (0.035)	−0.029*** (0.009)	0.270*** (0.041)	−0.025** (0.011)	0.251*** (0.038)	−0.054* (0.028)	0.284*** (0.029)	−0.039*** (0.013)
Random effects LPM	0.238*** (0.014)	−0.025*** (0.005)	0.212*** (0.034)	−0.023*** (0.008)	0.249*** (0.037)	−0.020** (0.010)	0.250*** (0.027)	−0.053*** (0.019)	0.247*** (0.026)	−0.028** (0.012)
Breusch-Pagan test	[0.000]		[0.000]		[0.000]		[0.000]		[0.000]	
Fixed effects LPM	0.152*** (0.021)	−0.012* (0.007)	0.128*** (0.046)	−0.009 (0.011)	0.173*** (0.052)	−0.012 (0.014)	0.238*** (0.044)	−0.053* (0.030)	0.115*** (0.039)	−0.003 (0.017)
Hausman-Wu test	[0.000]		[0.108]		[0.074]		[0.144]		[0.000]	

SOURCE: Authors' estimates using weighted data from the 2009–2011 CPS-FSS.

NOTES: Models control for household head's gender, age, age squared, race, ethnicity, nativity, marital status, education, and employment status; numbers of adults, children, and disabled members in household; age of youngest member (households with children); elderly members; residence in urban area; state unemployment rate; log of household income; homeownership; log of food needs; missing food needs; and state and year fixed effects. Models for all households also control for household type. Robust standard errors appear in parentheses. *P* values are in brackets.

* Significant at 0.10 level.
** Significant at 0.05 level.
*** Significant at 0.01 level.

contrast to the participant/nonparticipant analyses, the Hausman-Wu tests fail to reject the random-effect LPM for all-elderly households. For unmarried parent households, the Hausman-Wu test still fails to reject random-effect LPM; however, the *P*-value is very close to the 10 percent confidence level. The random-effect LPM is rejected for all other groups.

SENSITIVITY ANALYSES

The replication analysis is based on a sample of households with incomes at or below 130 percent of the federal poverty line. However, several previous studies estimate models with larger income cutoffs. A concern in these studies is that marginally eligible households will adjust their labor supply to ensure program eligibility, potentially affecting the observed relationship between SNAP and food insecurity. We examined the sensitivity of our findings to the choice of income limits by estimating models with a sample that restricted household income to 185 percent of the federal poverty line. We used the 185 percent of the federal poverty line threshold because it is the income screen used by the CPS-FSS for the food security questions. Models estimated using the 185 percent of the federal poverty line threshold (results not shown) were very similar to those using our primary (130 percent) sample.

Another potential concern is the use of a single binary measure of food insecurity. For the replication analysis we concentrate on a binary measure of food insecurity, which is consistent with most of the previous studies. As DePolt and colleagues (2009), Gundersen and colleagues (2011), and others have pointed out, these comparisons cast aside a considerable amount of information. To examine how the findings are affected by the choice of the food insecurity measure we reestimated models using the count of affirmed food security questions, which under the assumptions of the measurement model used to determine food security status should be a sufficient statistic of the underlying food security scale. Estimating models with the count of affirmed food security questions generated results that were consistent with our reported findings using the binary food insecurity measure.

The replication analysis uses an annual measure of SNAP benefits to examine the dose response of SNAP on food insecurity. An alternative to the dollar amount of SNAP benefits is the number of months of program receipt. We tested the sensitivity of our dose response findings to the choice of dose variable by estimating models with the count of months of SNAP receipt. A comparison of the estimates suggests our findings are robust to the choice of dose variable. All our sensitivity analyses are available on request.

CONCLUSIONS

It would be hard to overstate the importance of SNAP in the food assistance landscape. It is the largest food assistance program administered by the U.S. Department of Agriculture in terms of expenditures and participation. However, despite recent research that suggests SNAP reduces food insecurity, the evidence taken as a whole is somewhat inconsistent. In an effort to understand conflicting empirical results around the effect of SNAP's effectiveness against food insecurity, we have examined theory, literature, and empirical evidence that looks at this question and have replicated methods used in previous research.

The main finding of this study is that recent results showing that food assistance reduces food insecurity may not be robust to specification choice or data. As in other research, most of our simple models suggest a higher conditional mean of food security prevalence associated with SNAP. Moreover, our results for propensity score and longitudinal models mirror those in the empirical literature in showing, quite counterintuitively, that SNAP is associated with increases in food security prevalence. Our 2SLS results are a bit more consistent with recent findings, although the estimated sizes of the effects are statistically insignificant. Similarly, our findings using dummy endogenous approaches yield somewhat inconsistent results, with many of the statistically significant results being for two-parent households with children. We note that most of the results using this method yield parameter estimates with the appropriate sign, even when they are not significant. Our dose-response models are consistent with previous research in that they suggest larger amounts of SNAP benefits are associated with a reduction in the likelihood of food insecurity. Finally, although we did not try to replicate the methods of Gundersen and Kreider (2008) or Kreider and colleagues (2012), which involve using data and logical assumptions to identify plausible bounds for the effect of food assistance on food insecurity, our results are, broadly speaking, within the bounds for their least restrictive models. This is true both for models that do take account of measurement error and for those that do not.

Taken together, these results suggest some directions for future research. For example, some models that have most consistently found that SNAP reduces food insecurity share an assumption about the functional form of the residuals in selection and outcome processes—bivariate normal. A next step could be to examine similar models while relaxing the bivariate normal assumption, perhaps by use of maximum simulated likelihood methods and factor structures—both discrete and continuous. Additionally, such a consideration should take into account that a full switching regression framework—in which the outcome is estimated separately for each treatment state but simultaneously with treatment—may yield different results.[10]

Several of the 2SLS models in this chapter and in a few other studies have led to estimated associations between SNAP and food insecurity that are consistent with expectations but statistically imprecise and indistinguishable from zero. The precision of these estimates could be increased by using statistical approaches, such as ordered categorical models, continuous models based on Rasch scores, and Rasch behavioral models, that use more of the information from the food security scale. The precision might also be increased by using alternative policy variables as instruments that are better measured. Refinements and expansions of existing policy databases should be encouraged. Similarly, to the degree possible, studies using indirect methods and natural experiments should also be encouraged.

Finally, given that the results of our dose-response models are consistent with both the literature and with economic intuition about the effect of SNAP, further exploration into the uses of these methods and the design of surveys to exploit these relationships should be a priority. Nord and Prell (2011), Mabli and colleagues (2013), and Nord (2013) offer recent examples of this kind of work.

APPENDIX: QUESTIONS IN THE FOOD SECURITY MODULE

Questions asked of all households:

1. "We worried whether our food would run out before we got money to buy more." Was that **often, sometimes,** or never true for you in the last 12 months?

2. "The food that we bought just didn't last and we didn't have money to get more." Was that **often, sometimes,** or never true for you in the last 12 months?

3. "We couldn't afford to eat balanced meals." Was that **often, sometimes,** or never true for you in the last 12 months?

4. In the last 12 months, did you or other adults in the household ever cut the size of your meals or skip meals because there wasn't enough money for food? (**Yes**/No)

5. (If yes to question 4) How often did this happen—**almost every month, some months but not every month,** or in only 1 or 2 months?

6. In the last 12 months, did you ever eat less than you felt you should because there wasn't enough money for food? (**Yes**/No)

7. In the last 12 months, were you ever hungry, but didn't eat, because there wasn't enough money for food? (**Yes**/No)

8. In the last 12 months, did you lose weight because there wasn't enough money for food? (**Yes**/No)

9. In the last 12 months did you or other adults in your household ever not eat for a whole day because there wasn't enough money for food? (**Yes**/No)

10. (If yes to question 9) How often did this happen—**almost every month, some months but not every month,** or in only 1 or 2 months?

Questions asked only of households with children under 18 years of age:

1. "We relied on only a few kinds of low-cost food to feed our children because we were running out of money to buy food." Was that **often, sometimes,** or never true for you in the last 12 months?

2. "We couldn't feed our children a balanced meal, because we couldn't afford that." Was that **often, sometimes,** or never true for you in the last 12 months?

3. "The children were not eating enough because we just couldn't afford enough food." Was that **often, sometimes,** or never true for you in the last 12 months?

4. In the last 12 months, did you ever cut the size of any of the children's meals because there wasn't enough money for food? (**Yes**/No)

5. In the last 12 months, were the children ever hungry but you just couldn't afford more food? (**Yes**/No)

6. In the last 12 months, did any of the children ever skip a meal because there wasn't enough money for food? (**Yes**/No)

7. (If yes to question 16) How often did this happen—**almost every month, some months but not every month,** or in only 1 or 2 months?

8. In the last 12 months did any of the children ever not eat for a whole day because there wasn't enough money for food? (**Yes**/No)

Note: "Affirmative" responses indicated in **bold**.

TABLE 3.A.1

Definitions of food security status for households with and without children

Food security status	Households with children	Households without children
Food secure	0–2 affirmative responses	0–2 affirmative responses
Low food security	3–7 affirmative responses	3–5 affirmative responses
Very low food security	8–18 affirmative responses	6–10 affirmative responses

TABLE 3.A.2

Characteristics of analysis households

	Households with children and unmarried parents			Households with children and married parents			Households with all elderly members			Other adult-only households		
	No SNAP last year	Received SNAP last year	Received SNAP last month	No SNAP last year	Received SNAP last year	Received SNAP last month	No SNAP last year	Received SNAP last year	Received SNAP last month	No SNAP last year	Received SNAP last year	Received SNAP last month
Food insecure	0.347 (0.476)	0.534 (0.499)	0.525 (0.499)	0.287 (0.453)	0.524 (0.500)	0.511 (0.500)	0.135 (0.342)	0.425 (0.495)	0.415 (0.493)	0.270 (0.444)	0.584 (0.493)	0.579 (0.494)
Real SNAP benefit ($000)	0.000 (0.000)	3.153 (1.753)	3.376 (1.670)	0.000 (0.000)	3.020 (1.841)	3.297 (1.767)	0.000 (0.000)	1.119 (0.880)	1.170 (0.880)	0.000 (0.000)	1.593 (1.183)	1.708 (1.181)

STANDARD EXPLANATORY VARIABLES

	Households with children and unmarried parents			Households with children and married parents			Households with all elderly members			Other adult-only households		
	No SNAP last year	Received SNAP last year	Received SNAP last month	No SNAP last year	Received SNAP last year	Received SNAP last month	No SNAP last year	Received SNAP last year	Received SNAP last month	No SNAP last year	Received SNAP last year	Received SNAP last month
Female head	0.750 (0.433)	0.858 (0.349)	0.863 (0.344)	0.435 (0.496)	0.469 (0.499)	0.464 (0.499)	0.643 (0.479)	0.706 (0.456)	0.709 (0.454)	0.453 (0.498)	0.567 (0.496)	0.574 (0.495)
Age	38.597 (12.940)	35.336 (11.567)	35.323 (11.530)	40.767 (11.107)	36.831 (10.174)	37.001 (10.284)	73.407 (8.140)	70.468 (7.756)	70.580 (7.821)	42.668 (15.743)	47.443 (13.173)	47.790 (12.973)
White (reference)	0.663 (0.473)	0.587 (0.492)	0.585 (0.493)	0.796 (0.403)	0.797 (0.403)	0.796 (0.403)	0.815 (0.388)	0.729 (0.445)	0.734 (0.442)	0.735 (0.441)	0.639 (0.480)	0.647 (0.478)
Black	0.268 (0.443)	0.359 (0.480)	0.362 (0.481)	0.111 (0.314)	0.127 (0.333)	0.123 (0.329)	0.139 (0.346)	0.225 (0.418)	0.222 (0.416)	0.184 (0.388)	0.304 (0.460)	0.298 (0.457)
Other	0.069 (0.254)	0.053 (0.225)	0.053 (0.224)	0.093 (0.290)	0.076 (0.266)	0.080 (0.271)	0.046 (0.209)	0.046 (0.210)	0.044 (0.204)	0.081 (0.272)	0.057 (0.231)	0.055 (0.229)
Hispanic	0.309 (0.462)	0.240 (0.427)	0.236 (0.425)	0.403 (0.491)	0.360 (0.480)	0.344 (0.475)	0.088 (0.283)	0.162 (0.368)	0.157 (0.364)	0.157 (0.363)	0.137 (0.344)	0.141 (0.348)
Married, spouse present	0.000	0.000	0.000	1.000	1.000	1.000	0.238 (0.426)	0.099 (0.298)	0.098 (0.298)	0.207 (0.405)	0.139 (0.346)	0.134 (0.340)
Less than high school (reference)	0.265 (0.441)	0.302 (0.459)	0.306 (0.461)	0.316 (0.465)	0.352 (0.478)	0.354 (0.479)	0.352 (0.478)	0.460 (0.499)	0.460 (0.499)	0.192 (0.394)	0.325 (0.468)	0.337 (0.473)
Some college	0.651 (0.477)	0.661 (0.474)	0.661 (0.474)	0.562 (0.496)	0.592 (0.492)	0.590 (0.492)	0.555 (0.497)	0.475 (0.500)	0.481 (0.500)	0.642 (0.479)	0.620 (0.485)	0.609 (0.488)
College graduate	0.084 (0.278)	0.038 (0.190)	0.033 (0.179)	0.122 (0.327)	0.056 (0.231)	0.055 (0.229)	0.093 (0.290)	0.064 (0.246)	0.059 (0.236)	0.166 (0.372)	0.055 (0.227)	0.055 (0.227)
Immigrant	0.271 (0.445)	0.156 (0.363)	0.146 (0.354)	0.465 (0.499)	0.366 (0.482)	0.355 (0.479)	0.138 (0.345)	0.204 (0.403)	0.196 (0.397)	0.189 (0.391)	0.103 (0.303)	0.106 (0.308)
Number of adults in household	1.882 (1.087)	1.639 (0.890)	1.617 (0.870)	2.535 (0.918)	2.432 (0.838)	2.426 (0.842)	1.282 (0.467)	1.160 (0.410)	1.161 (0.415)	1.813 (0.974)	1.688 (0.881)	1.678 (0.875)
Number of children in household	1.845 (1.034)	2.125 (1.149)	2.133 (1.146)	2.241 (1.230)	2.602 (1.319)	2.637 (1.326)	0.000	0.000	0.000	0.000	0.000	0.000
Number of disabled in household	0.124 (0.389)	0.200 (0.466)	0.208 (0.475)	0.127 (0.402)	0.245 (0.565)	0.261 (0.587)	0.138 (0.374)	0.416 (0.562)	0.429 (0.570)	0.235 (0.514)	0.654 (0.684)	0.678 (0.679)

Age of youngest in household	7.250 (5.334)	5.713 (4.916)	5.705 (4.899)	6.208 (4.929)	4.691 (4.264)	4.706 (4.273)	1.000	1.000	1.000	0.107 (0.310)	0.104 (0.305)	0.104 (0.306)
Any elderly in household	0.071 (0.257)	0.041 (0.199)	0.041 (0.199)	0.065 (0.246)	0.034 (0.181)	0.038 (0.191)						
Urban residence	0.828 (0.377)	0.812 (0.391)	0.807 (0.395)	0.821 (0.384)	0.771 (0.420)	0.768 (0.422)	0.739 (0.439)	0.765 (0.424)	0.760 (0.427)	0.817 (0.387)	0.777 (0.416)	0.771 (0.420)
State unemployment rate	9.427 (1.750)	9.274 (1.696)	9.246 (1.697)	9.583 (1.796)	9.459 (1.698)	9.440 (1.715)	9.278 (1.727)	9.014 (1.519)	8.989 (1.521)	9.364 (1.757)	9.177 (1.622)	9.163 (1.618)
ECONOMIC EXPLANATORY VARIABLES												
Head employed	0.588 (0.492)	0.421 (0.494)	0.406 (0.491)	0.604 (0.489)	0.445 (0.497)	0.427 (0.495)	0.100 (0.301)	0.043 (0.204)	0.038 (0.192)	0.489 (0.500)	0.212 (0.409)	0.187 (0.390)
Real total household income ($0000)	1.611 (0.869)	1.215 (0.810)	1.187 (0.805)	2.107 (0.965)	1.782 (0.931)	1.761 (0.936)	0.997 (0.373)	0.896 (0.329)	0.905 (0.322)	1.022 (0.584)	0.909 (0.519)	0.896 (0.514)
Own home	0.341 (0.474)	0.188 (0.391)	0.187 (0.390)	0.533 (0.499)	0.343 (0.475)	0.341 (0.474)	0.624 (0.484)	0.300 (0.458)	0.306 (0.461)	0.365 (0.481)	0.251 (0.434)	0.246 (0.431)
Real subjective food needs	116.430 (88.146)	139.683 (104.475)	141.283 (104.762)	134.392 (92.598)	152.152 (102.766)	153.790 (104.168)	53.291 (48.859)	62.534 (53.454)	60.721 (51.295)	77.360 (63.508)	90.319 (75.075)	90.299 (75.285)
Missing food needs	0.085 (0.279)	0.054 (0.227)	0.053 (0.224)	0.069 (0.253)	0.040 (0.196)	0.038 (0.190)	0.167 (0.373)	0.097 (0.296)	0.099 (0.299)	0.094 (0.291)	0.070 (0.256)	0.065 (0.247)
OTHER ASSISTANCE												
SBP last month	0.314 (0.464)	0.589 (0.492)	0.598 (0.490)	0.307 (0.461)	0.597 (0.491)	0.612 (0.488)						
NSLP last month	0.396 (0.489)	0.698 (0.459)	0.709 (0.454)	0.399 (0.490)	0.723 (0.448)	0.733 (0.443)						
WIC last month	0.135 (0.342)	0.303 (0.460)	0.307 (0.461)	0.157 (0.364)	0.366 (0.482)	0.380 (0.486)						
Food bank last month	0.098 (0.297)	0.264 (0.441)	0.274 (0.446)	0.086 (0.281)	0.250 (0.433)	0.261 (0.439)	0.054 (0.226)	0.265 (0.441)	0.262 (0.440)	0.097 (0.295)	0.369 (0.483)	0.376 (0.484)
Soup kitchen last month	0.004 (0.062)	0.023 (0.150)	0.025 (0.157)	0.004 (0.063)	0.013 (0.113)	0.014 (0.117)	0.007 (0.086)	0.022 (0.146)	0.021 (0.143)	0.016 (0.126)	0.078 (0.268)	0.079 (0.270)
INSTRUMENTS												
Noncitizen	0.185 (0.388)	0.104 (0.306)	0.095 (0.294)	0.305 (0.461)	0.274 (0.446)	0.266 (0.442)	0.038 (0.191)	0.036 (0.185)	0.037 (0.190)	0.113 (0.316)	0.037 (0.188)	0.037 (0.190)
Median state certification interval	9.121 (2.987)	9.170 (2.979)	9.233 (2.975)	9.114 (2.982)	9.021 (2.984)	9.094 (2.982)	9.220 (2.980)	9.268 (2.981)	9.256 (2.985)	9.128 (2.987)	9.227 (2.977)	9.292 (2.971)
Observations N	2,266	3,529	3,130	2,655	1,591	1,344	4,391	1,090	1,004	6,523	2,824	2,489

SOURCE: Authors' estimates of means and standard deviations (in parentheses) using weighted household data from the 2009–2011 Current Population Survey Food Security Supplement.

NOTE: Means and standard deviations (in parentheses).

NOTES

Earlier versions of this paper were presented at the Five Decades of Food Stamps Conference, September 20, 2013, in Washington, DC, and at the 16th Labour Econometrics Workshop, August 10, 2013, in Melbourne, Australia. The authors thank Craig Gundersen, John Pepper, Steven Stillman, James Ziliak, and conference participants for helpful comments. The views expressed in this paper are those of the authors and not necessarily those of the ERS or USDA.

1. There is a concern that a unidimensional scale might not be appropriate for measuring food security among households with children. Nord and Coleman-Jensen (2014) provide an alternate classification to address this concern.

2. Gundersen and Gruber (2001), Gundersen and Oliveira (2001), Huffman and Jensen (2003), Ribar and Hamrick (2003), Meyerhoefer and Yang (2011), and Caswell and Yaktine (2013) also provide conceptual models.

3. In addition to these reviews, Meyerhoefer and Yang (2011) have summarized research on the association of SNAP with people's body weight and health.

4. Borjas's 2004 multivariate analysis is a notable exception.

5. The researchers used sampling weights to address this issue.

6. A fuller discussion of these issues in relation to food assistance programs can be found in Meyerhoefer and Yang (2011).

7. We focus on 2009–2011 because it is the most recent period available with consistent federal policies. The period includes the 15 percent benefit increase and other provisions from the American Recovery and Reinvestment Act of 2009. Extending the analysis further back would entail accounting for these policy changes.

8. We also estimate asymptotic standard errors following Terza (2012); however, we report the delta method standard errors to increase the replicability of our analysis.

9. In preliminary analyses, we also experimented with state-level measures of broad-based categorical eligibility policies and standard utility allowance provisions (two policies that are the focus of debate as the U.S. Congress considers the reauthorization of the Farm Bill, which includes funding for SNAP). However, neither of these policy variables was predictive of SNAP receipt in our samples.

10. This has recently been reported by Gregory and Coleman-Jensen (2013), who found that the ATE for SNAP participation is positive in a switching regression framework with bivariate normal errors, but negative in a simple bivariate probit.

REFERENCES

Alaimo, K, R. R. Briefel, E. A. Frongillo, and C. M. Olson. 1998. "Food Insufficiency Exists in the United States: Results from the Third National Health and Nutrition Examination Survey (NHANES III)." *American Journal of Public Health* 88(3): 419–426.

Barrett, C. B. 2002. "Food Security and Food Assistance Programs." In B. L. Gardner and G. C. Rausser, eds., *Handbook of Agricultural Economics*, vol. 2B. Amsterdam: Elsevier Science B.V.

Bartfeld, J., and R. Dunifon. 2006. "State-Level Predictors of Food Insecurity among Households with Children." *Journal of Policy Analysis and Management* 25(4): 921–942.

Becker, G. S. 1965. "A Theory of the Allocation of Time." *Economic Journal* 75(299): 493–517.

Bernell, S. L., B. A. Weber, and M. E. Edwards. 2006. "Restricted Opportunities, Personal Choices, Ineffective Policies: What Explains Food Insecurity in Oregon?" *Journal of Agricultural and Resource Economics* 31(2): 193–211.

Bhattacharya, J., and J. Currie. 2001. "Youths at Nutritional Risk: Malnourished or Misnourished?" In J. Gruber, ed., *Risky Behavior among Youths: An Economic Analysis*. Chicago: University of Chicago Press.

Bhattacharya, J., J. Currie, and S. Haider. 2004. "Poverty, Food Insecurity, and Nutritional Outcomes in Children and Adults." *Journal of Health Economics* 23(4): 839–862.

Borjas, G. J. 2004. "Food Insecurity and Public Assistance." *Journal of Public Economics* 88(7–8): 1421–1443.

Caswell, J. A., and A. L. Yaktine (eds.). 2013. *Supplemental Nutrition Assistance Program: Examining the Evidence to Define Benefit Adequacy*. Washington, DC: National Academies Press.

Cohen, B., J. Ohls, M. Andrews, M. Ponza, L. Moreno, A. Zambrowski, and R. Cohen. 1999. "Food Stamp Participants' Food Security and Nutrient Availability: Final Report." Report submitted to U.S. Department of Agriculture Food and Nutrition Service. Princeton, NJ: Mathematica Policy Research, Inc.

Coleman-Jensen, A., M. Nord, M. Andrews, and S. Carlson. 2012. *Household Food Security in the United States in 2011*. Economic Research Report no.141. Washington, DC: Economic Research Service, U.S. Department of Agriculture.

Currie, J. 2003. "U.S. Food and Nutrition Programs." In R. A. Moffitt, ed., *Means-Tested Transfer Programs in the United States*, 199–289. Chicago: University of Chicago Press.

DePolt, R. A., R. A. Moffitt, and D. C. Ribar. 2009. "Food Stamps, Temporary Assistance for Needy Families and Food Hardships in Three American Cities." *Pacific Economic Review* 14(4): 445–473.

Fox, M. K., W. Hamilton, and B. H. Lin (eds.). 2004. *Effects of Food Assistance and Nutrition Programs on Nutrition and Health: Vol. 3, Literature Review*. Food Assistance and Nutrition Research Report no. 19-3. Washington, DC: U.S. Department of Agriculture, Economic Research Service.

Fram, S. F., E. A. Frongillo Jr., S. J. Jones, R. C. Williams, M. P. Burke, K. P. DeLoach, and C. E. Blake. 2011. "Children Are Aware of Food Insecurity and Take Responsibility for Managing Food Resources." *Journal of Nutrition* 141(6): 1114–1119.

Gibson-Davis, C. M., and E. M. Foster. 2006. "A Cautionary Tale: Using Propensity Scores to Estimate the Effect of Food Stamps on Food Insecurity." *Social Service Review* 80(1): 93–126.

Greenhalgh-Stanley, N., and K. Fitzpatrick. 2013. "Food Stamps, Food Sufficiency, and Diet-Related Disease among the Elderly." Institute for Research on Poverty Discussion Paper no. 1407-13. Madison: University of Wisconsin.

Gregory, C. A., and A. Coleman-Jensen. 2013. "Do Higher Food Prices Mean Higher Food Insecurity in the US?" *Applied Economic Perspectives and Policy* 35(4): 679–707.

Gronau, R. 1977. "Leisure, Home Production, and Work—The Theory of the Allocation of Time Revisited." *Journal of Political Economy* 29(6): 1099–1123.

Grossman, M. 1972. "On the Concept of Health Capital and the Demand for Health." *Journal of Political Economy* 80(2): 223–255.

Gundersen, C., and J. Gruber. 2001. "The Dynamic Determinants of Food Insufficiency." In M. S. Andrews and M. A. Prell, eds., *Second Food Security Measurement and Research Conference, Vol. 2: Papers.* Food Assistance and Nutrition Research Report no. 11-2. Washington, DC: U.S. Department of Agriculture, Economic Research Service.

Gundersen, C., and B. Kreider. 2008. "Food Stamps and Food Insecurity: What Can Be Learned in the Presence of Non-Classical Measurement Error?" *Journal of Human Resources.* 43(2): 352–382.

Gundersen, C., B. Kreider, and J. Pepper. 2011. "The Economics of Food Insecurity in the United States." *Applied Economic Perspectives and Policy* 33(3): 281–303.

Gundersen, C., and V. Oliveira. 2001. "The Food Stamp Program and Food Insufficiency." *American Journal of Agricultural Economics* 83(4): 875–887.

Gundersen, C., and D. C. Ribar. 2011. "Food Insecurity and Insufficiency at Low Levels of Food Expenditures." *Review of Income and Wealth* 57(4): 704–726.

Hamilton, W. L., J. T. Cook, W. W. Thompson, L. F. Burton, E. A. Frongillo Jr., C. M. Olson, and C. A. Welder. 1997. *Household Food Security in the United States in 1995: Summary Report of the Food Security Measurement Project.* Washington, DC: U.S. Department of Agriculture, Economic Research Service.

Huffman, S. K., and H. H. Jensen. 2003. "Do Food Assistance Programs Improve Household Food Security? Recent Evidence from the United States." Working paper 03-WP 335. Ames: Iowa State University.

Jolliffe, D., and J. P. Ziliak, eds. 2008. *Income Volatility and Food Assistance in the United States.* Kalamazoo, MI: The W. E. Upjohn Institute for Employment Research.

Joyce, K. M., A. Breen, S. Ettinger de Cuba, J. T. Cook, K. W. Barrett, G. Paik, N. Rishi, B. Pullen, A. Schiffmiller, and D. A. Frank. 2012. "Household Hardships, Public Programs, and Their Associations with the Health and Development of Very Young Children: Insights from Children's HealthWatch." *Journal of Applied Research on Children: Informing Policy for Children at Risk* 3(1): Article 4.

Kabbani, N. S., and M. Y. Kmeid. 2005. "The Role of Food Assistance in Helping Food Insecure Households Escape Hunger." *Review of Agricultural Economics* 27(3): 439–445.

Kreider, B., J. V. Pepper, C. Gundersen, and D. Joliffe. 2012. "Identifying the Effects of SNAP (Food Stamps) on Child Health Outcomes when Participation Is Endogenous and Misreported." *Journal of American Statistical Association* 107(499): 958–975.

Mabli, J., J. Ohls, L. Dragoset, L. Castner, and B. Santos. 2013. *Measuring the Effect of Supplemental Nutrition Assistance Program (SNAP) Participation on Food Security*. Nutrition Assistance Program Report. Washington, DC: U.S. Department of Agriculture, Food and Nutrition Service.

Manski, C. F. 1995. *The Identification Problem in the Social Sciences*. Cambridge, MA: Harvard University Press.

Meyerhoefer, C. D., and M. Yang. 2011. "The Relationship between Food Assistance and Health: A Review of the Literature and Empirical Strategies for Identifying Program Effects." *Applied Economic Perspectives and Policy* 33(3): 304–344.

Mykerezi, E., and B. Mills. 2010. "The Impact of Food Stamp Program Participation on Household Food Insecurity." *American Journal of Agricultural Economics* 92(5): 1379–1391.

Nord, M. 2013. *Effects of the Decline in the Real Value of SNAP Benefits from 2009–2011*. Economic Research Report 151. Washington, DC: U.S. Department of Agriculture, Economic Research Service.

Nord, M., and A. Coleman-Jensen. 2014. "Improving Food Security Classification of Households with Children." *Journal of Hunger and Environmental Nutrition* 9(3): 318–333.

Nord, M., and A. M. Golla. 2009. *Does SNAP Decrease Food Insecurity? Untangling the Self-Selection Effect*. Economic Research Report No. 85. Washington, DC: U.S. Department of Agriculture, Economic Research Service.

Nord, M., and M. Prell. 2011. *Food Security Improved Following the 2009 ARRA Increase in SNAP Benefits*. Economic Research Report No. 116. Washington, DC: U.S. Department of Agriculture, Economic Research Service.

Ratcliffe, C., S. McKernan, and S. Zhang. 2011. "How Much Does the Supplemental Nutrition Assistance Program Reduce Food Insecurity?" *American Journal of Agricultural Economics* 93(4): 1082–1098.

Ribar, D. C., and M. Edelhoch. 2008. "Earnings Volatility and the Reasons for Leaving the Food Stamp Program." In D. Jolliffe and J. P. Ziliak, eds., *Income Volatility and Food Assistance in the United States*, 63–102. Kalamazoo, MI: W. E. Upjohn Institute for Employment Research.

Ribar, D. C., M. Edelhoch, and Q. Liu. 2008. "Watching the Clocks: The Role of Food Stamp Recertification and TANF Time Limits in Caseload Dynamics." *Journal of Human Resources* 43(1): 208–239.

———. 2010. "Food Stamp Participation and Employment among Adult-Only Households." *Southern Economic Journal* 77(2): 244–270.

Ribar, D. C., and K. S. Hamrick. 2003. *Dynamics of Poverty and Food Sufficiency*. Food Assistance and Nutrition Research Report No. 36. Washington, DC: U.S. Department of Agriculture, Economic Research Service.

Rose, D., C. Gundersen, and V. Oliveira. 1998. "Socio-Economic Determinants of Food Insecurity in the United States: Evidence from the SIPP and CSFII Datasets." Technical Bulletin 1869. Washington, DC: Economic Research Service, U.S. Department of Agriculture.

Rosenbaum, P., and D. Rubin. 1983. "The Central Role of the Propensity Score in Observational Studies for Causal Effects." *Biometrika* 70(1): 41–55.

Shaefer, H. L., and I. Gutierrez. 2012. "The Supplemental Nutrition Assistance Program and Material Hardships among Low-Income Households with Children." Unpublished manuscript. Ann Arbor: University of Michigan.

Terza, J. V. 2012. "Correct Standard Errors for Multi-Stage Regression-Based Estimators: A Practitioner's Guide with Illustrations." Unpublished manuscript. Indianapolis: Indiana University-Purdue University Indianapolis.

Van Hook, J., and K. S. Balistreri. 2006. "Ineligible Parents, Eligible Children: Food Stamps Receipt, Allotments, and Food Insecurity among Children of Immigrants." *Social Science Research* 35(1): 228–251.

Watson, T., L. Shore Sheppard, and L. Schmidt. 2012. "The Effect of Safety Net Programs on Food Insecurity." DP 2012-12. Lexington: University of Kentucky Center for Poverty Research.

Wilde, J. 2000. "Identification of Multiple Equation Probit Models with Endogenous Dummy Regressors." *Economics Letters* 69(3): 309–312.

Wilde, P. E. 2007. "Measuring the Effect of Food Stamps on Food Insecurity and Hunger: Research and Policy Considerations." *Journal of Nutrition* 137(2): 307–310.

Wilde, P. E., and M. Nord. 2005. "The Effect of Food Stamps on Food Security: A Panel Data Approach." *Review of Agricultural Economics* 27(3): 425–432.

Wilde, P. E., and C. K. Ranney. 2000. "The Monthly Food Stamp Cycle: Shopping Frequency and Food Intake Decisions in an Endogenous Switching Regression Framework." *American Journal of Agricultural Economics* 82(1): 200–213.

Wunderlich, G. S., and J. L. Norwood (eds.). 2006. *Food Insecurity and Hunger in the United States: An Assessment of the Measure.* Washington, DC: National Academies Press.

Yen, S. T., M. Andrews, Z. Chen, and D. B. Eastwood. 2008. "Food Stamp Program Participation and Food Insecurity: An Instrumental Variables Approach." *American Journal of Agricultural Economics* 90(1): 117–132.

CHAPTER FOUR

SNAP and Food Consumption

Hilary W. Hoynes
Leslie McGranahan
Diane W. Schanzenbach

Economists have a robust theoretical framework, as described in the following pages, through which to predict consumption responses to in-kind transfers such as SNAP. In this chapter, we review this framework and then present new evidence on food spending patterns among households that are eligible for SNAP, as well as other population groups. We compare these spending patterns to parameters used in the SNAP benefit formula and to average benefit levels. These data provide a rich description of the food spending patterns of low-income families and, importantly, an evaluation of the adequacy of the SNAP program. Additionally, they allow us to present new evidence on one of the oldest questions in the analysis of the program—how the provision of food benefits *in-kind* affects food spending in an absolute sense and relative to providing these benefits in cash.

SNAP is designed to supplement a family's ability to purchase food so that they are able to purchase at least a minimal-cost, nutritious diet. The cost of this diet is referred to as the "needs standard" and as described in the following discussion is an important parameter in the formula by which benefits are awarded. We find that the program's needs standard is close to median food spending among eligible and recipient households but that a substantial fraction of SNAP households spend more on food than the needs standard. We also show that the relationship between family size and food spending is steeper than the slope of the SNAP needs parameter. In other words, the actual spending of smaller families is higher compared with larger families than is assumed in the benefits calculation. This suggests that benefits may be relatively more generous for larger households. Finally, we show that most families spend more on food than their predicted benefit allotment. In this case, the neoclassical model implies that SNAP benefits are treated like cash.

A FRAMEWORK FOR CONSUMPTION RESPONSES TO SNAP

The Neoclassical Theory

We begin by presenting the neoclassical model of consumer choice and use this to discuss predictions for the effects of SNAP on family spending patterns.[1] Figure 4.1a presents the standard Southworth (1945) model, in which a consumer chooses to allocate a fixed budget between food and all other goods. The slope of the budget line is the relative price of food to other goods. In the absence of SNAP, the budget constraint is represented by the line AB. When SNAP is introduced, it shifts the budget constraint out by the food benefit amount B_F to the new budget line labeled ACD. The first, and most important, prediction of the neoclassical model is that the presence of, or increase in the generosity of, the SNAP transfer leads to a shift out in the budget constraint. The transfer does not alter the relative prices of different goods, so in the economic model it can be analyzed as a pure income effect, and as a result we predict an increase in the consumption level of all normal goods. Thus, the central prediction is that food stamps, like an increase in disposable income or a cash transfer, will increase both food spending and nonfood spending.

However, SNAP benefits are provided as a voucher that can be used only toward food purchases. Canonical economic theory predicts that in-kind transfers like SNAP are treated as if they are cash as long as their value is no larger than the amount that a consumer would spend on the good if she had the same total income in cash. Stated differently, SNAP benefits are like cash as long as the household wants to spend at least the benefit amount on food. Returning to our figure, there is a portion of the budget set that is not attainable with SNAP that would be attainable with the equivalent-value transfer in cash. In other words, because the benefits B_F are provided in the form of a food voucher, this amount is not available to purchase other goods, and thus we would expect a consumer to purchase at least B_F amount of food. As shown in Figure 4.1, paying benefits in the form of a food voucher leads to a nonlinear budget constraint, labeled ACD in our figure, which has a kink point at C.

Figure 4.1b illustrates how consumption responds to SNAP benefits. In accordance with standard economic theory, we assume that consumers have well-defined preferences that can be represented in a utility curve. In the absence of SNAP, a typical consumer purchases some mix of food and nonfood goods, choosing the bundle that maximizes her utility and exhausts her budget constraint. This is represented in panel B as point $A_0{}^*$, with the consumer purchasing food in the amount F_0. After SNAP is introduced, the budget constraint shifts outward and the consumer chooses the consumption bundle represented by point $A_1{}^*$. Note that consumption of both goods

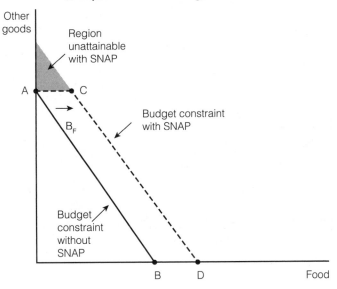

a. Impact of SNAP on budget constraints

Other goods

Region unattainable with SNAP

A — — — C

B_F

Budget constraint with SNAP

Budget constraint without SNAP

B   D   Food

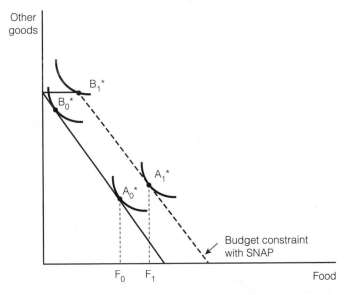

b. Consumption decisions in response to SNAP

Other goods

B_1^*

B_0^*

A_1^*

A_0^*

Budget constraint with SNAP

F_0 F_1 Food

Figure 4.1. Economic frameworks for analyzing SNAP.

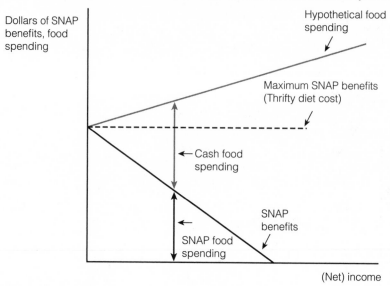

c. **Stylized relationship among income, benefits, and food spending**

Dollars of SNAP
benefits, food
spending

Hypothetical food
spending

Maximum SNAP benefits
(Thrifty diet cost)

←Cash food
spending

SNAP
benefits

←

SNAP food
spending

(Net) income

Figure 4.1.   (continued)

increases, and food consumption goes up by less than the full SNAP benefit amount. Such a consumer is termed *inframarginal* because the preferred consumption bundle is below the margin where the in-kind benefits would need to be spent on food. The canonical model predicts that for these consumers SNAP will increase food spending by the same amount as if the benefits were paid in cash. As discussed further in the following pages, the predicted impacts of proposed policy changes, such as increases in benefit levels and calls to restrict purchases of certain goods with SNAP benefits, hinges on what proportion of recipients is inframarginal. We will show that the vast majority of SNAP recipients are inframarginal, meaning they spend more than their benefit amount on food.

There are two important exceptions to the SNAP-as-cash model, though. The first is for consumers who prefer relatively little food consumption. In the absence of SNAP, such a consumer may choose the consumption bundle labeled $B_0{}^*$ in Figure 4.1b. When SNAP is introduced, this consumer spends only his benefit amount on food, preferring to use all available cash resources to purchase other goods as represented at point $B_1{}^*$. If benefits were paid in cash instead of as a food voucher, the consumer would opt to purchase less food and more of other goods and could obtain a higher level of utility. As a result, for this type of consumer, the canonical model predicts that SNAP will increase food spending by more than an equivalent cash transfer would. Another exception to the standard model comes from behavioral economics and predicts that SNAP may not be equivalent to cash if households use a mental accounting framework that puts the benefits in a separate "category."[2]

The Benefit Formula

A stylized version of the benefit formula is presented in Figure 4.1c for a family of a fixed size. A key parameter of the formula is the cost of food under the USDA's Thrifty Food Plan, which we term the "needs standard" in this chapter. The maximum SNAP benefit amount (the horizontal line in the figure) is typically set equal to the needs standard, although sometimes Congress sets maximum benefits equal to some multiple of the needs standard. For example, the American Recovery and Reinvestment Act of 2009 temporarily raised maximum benefits to be 113.6 percent of the needs standard.

SNAP is designed to fill the gap between the needs standard and the cash resources available to a family that can be used to purchase food. A family with no income receives the maximum benefit amount and is expected to contribute nothing out-of-pocket to food purchases. Thus, total food spending (depicted by the upward sloping line "hypothetical food spending") equals maximum benefits for a family with no other income source. The food spending line is upward sloping based on the assumption that, as income increases, desired spending on food (and all other normal goods) increases. As a family's income increases, the SNAP formula expects them to be able to spend more of their own cash on food purchases, and SNAP benefits are reduced accordingly. The slope of the SNAP benefits line in Figure 4.1c is known as the benefit reduction rate and is currently set at 0.3. Therefore, the benefit formula can be described mathematically as follows:

$$\text{Benefits} = \text{Max\_Benefit} - 0.3 * \text{Income} \tag{1}$$

The SNAP benefit as a function of net family income is represented by the downward-sloping line on the figure. Finally, the family's out-of-pocket spending on food is the vertical distance between the SNAP benefits line and the food spending line. Important policy issues include whether the needs standard is set at an appropriate level and whether the benefit reduction rate is appropriate. We explore these issues in more detail in the empirical results following.

In practice, the SNAP benefit formula is somewhat more complicated than we have described, because benefit levels are a function of net income and not total income. Net income is calculated as total earned income plus any unearned income minus the following deductions: a standard deduction, a deduction of some of the earned income, an excess-housing-cost deduction, a deduction for child care costs associated with working/training, and a medical-cost deduction that is available only to the elderly and disabled. Because of the mechanics of these deductions, in practice the benefit reduction rate out of gross income is somewhat lower than 0.3. It is worth pointing out that the SNAP benefit reduction rate is much lower than that used in other safety net programs such as disability and Temporary Assistance for Needy Families (TANF).

PRIOR RESEARCH ON CONSUMPTION RESPONSES TO SNAP

The first-order prediction of the model is that SNAP, by shifting out the budget set, should lead to an increase in food (and nonfood) spending. This is confirmed in the empirical literature. A large literature, mostly using data from more than twenty years ago, focuses on whether SNAP leads to larger increases in food spending than a similar sized cash transfer. Many papers have found that SNAP recipients consume more food out of their SNAP benefits than they would with an equivalent cash transfer. More recent papers, however, based on research designs that are better able to isolate causality, have found evidence of results more consistent with the standard predictions, namely, that SNAP benefits lead to consumption changes comparable to similar cash benefits for inframarginal households (Hoynes and Schanzenbach 2015).

Early observational studies (summarized in Fraker 1990 and Levedahl 1995) typically estimate the marginal propensity to consume food using the following linear equation (or a comparable one using log of food spending and/or log of income):

$$fspend_i = \beta_0 + \beta_1 cash_i + \beta_2 fstamp_i + Z_i\gamma + \varepsilon_i \tag{2}$$

where $fspend_i$ is expenditure on food for household i; $cash_i$ and $fstamp_i$ are income in cash and from food stamps, respectively; Z_i is a vector of covariates such as household size and age/gender makeup; and ε_i is an error term. Here the primary impact of food stamps is measured as the increased consumption out of food stamps compared to cash income, as measured by the differences in estimated coefficients by income type in equation (2).

This literature suffers from many of the standard shortcomings of observational studies conducted in the 1970s and 1980s. It is important that food stamp participation is taken as exogenous and the estimates are identified by comparing food stamp recipients to "similar" nonrecipients. Standard models of program participation (Moffitt 1983; Currie 2006), however, show that program participation is a choice variable and—in this case—positively correlated with tastes for food consumption. Critically, then, these naïve comparisons between participants and nonparticipants are expected to *overstate* the impact of the program on food consumption.

This upward bias seems evident in the literature. Fraker (1990), in his summary of the literature, reports that the estimates of the marginal propensity to consume (MPC) food out of food stamps are two to ten times higher than the estimated MPC food out of cash income. The median study in Fraker's literature review reports a marginal propensity to consume food out of food stamp income that is 3.8 times as large as that from cash income.[3] These findings are often interpreted as evidence that food stamps increase food spending by more than an equivalent cash-transfer system.

Another set of evidence comes from randomized experiments conducted by the USDA in the early 1990s. In those experiments, the treatment group received its food stamp benefits in cash while the controls received the standard food stamp voucher. The results of these experiments indicate that spending on food was only about 5 percent higher among the group that received benefits paid in stamps (Ohls et al. 1992; Fraker, Martini, and Ohls 1995). Schanzenbach (2007) finds that the mean treatment effect is a combination of no difference in food spending among inframarginal recipients and a substantial shift in consumption toward food for stamp recipients at the margin—that is, among those who would prefer to spend less on food than their benefit. Thus the experimental literature concludes that SNAP and cash payments would provide very similar effects on food spending. These experiments provide evidence on the difference between cash and vouchers but do not provide estimates for the broader question of how providing SNAP benefits, by increasing family disposable income, affects food spending or consumption more broadly.

Recent work by two of us (Hoynes and Schanzenbach 2009) provides the first quasi-experimental research on the effects of SNAP on food spending. We use the initial rollout of the program, which took place across the approximately 3,000 U.S. counties between 1961 and 1975. Our estimates use this "program introduction" design by comparing differences across counties over time in a difference-in-differences approach. We find that the introduction of the program leads to a decrease in out-of-pocket food spending and an increase in overall food expenditures, just as the model described in Figure 4.1 predicts. The estimated marginal propensity to consume food out of food stamp income is close to the marginal propensity to consume out of cash income. In addition, those predicted to be constrained (at the kink in Figure 4.1) experience larger increases in food spending with the introduction of food stamps.

Measuring Spending Patterns

The preceding discussion suggests that to understand the effect of SNAP on consumption we need to know the relationship between desired food spending and the magnitude of SNAP benefits. Although there is little such evidence in the literature, we aim to address this by presenting a comprehensive description of the overall food spending patterns of SNAP households and how those have evolved over time. In particular, we analyze a time series of data from the Consumer Expenditure Survey, the most comprehensive source of microdata on spending in the United States. We document trends in spending on food among SNAP recipients and SNAP-eligible households and compare these both to the program's assumed needs standards and to benefit levels. Of course, we are not investigating the causal impact of the food stamp program because doing so would require a research design that accounts for selection into the program (for a discussion of issues related to selection into the program, see Chapters Three and Five in this volume), and we have not found a suitable approach to do so. Rather, we present the underlying consumption patterns to inform the predictions of the economic model.

We are interested in measuring how well the food stamp program's benefit formula matches the food consumption patterns of households. We investigate both how the needs standards and average benefit amounts correspond to food consumption patterns and more nuanced aspects of the program such as how family size adjustments correspond to observed consumption across different family sizes.

Measures of Food Consumption

The Consumer Expenditure Survey (CEX) tracks the expenditure patterns of a representative sample of Consumer Units, a unit conceptually similar to a household. In the survey, expenditures are included independent of the method of payment (for example, food stamps, cash out of pocket). Importantly for our analysis, the instructions specify that households are to include items paid for with SNAP. However, we cannot link individual items to their source of payment. In other words, we cannot identify which particular food items are purchased with SNAP benefits and which are purchased with other family resources. Note that the CEX measures expenditure, not consumption, so it does not capture food provided free of charge through other programs (school meals, emergency food) or by nonprofits and does not account for the fact that some food is thrown out or consumed at a later date. There are two subsurveys in the CEX—the Interview and the Diary. We rely almost exclusively on the Interview Survey because it asks about food expenditures over a longer time horizon (three months) than the Diary (one week), and we want to smooth over the substantial week-to-week variation in food purchases.[4]

We calculate three measures of monthly food expenditures for households in the survey. First is spending on food for at-home consumption.

SNAP benefits can be used only to purchase food intended for preparation and consumption at home. Prepared hot foods, fast food, or restaurant foods cannot be purchased with SNAP benefits. The CEX "food-at-home" concept is the one that is the closest (but still imperfect) match to the items that can be purchased with SNAP benefits.[5] This measure collects information on spending on food at grocery stores, convenience stores, specialty stores, farmers' markets, and home delivery services, minus the cost of paper products, cleaning supplies, pet food, and alcohol.

The second measure is total food spending, including both food at home and food away from home. Food away from home includes food purchased at restaurants, fast-food establishments, and cafeterias. Total food spending shows the role of food spending in the household's budget.

The third measure we use is an *adjusted* total food spending measure. Food away from home is typically more expensive than food at home, because the price of food away from home implicitly includes costs of preparation and service, whereas households typically provide their own labor to prepare and serve food at home. Although higher-income households spend a higher percentage of their food dollars away from home, low-income households also spend some money on food away from home. We would like to construct a measure that accounts for all food spending but adjusts the price of food away from home to a food-at-home equivalent. In other words, spending on dining out can be thought of as a combination of spending on food, preparation, and service, and our goal is to extract solely the food portion of away-from-home spending. Based on tabulations from Morrison, Mancino, and Variyam (2011) that provide information on the per calorie cost of food at home and away from home, we divide total spending on food away from home into the cost of preparation and service (37 percent) and the cost of food (63 percent). We then calculate our measure of "adjusted total food spending" as the cost of food at home plus the cost of only the food portion of spending on food away from home. We prefer this adjusted total food spending measure because we think it is the most accurate and comprehensive measure of food expenditure.

MEASURES OF SNAP

The CEX directly asks households about SNAP benefit receipt; however, total benefits received and participation are severely understated relative to administrative totals. The fraction of dollars reported in the interview surveys in the CEX ranges from 35 to 75 percent of administrative totals since 1990 (see McGranahan 2014). We provide some evidence on the relationship between spending and reported SNAP benefits, but, due to this underreporting, we focus our analysis on other SNAP measures.

We use four different concepts when considering SNAP benefit amounts. First is the needs standard, which is based on the Thrifty Food Plan budget for a family of four in a given year and is then adjusted by family size (we return to this family size adjustment later). Second is the maximum benefit level (MAXBEN), which is typically set by Congress to equal 99 to 103 percent of the needs standard. As part of the ARRA stimulus, maximum benefits were temporarily increased by 13.6 percent beginning in April 2009. Third, we use SNAP benefits reported by households in the survey, even though we are aware that this includes some underreporting of benefits. We call households that report benefit receipt "SNAP-recipient" households. Fourth, we impute benefits according to the SNAP benefit formula using information on a household's income, family size, age, disability status, and spending on child care, medical care, and shelter. We call households for which there is a positive imputed benefit level "SNAP-eligible" households.

Overall, our imputation procedure leads to an overestimate of total spending on the SNAP program compared to actual programmatic spending reported by the U.S. Department of Agriculture (USDA 2014). This is partly due to the fact that in the imputations we assume all eligible households receive benefits. This is a substantial overstatement of benefit receipt because on average over the years covered in this chapter only 63 percent of eligible households participated in the program.[6] People who are eligible for relatively small benefits are less likely to enroll in the program—on average participants took up approximately 80 percent of available benefits (Eslami 2014). However, our imputed SNAP spending is still higher than estimates of what programmatic spending would have been had all eligible households taken up all available benefits. We attribute the higher imputed benefits in the CEX to income underreporting. As a result, we impute benefit levels (as a function of reported income) that are too high, and we also deem some households to be income eligible based on reported income that would not have been eligible if we could observe actual income. A strength of our approach is presenting these four approaches that have different advantages and disadvantages.

Spending in Relation to the Needs Standard

An important parameter for SNAP benefit allotments is the needs standard, which is the level of expenditures necessary to purchase a "healthful and minimal cost meal plan." The needs standard is based on the USDA's Thrifty Food Plan (TFP), and the maximum benefit is a function of the TFP needs standard. We begin by comparing how *actual* spending compares with the needs standard in Figure 4.2. We tabulate adjusted total food spending— that is, food at home plus a fraction of food away from home as previously described—relative to the needs standards. Note that we use the needs standard instead of maximum benefit levels to abstract from the temporary 2009 ARRA benefit increase.

Figure 4.2a shows results for all households from 1990 to 2013. Approximately 32 percent of households spend less on food than the needs standard over the time period covered by our data. Another 30 percent spend between 100 and 150 percent of the needs standard. Eighteen and 20 percent of households, respectively, spend between 150 and 200 percent, and more than 200 percent of the needs standards.[7] Figure 4.2b limits the results to households with incomes less than 200 percent of the poverty line. Because these households have lower levels of income, we expect them to spend less on food (and other goods). Indeed, compared to panel A, a higher share—48 percent—report spending less than the needs standard, and 23 percent spend more than 150 percent of it. Among households that report receiving SNAP income (panel C), approximately 62 percent spend less than the needs standard, and only 12 percent spend more than 150 percent of it.

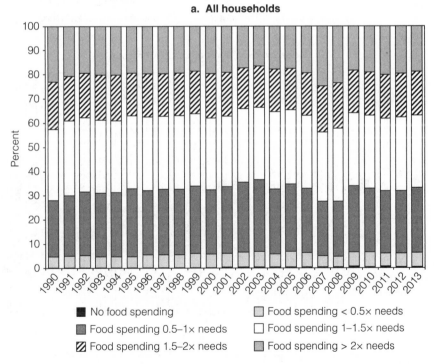

Figure 4.2. Adjusted total food spending relative to needs standards. Note: Adjusted total food spending includes spending on food at home plus 0.63 times food away from home.

SOURCE: Authors' calculations using CEX data.

b. Households with income less than 200 percent of the federal poverty line

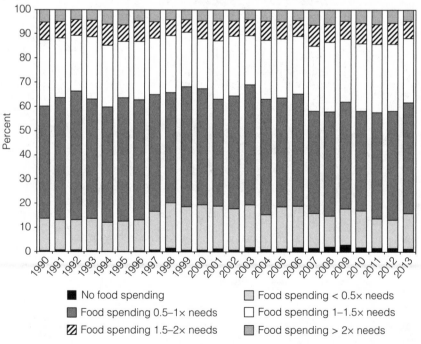

c. Households with reported SNAP receipt

Figure 4.2. (*continued*)

TABLE 4.1

Adjusted food spending as a percentage of the needs standard, 1990–2013

	All households	Households less than 200 percent of federal poverty line	Households eligible for SNAP			
			Overall	HH with children	Elderly member	SNAP recipients
	(1)	(2)	(3)	(4)	(5)	(6)
No reported spending	0.3%	0.8%	1.0%	0.5%	1.2%	1.2%
0–50	5.5%	10.6%	13.0%	16.2%	8.8%	14.4%
50–100	26.4%	36.9%	38.4%	50.8%	32.5%	46.4%
100–150	30.2%	28.8%	26.8%	23.4%	30.0%	25.6%
150–200	17.9%	12.5%	11.1%	5.9%	14.3%	7.4%
200+	19.7%	10.4%	9.7%	3.2%	13.2%	4.9%
Sample size N	1,695,679	599,447	336,176	134,465	100,327	117,653

SOURCE: Authors' calculations using Consumer Expenditures Survey (CEX) data.

The percentage of households falling into each expenditure bin (averaged across all years) is shown in Table 4.1.

In Figure 4.3, we display median adjusted total food spending relative to the needs standards for all households and various subsets of interest. For SNAP-eligible households, at the median, food spending is fairly close to the needs standard throughout the sample period. The ratio rises above 1.0 (higher food spending) when the measures of spending on food away from home are improved beginning in 2007. Spending among all households with income less than 200 percent of the poverty line follows a similar pattern, with median spending ratios that hover around 1.0. Mean benefit ratios are quite a bit higher reflecting the fact that the distribution is skewed—that is, there is a small group of households that spend substantially more than the needs standard.

Figure 4.4a displays the distribution of spending relative to the needs standard among the population eligible for SNAP and those reporting SNAP receipt. In Figure 4.4b, we show the distribution of the ratio of food to needs for SNAP-eligible households with children and those with an elderly member. This graph shows that elderly households are more likely to have food spending above the needs threshold. Overall, these results document that the needs standards are fairly close to the median food expenditure patterns of SNAP-eligible households and low-income households more broadly. We also document that a substantial fraction of households spends more than the needs standard and that this fraction differs across household type.

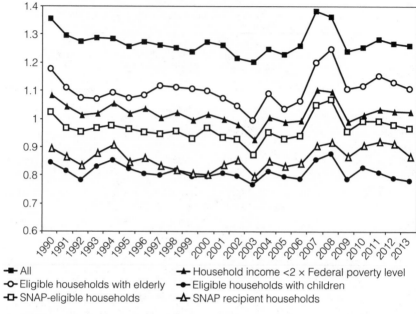

Figure 4.3. Ratio of median adjusted total food spending to needs standard, by household type.

SOURCE: Authors' calculations using CEX data.

Food spending in the CEX is widely thought to be underreported. For example, only 64 percent of reported food spending in the personal consumption expenditures (PCE) portion of the National Income and Product Accounts (which are part of the official GDP calculations) is picked up in the CEX measures (Bureau of Labor Statistics 2014).[8] If we could account for this measurement error, it would imply that even *fewer* families spend less than the needs standard.

Family-Size Adjustments

Because each member of a household has food needs, the SNAP needs standards for a household increase as family size increases. However, the needs standard increases by less than an amount that would keep the per capita needs standard fixed because there are assumed to be economies of scale in the consumption and preparation of meals at home. For example, the needs standard for a household with four people is 182 percent of the level of a household with two people, or about 9 percent less per person. In this section, we document how the family size adjustments used in the SNAP benefit formula compare to the observed differences in the spending amounts of households of different sizes.

a. SNAP-eligible and SNAP-receiving households

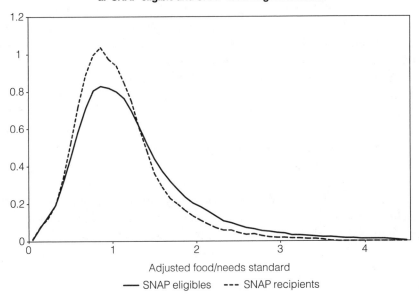

Adjusted food/needs standard

—— SNAP eligibles   --- SNAP recipients

b. SNAP-eligible households with children or with elderly head

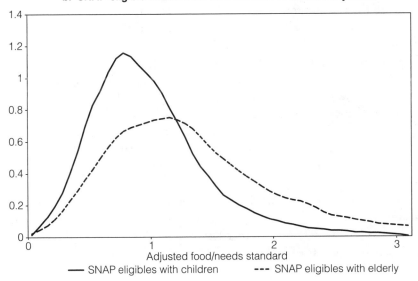

Adjusted food/needs standard

—— SNAP eligibles with children   --- SNAP eligibles with elderly

Figure 4.4. Distribution of total adjusted food spending as a fraction of needs standard, 1990–2013.

NOTE: Figure represents the kernel density of the 1st to 99th percentile of each distribution.

SOURCE: Authors' calculations using CEX data.

Table 4.2 lays out the SNAP program benefit multipliers across different family sizes (in columns 1 to 3) for 2010. The reference family contains four persons, and the TFP is estimated to cost $588 per month (that is, $139.50 per person per month). Because of the ARRA increase, benefits in 2010 were set at 113.6 percent of the needs standard, so maximum benefits for a four-person family were increased to $668 per month or $167 per person. To account for economies of scale, the SNAP formula multiplies the *per person* benefit in the reference family by different multipliers for each family size. For example, the multiplier for a one-person family is 1.2, so the maximum per-person benefit is 1.2 times the per person benefit in the reference family. All families with five or more people have the same per person multiplier (0.95). These multipliers have been the same for all the years of the modern food stamp program. Benefits for a family are equal to the per person benefit for a family of four, times the multiplier for the family's size, times the number of people in the family. The per person benefit level is displayed in column 2. Multiplying column 2 by the family size yields the maximum benefits (column 3).

In Figure 4.5a, we graph average adjusted total food spending per capita for families of sizes ranging from one to eight members relative to spending per capita of a four-person family for different types of families, averaging across all the years in the sample. (Although not shown here, these patterns have been similar over time.) We compare this to the multiplier used by the program to adjust benefits, which we label "program parameter." For example, the line for all families attains the value of 1.46 for a two-person household because, on a per person basis, the average two-person household spent 1.46 times the amount spent by a four-person family. The program multiplier allows individuals in a two-person household a budget that is only 1.1 times as much per person. We note that, for all family types, the spending gradient is far steeper, with respect to family size, than the program parameters capture. Households eligible for SNAP and those reporting receipt of SNAP follow a pattern similar to households overall. For families with children, we include data for family sizes of two or more because "child-only" cases are rare in the data. For small families with children, the gradient is less steep than for other family types. This may be the result of the lower food needs of children or due to a greater gap between the food expenditure and consumption of children due to other programs such as the Special Supplemental Nutrition Program for Women, Infants, and Children (WIC) and school lunch (which is not counted in CEX food expenditures). Figure 4.5b repeats the exercise using spending on food at home only because we are concerned that the pattern in Figure 4.5a may be driven by the propensity of small households to spend more on meals out. Although the

TABLE 4.2

Benefit formula multipliers, spending patterns, and food insecurity by household size

Household size	SNAP formula			Per-person spending relative to family of four						Food insecurity rate	Sample size (columns 4–7)
	SNAP formula multiplier	Maximum per person	Maximum monthly benefits	Average adjusted total food spending	Median adjusted total food spending	Average food at home spending	Median food at home spending				
	(1)	(2)	(3)	(4)	(5)	(6)	(7)			(8)	(9)
1	1.20	200	200	1.81	1.70	1.68	1.57			0.14	25,528
2	1.10	184	367	1.48	1.44	1.41	1.34			0.11	26,007
3	1.05	175	526	1.15	1.13	1.13	1.11			0.14	12,638
4 (reference)	—	167	668	1.00	1.00	1.00	1.00			0.16	11,390
5	0.95	159	793	0.83	0.83	0.85	0.82			0.21	5,387
6	0.95	159	952	0.74	0.74	0.79	0.72			0.22	2,210

SOURCES: Columns 4 through 7 are authors' calculations from CEX data. Column 8 is authors' calculations from the December 2010 Current Population Survey.

NOTES: Average (median) adjusted food spending for a family of four is $171 ($155) per person. Average (median) food-at-home spending for a family of four is $136 ($130) per person.

a. Average adjusted total food spending per capita, by selected household types

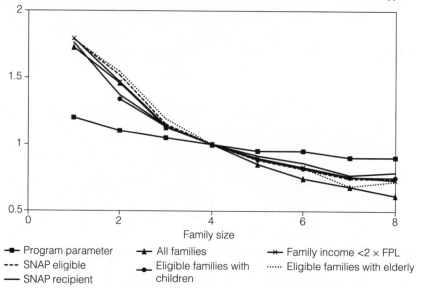

b. Average spending on food at home per capita, by selected household types

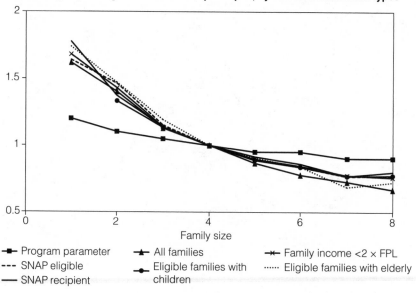

Figure 4.5. Spending per capita by family size, relative to four-person households.
SOURCE: Authors' calculations using CEX data.

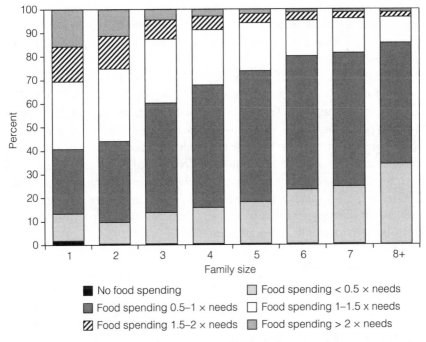

Figure 4.6.   Adjusted total spending relative to needs standards, by family size for eligible households.

<small>S O U R C E : Authors' calculations using CEX data.</small>

gradient here is flattened somewhat relative to total adjusted food spending, it continues to be substantially steeper than the benefits multipliers.

Returning to Table 4.2, in columns 4 through 7 we use the 2010 CEX and present average and median per person spending by family size, separately for adjusted total food spending and food-at-home spending, as a ratio of per person spending in a four-person family. Although the exact estimates vary somewhat across specifications, in all cases they reflect spending differentials that are steeper, with respect to family size, than those used to adjust SNAP benefits. Column 8 presents rates of food insecurity in 2010 by household size, which shows that larger families are not less likely to be food insecure than smaller families. This disparity likely reflects the fact that larger households are more likely to be poor (that is, have less non-SNAP income).

In Figure 4.6, we summarize adjusted total food spending relative to the needs standard, separately for each family size one through eight and up for those who are imputed to be SNAP eligible. We see that food spending is far more likely to be above the needs standards in smaller households. For some of the larger family sizes (six and up), the fraction that spends less than the needs standard is nearly twice as large as the level for the one- and two-person families. Note that the average SNAP household is fairly small, averaging 2.2 overall and 3.3 among households with children (Eslami, Filion, and Strayer 2011).

Our investigation into family size adjustments shows that per capita spending decreases with family size more dramatically than is assumed in the benefits calculation. This is true both for families overall and within family types. This finding does not necessarily imply that the benefit multipliers are inappropriate, because the multipliers are designed to account for economies of scale rather than to reflect actual spending patterns. We have furthermore documented that the relatively larger transfers to larger families does not translate into lower overall food insecurity rates for them. However, it does suggest that food stamp benefits may play a different role in the budgets of small and large households.

Estimated Benefits

We next compare imputed monthly SNAP benefits to both the maximum benefit level and food spending. Using data from the interview survey, we predict SNAP benefit levels based on the benefit formula. This prediction is based on the following information:

1. Program parameters from each year: maximum benefits, the standard deduction, minimum benefits for one- and two-person households, and the caps on dependent care and excess-shelter-cost deductions.

2. Household demographics and income: family size, family income, earnings, and indicators for whether household contains an elderly member or someone who is disabled or receives SSI or TANF.[9]

3. Expenditure patterns: spending on shelter, child care, and health care to calculate deductions for net income.

We do not use standard medical deductions (available to the elderly) as they vary by state and are implemented late in our sample time period. We also do not have consistent data on child support payments over time. However, we capture most of the other measures used to calculate benefits.

Figure 4.7 shows a smoothed version of the median of the ratio of predicted SNAP benefits to maximum benefits by year.[10] These are less than 1.0 because most families have positive net income and are therefore not eligible for the maximum benefit. Recall that these are predicted benefits (that is, assuming universal take-up), so variation over time is driven primarily by differences in income and deductions. As Ziliak shows in Chapter One, actual take-up rates are less than 100 percent and vary across the business cycle. In

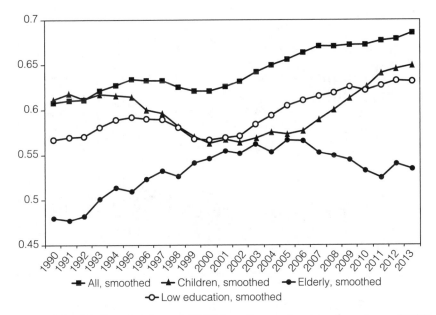

Figure 4.7. Median of estimated SNAP benefits as a fraction of maximum SNAP benefits.

SOURCE: Authors' calculations using CEX data.

the full sample of eligible households, the median predicted benefit has consistently been around 65 percent of the maximum benefit. There is a modest upward trend in this ratio due to increases in the value of the shelter and medical deductions and the temporary ARRA increase in benefits. The ratio of median predicted benefits to maximum benefits is lower for households with children and elderly households, reflecting higher net incomes among these groups. We estimate that nearly 30 percent of eligible households are predicted to qualify for the maximum benefit across all our years of data. The high share of households eligible for the maximum benefit is the result of the numerous deductions to net income, particularly the shelter deduction. SNAP program data report that 46 percent of participant households received the maximum benefit in FY2011 (Eslami 2014).

We next compare estimated benefits to adjusted total food spending among eligible households. This is of interest because, referring back to the economic framework outlined in Figure 4.1, it empirically shows how likely a household is to be inframarginal and therefore how likely a household is to treat their SNAP benefits as cash. Figure 4.8 shows that, overall, fewer than 30 percent of eligible households spend less on food than their predicted benefit amount and approximately a third of households spend more than twice their predicted benefit amount. Note that spending relative to average

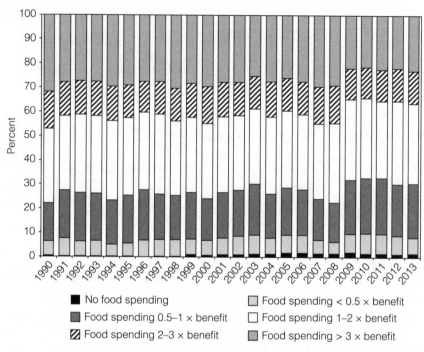

Figure 4.8. Adjusted total food spending relative to estimated benefits, all SNAP-eligible households.

SOURCE: Authors' calculations using CEX data.

TABLE 4.3

Adjusted total food spending as a percentage of SNAP benefits

	All eligible households	Eligible households with children	Eligible households with elderly	Eligible households less than 200 percent of federal poverty line	Recipient households (relative to reported benefits)
	(1)	(2)	(3)	(4)	(5)
No spending	1.0%	0.6%	1.2%	1.0%	1.2%
0–50	6.8%	7.3%	4.0%	6.8%	2.9%
50–100	19.8%	25.3%	14.8%	19.9%	12.1%
100–150	32.0%	34.8%	29.5%	32.1%	28.5%
150–200	13.9%	13.4%	14.3%	13.8%	11.6%
200+	26.5%	18.5%	36.2%	26.3%	43.7%
Sample size N	336,176	134,465	100,327	330,994	117,653

SOURCE: Authors' calculations using CEX data.

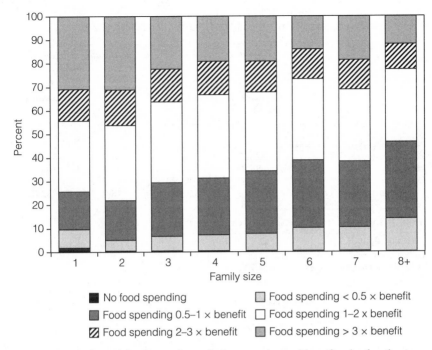

Figure 4.9.   Adjusted food spending relative to estimated benefits, by family size.
SOURCE: Authors' calculations using CEX data.

benefits falls sharply in 2009 when benefit allotments were raised as part of the economic stimulus. Table 4.3 shows the average ratio of adjusted total food spending to estimated benefit levels over all years pooled for different groups of SNAP households. Among eligible households with children, about a third of households spend less on food than their estimated benefits. Fewer than 20 percent of elderly spend less than their estimated food stamp allotment. Among households that report receiving food stamps, only 16 percent spend less than their reported allotment, and nearly half spend more than twice their reported allotment. Recall that because of measurement error, our data understate food spending and income (and thus overstate predicted benefits), and thus these are likely to be upper bounds on the fraction of families spending less than predicted benefit amounts. Figure 4.9 displays the relationship between adjusted total food spending and benefits by family size for SNAP-eligible households. Benefit levels are more likely to be above food spending for the larger households, but even among the largest families fewer than half of households spend less on food than their benefits are predicted to be worth.

These estimates indicate that most families spend more than their benefit amount. As discussed earlier, such families are considered "inframarginal,"

TABLE 4.4

Food spending by type of food and SNAP eligibility, 2010

	Households eligible for SNAP		Households ineligible for SNAP	
	Mean	Standard deviation	Mean	Standard deviation
	(1)	(2)	(3)	(4)
PANEL A: SPENDING LEVEL				
Food at home	226.7	308.6	345.8	338.8
Healthier foods	95.9	122.1	123.1	134.1
Unhealthy foods	27.2	45.8	39.2	56.1
Sugar-sweetened beverages	16.3	28.8	18.0	32.0
N	2,288		10,678	
PANEL B: SPENDING AS A PERCENTAGE OF FOOD-AT-HOME SPENDING				
Healthier foods	36.2%		35.8%	
Unhealthy foods	11.2%		11.9%	
Sugar-sweetened beverages	7.7%		6.2%	
N	1,973		9,642	

SOURCE: Authors' calculations using CEX data.

and this finding implies that policies to restrict purchase of certain foods with SNAP benefits (such as proposed bans of soda purchase) will do little to alter consumption behavior. The neoclassical model predicts no change in consumption behavior as long as the benefit level is less than preferred household spending on the allowable products (after any additional restrictions are enacted). In Table 4.4, we show the breakdown in food-at-home spending according to the 2010 CEX Diary data into healthful food, unhealthful food, and sugar-sweetened beverages for both SNAP-eligible households and ineligible households.[11] The "healthier foods" category includes bread (other than white), poultry, fish and shellfish, eggs, milk, cheese, other non–ice cream dairy foods, fruit (excluding juice), vegetables, dried fruit, nuts, prepared salads, and baby food. The "unhealthful foods" category comprises ice cream, candy, gum, hot dogs, potato chips and other snacks, and bakery goods and prepared desserts such as cakes, cupcakes, doughnuts, pies, and tarts. The sugar-sweetened beverages group includes colas, other carbonated drinks, and noncarbonated fruit-flavored and sports drinks. We note that sugar-sweetened beverages and unhealthful foods represent a small portion of the spending of both eligible and ineligible households. As a result, for the majority of eligible households, spending on allowable products is likely to exceed benefit levels, and therefore the proposed restrictions on the purchase of particular goods are unlikely to alter behavior.

CONCLUSIONS

This chapter presents new descriptive information on food consumption patterns among households overall, the SNAP-eligible population, and other subgroups of policy relevance. We begin by reviewing the neoclassical model's predictions for the food stamp program. The first-order effect of SNAP is to shift out the budget set, and thus the program will increase food and nonfood spending. For households that desire a low level of spending on food, providing the SNAP benefit as a food voucher may induce higher food consumption than would an ordinary cash transfer. Our results show that a substantial fraction of SNAP-eligible households spend an amount that is above the program benefit levels and also above the "needs-standard" level on which benefits are based. This suggests that many households are inframarginal and are therefore predicted to treat their benefits like cash. We also show that per capita food spending declines more sharply with increases in family size than the program assumes in its benefits formula and that large families are more likely to spend less on food than the needs standard amount.

NOTES

This paper was prepared for the Five Decades of Food Stamps Conference held at the Brookings Institution on September 20, 2013. The authors would like to thank Tom DeLeire, Jonathan Schwabish, and the editors for useful comments.

1. See also Currie and Gahvari (2008) for an excellent overview of the economics of in-kind transfer programs.

2. There are other reasons that may explain why SNAP leads to different effects on food consumption compared to ordinary case income. It is possible that the family member with control over food stamp benefits may be different from the person who controls earnings and other cash income. If the person with control over food stamps has greater preferences for food, then we may find that food stamps leads to larger increases in food consumption compared to cash income. Alternatively, families may perceive that food stamp benefits are a more permanent source of income compared to earnings. Finally, Shapiro (2005) finds evidence of a "food stamp cycle" whereby daily caloric and nutritional intake declines with weeks because their food stamp payment suggests a significant preference for immediate consumption.

3. The MPC out of cash is estimated to be 0.03 to 0.17 (with most estimates between 0.05 and 0.10), and the MPC out of food stamps is estimated to be 0.17 to 0.47.

4. We performed nearly all of the analysis using the Diary data as well, and patterns are similar.

5. For example, hot foods intended for immediate consumption such as rotisserie chickens cannot be purchased with SNAP benefits, but we cannot separate spending on such items in the CEX data.

6. Take-up rates vary over the business cycle and in response to policy changes.

7. The drop in 2007 and 2008 is the result of increases in reported spending on food away from home, which was the result of changes in the interview question rather than the result of a real increase in spending. The responses in 2007 and beyond are closer to the responses in the Diary and likely reflect an improvement in the survey instrument (Henderson 2014).

8. For food and beverages away from home the ratio was 60 percent. These ratios were measured in 2012, but they have not varied substantially over time. These ratios are primarily based on Diary data. Using information from Henderson (2014), we estimate that the 2012 ratios in the Interview portion of the CEX are approximately 80 percent (home) and 51 percent (away). Although some of this is due to coverage differences between the PCE and CEX, much is likely due to underreporting in the CEX. As already stated, the CEX measures food expenditures, not consumption. In particular, we do not capture the consumption of no-cost food such as school meals, emergency food, and so on. This suggests that expenditures understate consumption. But for our analysis here, and the implications for the adequacy of the SNAP benefit, it is important to point out that the unmeasured elements are absent from both the numerator (spending) and denominator (benefit level). Using aggregate statistics, we estimate that SNAP represents 76 percent of total food program benefits.

9. We use annual income data in the CEX that cover the same period as the expenditure data.

10. We calculate a five-year moving average.

11. The detailed expenditure data required for such breakdowns are available only in the Diary.

REFERENCES

Bureau of Labor Statistics. 2014. "Comparing Expenditures from the Consumer Expenditure Survey with the Personal Consumer Expenditures: Results of the CE/PCE Concordance." Tabulated June 4. Available at www.bls.gov/cex/cepceconcordance.htm.

Currie, J. 2006. "The Take-up of Social Benefits." In A. Auerbach, D. Card, and J. Quigley, eds., *Poverty, the Distribution of Income, and Public Policy*. New York: Russell Sage Foundation.

Currie, J., and F. Gahvari. 2008. "Transfers in Cash and In-Kind: Theory Meets the Data." *Journal of Economic Literature* 46(2): 333–383.

Eslami, E. 2014. "Trends in Supplemental Nutrition Assistance Program Participation Rates: Fiscal Year 2010 to Fiscal Year 2012." *Current Perspectives on SNAP Participation*. Washington, DC: USDA Food and Nutrition Service.

Eslami, E., K. Filion, and M. Strayer. 2011. *Characteristics of Supplemental Nutrition Assistance Program Households: Fiscal Year 2010*. Washington, DC: U.S. Department of Agriculture, Food and Nutrition Service, Office of Research and Analysis.

Fraker, T. 1990. *Effects of Food Stamps on Food Consumption: A Review of the Literature*. Washington, DC: Mathematica Policy Research, Inc.

Fraker, T. M., A. P. Martini, and J. C. Ohls. 1995. "The Effect of Food Stamp Cashout on Food Expenditures: An Assessment of the Findings from Four Demonstrations." *Journal of Human Resources* 30(4): 633–649.

Henderson, S. 2014 (September 18). "Comparing Global Questions and Answers to Results from Detailed Specific Questions: Data on Food Expenditures from the Consumer Expenditure Survey." Washington, DC: Bureau of Labor Statistics, Note.

Hoynes, H. W., and D. Whitmore Schanzenbach. 2009. "Consumption Responses to In-Kind Transfers: Evidence from the Introduction of the Food Stamp Program." *American Economic Journal: Applied Economics* 1(4): 109–139.

———. 2014. "U.S. Food and Nutrition Programs." NBER Working Paper.

Levedahl, J. 1995. "A Theoretical and Empirical Evaluation of the Functional Forms Used to Estimate the Food Expenditure Equation of Food Stamp Recipients." *American Journal of Agricultural Economics* 77 (November): 960–968.

McGranahan, L. 2014. "A Primer on the Food Stamp Information in the Consumer Expenditure Survey." Mimeo. Chicago: Federal Reserve Bank of Chicago.

Moffitt, R. 1983. "An Economic Model of Welfare Stigma." *American Economic Review* 73(5): 1023–1035.

Morrison, R., L. Mancino, and J. Variyam. 2011. "Will Calorie Labeling in Restaurants Make a Difference?" *Food Choices and Health*, US ERS, March 14.

Ohls, J. C., T. M. Fraker, A. P. Martini, and M. Ponza. 1992. *The Effects of Cash-Out on Food Use by Food Stamp Program Participants in San Diego*. Princeton, NJ: Mathematica Policy Research.

Schanzenbach, D. W. 2007. "What Are Food Stamps Worth?" Working Paper. Chicago: University of Chicago.

Shapiro, J. 2005. "Is There a Daily Discount Rate? Evidence from the Food Stamp Nutrition Cycle." *Journal of Public Economics* 89(2–3): 303–325.

Southworth, H. M. 1945. "The Economics of Public Measures to Subsidize Food Consumption." *Journal of Farm Economics* 27 (February): 38–66.

U.S. Department of Agriculture (USDA), Food and Nutrition Service. 2014. "Supplemental Nutrition Assistance Program Participation and Costs." November 7. Available at www.fns.usda.gov/sites/default/files/pd/SNAPsummary.pdf.

CHAPTER FIVE

The Health and Nutrition Effects of SNAP

Selection into the Program and a Review of
the Literature on Its Effects

Marianne P. Bitler

The goal of this chapter is to assess the state of knowledge about whether the Supplemental Nutrition Assistance Program improves health and nutrition outcomes. I begin by noting elements of the SNAP rules that might have important implications for nutrition and health. I then show descriptive data on the stark difference in health outcomes between SNAP participants and nonparticipants, even for characteristics that likely well predate SNAP participation. This illustrates the complicated selection problem that researchers face when studying SNAP: Recipients and nonrecipients vary in both observable and unobservable ways that complicate evaluation of the program. In other words, SNAP participants appear to have worse health than do nonparticipants before SNAP use takes place, suggesting there are differences in health by SNAP use that are not due to the effects of the program. I then move on to discuss the causal estimates of the effects of SNAP we have from the literature. These take advantage of various approaches that are more appropriate for producing causal estimates of the effects of SNAP on health and nutrition. They suggest some evidence that SNAP affects health positively in the short run and long run, although the counterfactual for the long-run effects might be different from today.

In an era of fiscal crisis, knowing whether SNAP has any significant causal effect on health and nutrition is crucial for informing policy decisions and policy makers. In this review, I pay particular attention to the challenges researchers face in overcoming selection bias and identifying causal effects of the SNAP program, and I assess the literature through that lens. The fundamental challenge in program evaluation in general, and in assessing the impact of SNAP in particular, is that participants are not selected at random from the population. Thus, comparisons of those who use SNAP and those who do not—even conditional on observable characteristics—may not be apples-to-apples comparisons. To the extent that those who choose to participate in SNAP are negatively selected, as one might expect, SNAP recipients are likely to be less healthy even before participating in the program, and thus naïve estimates comparing participants and nonparticipants could be biased downward and miss possible positive effects of SNAP. This is analogous to the challenges facing studies of the impact of SNAP on food insecurity, as discussed in Chapter Three.

I begin with descriptive evidence from pooled waves of the National Health Interview Survey (NHIS) that show the extent of negative selection according to health status and other characteristics for SNAP participants compared to nonparticipants. The NHIS is the only nationally representative large-sample survey that allows us to look at health insurance coverage, health care use, and self-reported health status and prevalence of chronic and acute conditions. In this analysis, I find that SNAP recipients are less healthy than are nonparticipants on many dimensions, including a number that likely predate SNAP participation. I then turn to the only nationally representative source of data on U.S. diet and nutrition, the National Health and Nutrition Examination Survey (NHANES). I then compare dietary outcomes for SNAP recipients and nonparticipants, finding that SNAP recipients eat differently and have different levels of nutrition than do nonrecipients. Like the NHIS, the NHANES data show strong evidence of selection into SNAP, raising questions about the usefulness of SNAP/no SNAP comparisons.

Then I go on to assess the evidence about the causal effects of SNAP on a host of outcomes, based on the set of papers using the best causal evidence from the existing SNAP literature. Do SNAP recipients have different diets than do nonrecipients, accounting for unobserved and observed differences? Does SNAP improve health and nutrition outcomes in a causal fashion? If so, which ones and by how much? Can SNAP improve birth outcomes (could we improve the health of infants if we assigned more to households getting SNAP)? I note that much of the convincing causal estimates are based on the rollout of the program during the War on Poverty in the 1960s. This raises additional questions, including whether there is useful evidence about infant health beyond the work showing that the introduction of SNAP leads to improvements in infant outcomes.

To answer these questions, I discuss and critically assess existing efforts in the literature to adjust for possible selection into the SNAP program. Methods used in the existing literature range from relatively simple comparisons of SNAP participants and nonparticipants (likely not causal); to methods that adjust for selection on observables (either via matching or similar methods or by regression); to those relying on policy changes and difference-in-differences estimation or event studies; to instrumental variables and other approaches that deal with selection on unobservables. I will also discuss experimental approaches and the use of bounding methods in this setting. Finally, I pose challenges for research and suggestions for experimentation to answer some of the remaining puzzles about the health and nutrition effects of SNAP.

PREDICTED EFFECTS ON NUTRITION

Studying the effects of SNAP on food choices depends on the role of program benefits in the household budget. Unlike a cash transfer like cash welfare for families with children, SNAP is an in-kind benefit that constrains families' choice of food. (For an in-depth discussion of the impacts of SNAP on food consumption, see Chapter Four by Hoynes, McGranahan, and Schanzenbach; for a broader discussion of in-kind benefits, see Currie and Gahvari 2008.) If the food households could buy with a SNAP Electronic Benefit Transfer (EBT) card were identical to that they would choose to buy with cash, then economic theory predicts that under typical assumptions about whether people would buy more food with more income (assuming food is a normal good), the only families influenced by the in-kind nature of the program (requirement to buy unprepared food) are those who would have spent less than their SNAP allotment on qualifying foods (so-called extramarginal or constrained participants). Chapter Four discusses some empirical findings on this topic (other references include Wilde, Troy, and Rogers 2009 and Meyerhoefer and Yang 2011).

Of course, SNAP also differs from a simple in-kind program in that it also requires individuals to buy food to prepare rather than food that is ready to eat immediately after purchase. (Thus, no food from restaurants or ready-to-eat food from stores can be purchased with SNAP benefits.) Preparing food has nontrivial time costs. Rose (2007) reports that making food using weekly food plans based on recipes and meal plans created to show how the 1999 Thrifty Food Plan—the USDA standard for a minimal-cost nutritious diet used as a basis for maximum food stamp benefits—could work took 16.1 hours per week (excluding clean-up and shopping), suggesting this restriction could have important effects.

The SNAP requirement to purchase unprepared ingredients or at least not ready-to-eat food at the store could also affect SNAP recipients' behavior, although less so now than perhaps in the past, as preparation time for all food has declined. Existing research finds evidence that SNAP reduces food insecurity (see Chapter Three of this volume for an in-depth discussion), but research does not generally find evidence of large and meaningful effects on diet quality. Attention has also focused on how SNAP affects the mix of food at home and away and whether summary measures of diet quality—like the USDA's Healthy Eating Index—are affected by SNAP use.

Recent discussion in some states has focused on excluding or taxing some foods such as sugar-sweetened beverages from the qualifying list of foods, although the USDA has refused to allow states to do this. At the same time, pilot studies have focused on the use of "carrots"—such as financial incentives to consume more fruits, vegetables, and other healthful foods (for example, the Healthy Incentives Pilot, authorized by the 2008 Farm Bill).

SNAP also includes a nutritional education component, like many federal food assistance programs. In the Healthy and Hunger Free Kids Act of 2010, Congress added obesity prevention to the program's nutritional education goals. State agencies have the option of providing this education to SNAP recipients. In fiscal year 2014, about $400 million in grants for education was available. The USDA also provides states with guidance about strategies for obesity prevention and control. It is possible that this nutritional education component could affect participants, although evidence is somewhat lacking. There is also variation across states in when they began participating in the nutritional education component. Cole and Fox (2008) report that in 1992 only seven states participated in the program. The relationship between SNAP and obesity is the focus of Chapter Six in this volume and thus not examined in this chapter.

PREDICTED EFFECTS OF SNAP ON HEALTH

Since the influential work of Grossman (1972), economists have viewed health as a capital good that is produced by individuals. That is, to put it in nontechnical language, maintaining one's health status requires that one make investments in health (that is, exert effort and spend money to remain healthy). These investments could be simply engaging in preventive care or, in this context, could mean eating an appropriate amount of healthful foods to stay healthy.

In the Grossman model of how persons choose health, the desire to remain healthy is a function of one's desire to be happy (or in economic terms, to maximize utility). Health is not an end in itself but a means to happiness or life satisfaction. And, as already noted, maintaining health requires one keep investing in it, as it decays across time. Thus, individuals must spend time and money to stay healthy, and this must be traded off with the other things they would like to consume with their money or use their time for. In this model, use of health care and healthy behaviors are investments people make to improve their own health. The desire among individuals to keep healthy derives both from the consumption aspect of health-related investments and from the investment nature of health (healthier persons can participate in more market activities and consume more leisure). The Grossman model also assumes that education increases the efficiency of nonmarket production and thus posits that the more educated may end up with higher optimal health stocks. (Or, in less technical terms, those with higher education may be able to get the same health effects for a lower investment [of money or time] compared to those with lower education levels.)

Finally, there are other key assumptions built into the Grossman model, namely, that individuals want to maximize lifetime well-being (or utility) rather than only current well-being and are exponential discounters with perfect information (individuals have a deterministic way of balancing future gains compared to current gains, which is modeled in this fashion) and that there are no insurance markets (one can't buy insurance to protect one's well-being in the future; one needs to invest now and in an ongoing sense). In this model, wages reflect one's own opportunity cost or the value of what one would otherwise be doing, and higher wages mean a higher value of healthy leisure time. This suggests that those with higher wages will demand more medical care. In this model, subsidies to goods that improve health and health education can improve health.

It is possible and even likely that not all the assumptions of the Grossman model hold, yet some of the insights of the model are helpful for considering the health impacts of a program like SNAP. First, if health is a stock variable (like wealth), which requires investment to maintain, then it is unlikely that brief exposure to SNAP is going to improve health. In fact, it might take sustained exposure to a program before health responds. Health care use, by contrast, can change quickly in response to changing circumstances. Thus, a comparison of long-ago-determined health outcomes of SNAP recipients and nonrecipients is unlikely to reveal differences that are due to SNAP. Instead, such differences likely show evidence of selection into SNAP.

At the same time, there is clearly a possibility that SNAP can improve nutrition and thus health. At baseline, if individuals were constrained in their access to healthful food, which is itself an investment good used to produce health, then SNAP use could alleviate these constraints and could have positive effects on health. It is certain that at the time the program was first implemented as part of the War on Poverty, many individuals who would likely be eligible for what was then known as the Food Stamp Program did not have adequate access to food and suffered from anemia and other nutritional health issues. In fact, the Ten-State Nutrition Survey conducted from 1968 to 1970 found wasting among low-income children, as well as widespread prevalence of iron-deficiency anemia and deficiencies in vitamin A (Lowe et al. 1973).

Next, we turn to the NHIS and NHANES to get a sense of the descriptive associations between SNAP use, demographics, income, and health and nutrition. These analyses are intended to illustrate the underlying selection into SNAP. We examine in great depth the degree of health selection in SNAP. Then, we look at differences in nutrition between SNAP recipients and nonrecipients.

NHIS

The NHIS is a large cross-sectional survey done since 1957 to monitor the health of the nation. The current incarnation of the NHIS is a household interview survey, which samples households and those in noninstitutional group quarters. Blacks and Hispanics, and more recently Asians, are oversampled, and thus weights must be applied to obtain population-representative results. The sample is drawn from each state and the District of Columbia. Since 1997, the survey has consisted of a core set of questions asked every year. The core includes household and family components, which collect information on demographics, health status and limitations, injuries, health access and use, health insurance, and income and assets; these are collected from everyone. The core also includes a sample adult and a sample child component, which include data on health status, health care services, and health behaviors, asked only for a random adult or child, if a child is present. In some years, supplements are used to collect specific health data. Our limited NHIS data on nutritional outcomes come from such a supplement. The public-use version of NHIS does not report state or a finer geographic area than four regions due to a combination of concerns about privacy and the fact that the individual data are not statistically representative of states. That said, the fact that the NHIS does not provide representative state-specific estimates in no way invalidates it as a data source, and it is the premier source of information on self-reports of health, health insurance status, and use of health care, with samples that are as large as many other important surveys such as the Annual Social and Economic Supplement to the Current Population Survey, which is the source of the official poverty statistics as well as our estimates of the unemployment rate. This chapter uses NHIS data from 1998 to 2010, spanning several recessions, including the Great Recession and the recent anemic recovery. In our sample, data on SNAP use are collected from 1998 through 2010 in the NHIS family questionnaire. Thus, any family where some member is reported to be an authorized SNAP user in the last year is coded as having gotten SNAP. As in many other large survey sample data sets, SNAP use is underreported in the NHIS.[1] However, the NHIS is no worse and in some cases is better on this front than most large survey data sets, showing less underreporting than does the CPS ASEC.

NHANES

The NHANES is a set of surveys designed to measure the health and nutritional status of children and adults. Although it was started in the 1960s as a periodic survey, the current incarnation is a continuous program that measures outcomes for a nationally representative sample of 5,000 persons a year from about fifteen counties. In addition to collecting demographics and socioeconomic outcomes, NHANES collects information on dietary and health-related measures. Additionally, a key aspect of NHANES is the examination component, where individuals are given medical, dental, and physiological examinations and administered laboratory tests. Unlike almost all other large U.S. health data sets, which rely on self-reports of conditions and medical experiences, the NHANES provides objective measures of these outcomes. (That is, it does not rely on self-reports of any health measures but collects objective information through extensive examinations.) Further, most other data sets include data only on conditions that individuals have been told by a medical professional that they have. For example, even for an event like a heart attack, some 15 percent of persons may not know they have had such an event. Thus, these individuals would not report that they have been told by a doctor they had this condition, and it is likely that low-SES individuals and those with limited interaction with medical professionals might be more likely to not know about such conditions. Like NHIS, NHANES oversamples blacks, Hispanics, and some older individuals. Also like NHIS, the public use version of the data does not include detailed geographic information. NHANES is also the only nationally representative source of dietary intake data (and has associated information on the levels of various nutrients contained in the diet). The NHANES data we use are for 2007 to 2008, spanning the beginning of the Great Recession. Thus, comparisons of our NHIS and NHANES results should note this.

Mean Differences between SNAP Recipients and Nonrecipients in the NHIS

Table 5.1 presents summary statistics for 1997 to 2010 for demographics, health insurance coverage, cash income and in-kind benefits, and home-ownership for the full sample (column 1). Columns 2 and 3 show means for those reporting SNAP use or no SNAP use in the last year. (Data for a small share of persons who do not respond to the SNAP question are excluded from columns 2 and 3.) This table clearly shows the degree of selection into SNAP use that exists; SNAP recipients are systematically different from

TABLE 5.1
Summary statistics for National Health Interview Survey, full sample

	Full sample	SNAP	No SNAP
Male	0.49	0.36	0.5
Age	36	29	36
Household size	3.3	3.7	3.3
Number of children	1.2	1.9	1.1
Hispanic	0.14	0.21	0.13
White	0.71	0.52	0.72
Black	0.11	0.28	0.1
Asian	0.04	0.02	0.04
American Indian/Alaska Native	0.01	0.01	0.01
Race other/miscellaneous	0.13	0.17	0.13
Citizen	0.93	0.95	0.93
In U.S. less than 5 years	0.02	0.02	0.02
Poor	0.1	0.57	0.08
Uninsured now	0.15	0.18	0.14

OWN HEALTH INSURANCE FROM FOLLOWING SOURCE:

	Full sample	SNAP	No SNAP
Private insurance	0.67	0.09	0.7
Medicaid	0.1	0.62	0.07
SCHIP	0.01	0.03	0.01
Other state plan	0.003	0.006	0.003
Medicare	0.13	0.12	0.13
Military coverage	0.03	0.01	0.03
Indian Health Service	0.003	0.005	3

FAMILY IN-KIND BENEFIT LAST YEAR FROM:

	Full sample	SNAP	No SNAP
SNAP	0.05	1	0
SNAP don't know or refused to answer	0.02	0	0
Housing assistance	0.03	0.27	0.003
TANF/AFDC noncash	0.01	0.06	0.02

FAMILY INCOME LAST YEAR FROM:

	Full sample	SNAP	No SNAP
Wages	0.47	0.27	0.49
Self-employment	0.07	0.02	0.07
Social Security, old age or retirement	0.11	0.08	0.12
Social Security disability	0.01	0.05	0.01
Supplemental Security Income disability	0.02	0.11	0.01
Supplemental Security Income nondisability	0.004	0.03	0.003
Child support	0.02	0.08	0.02
TANF/AFDC cash	0.02	0.22	0.005

HOUSING:

	Full sample	SNAP	No SNAP
Own/buying	0.68	0.26	0.72
Renting	0.28	0.69	0.26
N	1,279,344	74,369	1,173,583

SOURCE: Author's calculations using National Health Interview Survey (NHIS) data.

NOTES: Table reports means for full sample (column 1), for those reporting SNAP last year (column 2), and for those reporting no SNAP last year (column 3). Health insurance measures reported are Integrated Health Interview Series (IHIS) recodes and are not mutually exclusive. All differences between columns 2 and 3 are significant at the 1 percent level. Statistics weighted with person weight, and variances for tests of equality allow for stratification and clustering within primary sampling units (PSUs) in the original sample with the public use NHIS stratum and PSU variables.

nonrecipients on many dimensions, and a large number of these differences plausibly extend before SNAP receipt.

It is obvious from this table that SNAP recipients are more disadvantaged on many dimensions than those not getting SNAP. They live in larger households and are less likely to be white or Asian and more likely to be black or Hispanic. They are more likely to live in households with children and much more likely to be under the poverty threshold (57 percent are in poverty compared to 8 percent of the non-SNAP population). SNAP recipients are much less likely to have private insurance coverage than are nonrecipients (9 percent versus 70 percent) and much more likely to have Medicaid coverage (62 percent versus 7 percent).

They are also much more likely to be getting other in-kind public assistance, like public housing. Twenty-seven percent of SNAP recipients were in families with wage and salary income in the previous year, compared to 49 percent of non-SNAP recipients. SNAP recipients are also more likely to participate in other safety-net programs like AFDC/TANF[2] (22 percent versus 0.5 percent of non-SNAP recipients) and SSI (14 percent versus 1 percent). Due in part no doubt to the fact that many SNAP recipients are single parents, SNAP recipients are also more likely than nonparticipants to receive private transfers (8 percent received child support compared to 2 percent of non-SNAP recipients). Finally, they are much more likely to be renters than are nonrecipients and more likely to be citizens (not surprising given eligibility requirements). These differences are all statistically significant at the 1 percent level. (Note that the test statistics use weights and are adjusted for the complex sample design.) All these comparisons suggest that SNAP use is correlated both with observed characteristics and possibly with unobserved characteristics, raising questions about a causal interpretation of the effects of SNAP use.

Table 5.2 reports further statistics for demographics, self-rated health and presence of family members with limitations, and health care use for adults. (Recall that the NHIS definition of adult is age eighteen or older.) Again, column 1 reports results for the full sample, column 2 for SNAP recipients, and column 3 for non-SNAP recipients. Again, the fact that SNAP recipients are more disadvantaged than are nonrecipients is clear; SNAP recipients are less likely to be married, more likely to have a low level of education, and much less likely to be in excellent or very good health. They are also much more likely to have a family member with a functional limitation and to have a child who is in special education or whose parent has been told he or she has a developmental delay. The SNAP recipients are more likely to live in families with children and have more contact with the medical system. They are also much more likely to report a family member needed medical

TABLE 5.2
Summary statistics for NHIS, adults (age eighteen and older)

	Full sample	*SNAP*	*No SNAP*
Age	45	41	46
MARITAL STATUS:			
Married now	0.57	0.28	0.59
Widowed/divorced/separated	0.18	0.36	0.18
Never married	0.23	0.36	0.23
COMPLETED EDUCATION:			
High school dropout	0.16	0.4	0.15
High school graduate/GED	0.29	0.33	0.29
More than high school	0.52	0.26	0.54
SELF-RATED HEALTH:			
Excellent/very good	0.62	0.34	0.63
Good	0.26	0.31	0.26
Fair/poor	0.12	0.34	0.11
FAMILY MEMBER LIMITED:			
Any	0.26	0.54	0.25
Number	0.33	0.76	0.31
CHILD IN SPECIAL EDUCATION OR WITH OTHER DEVELOPMENTAL DELAY:			
Any	0.09	0.17	0.09
No child in family	0.61	0.41	0.62
HEALTH CARE USE IN FAMILY LAST TWO WEEKS:			
At least one doctor visit	0.34	0.43	0.34
Number of persons in hospital overnight	0.23	0.39	0.22
HEALTH CARE USE IN FAMILY LAST YEAR:			
At least someone needed care could not afford	0.1	0.25	0.1
N	922,970	45,293	855,514

SOURCE: Author's calculations using NHIS data.

NOTES: Table reports means for all adults (age eighteen and older, column 1), for adults reporting SNAP last year (column 2), and for adults reporting no SNAP last year (column 3). All differences between columns 2 and 3 are significant at the 1 percent level. Statistics weighted with person weight, and variances for tests of equality allow for stratification and clustering within PSU in the original sample with the public use NHIS stratum and PSU variables.

care he or she did not get because he or she couldn't afford it. Again, all these differences are statistically significant at the 1 percent level.

Table 5.3 reports similar measures for children (ages zero to seventeen). SNAP-recipient children live in larger families and are younger than are nonrecipient children. They are also more likely to have parents with less education or no reported information on education and have worse parent-rated health for the child. They are much more likely than are nonrecipient children to themselves be in special education (9 percent versus 6 percent)

TABLE 5.3
Summary statistics for NHIS, children (age zero to seventeen)

	Full sample	SNAP	No SNAP
Age	8.5	7.6	8.6
Under five	0.28	0.33	0.27
Family number of children	2.5	2.9	2.4
MOTHER'S COMPLETED EDUCATION:			
High school dropout	0.15	0.36	0.13
High school graduate/GED	0.25	0.3	0.24
More than high school	0.52	0.26	0.55
Missing	0.08	0.08	0.07
FATHER'S COMPLETED EDUCATION:			
High school dropout	0.11	0.16	0.11
High school graduate/GED	0.2	0.13	0.21
More than high school	0.41	0.09	0.45
Missing	0.27	0.62	0.24
SELF-RATED HEALTH:			
Excellent/very good	0.82	0.7	0.84
Good	0.16	0.26	0.15
Fair/poor	0.02	0.05	0.02
FAMILY MEMBER LIMITED:			
Any	0.23	0.4	0.22
Number	0.33	0.63	0.3
CHILD IN SPECIAL EDUCATION OR WITH OTHER DEVELOPMENTAL DELAY:			
Self	0.06	0.09	0.06
Any	0.12	0.2	0.11
HEALTH CARE USE IN FAMILY LAST TWO WEEKS:			
At least one doctor visit	0.38	0.4	0.38
Number in hospital overnight	0.31	0.41	0.31
HEALTH CARE USE IN FAMILY LAST YEAR:			
At least someone needed care could not afford	0.11	0.23	0.11
N	356,378	30,176	318,069

SOURCE: Author's calculations using NHIS data.

NOTES: Table reports means for all children (age seventeen and younger, column 1), for children reporting SNAP last year (column 2), and for children reporting no SNAP last year (column 3). All differences between columns 2 and 3 are significant at the 1 percent level except mother's education missing, which is significant at the 5 percent level. Statistics weighted with person weight, and variances for tests of equality allow for stratification and clustering within PSU in the original sample with the public use NHIS stratum and PSU variables.

and to live in a family with some child in special education (20 percent versus 11 percent).

Tables 5.4 and 5.5 present similar breakdowns for many of the health conditions and disability measures in the NHIS for adults and children, respectively, along with some health behaviors and a small number of

TABLE 5.4
Health conditions for adults on and off SNAP

	SNAP	No SNAP
Height (inches)	67	68
Weight (pounds)	185	178
BED DISABILITY DAYS IN THE LAST YEAR:		
None	0.51	0.63
One to seven	0.28	0.29
Eight to thirty	0.1	0.05
Thirty-one to 180	0.1	0.023
181 or more	0.02	0.004
Missing	0.03	0.01
DIAGNOSED WITH/HAS HEALTH CONDITION:		
ADD ever	0.07	0.03
Asthma ever	0.19	0.1
Asthma still	0.12	0.05
Vision problem	0.18	0.09
Blind	0.01	0.004
Chronic bronchitis	0.1	0.04
Diabetes	0.12	0.07
Heart attack	0.12	0.03
Stroke	0.05	0.02
Ulcer	0.13	0.07
HEALTH CONDITIONS IN LAST THREE MONTHS:		
Lower back pain	0.45	0.27
Lower back and leg pain	0.21	0.08
Neck pain	0.24	0.14
Migraines frequently	0.32	0.14
HEALTH CONDITIONS IN LAST YEAR:		
Hay fever	0.08	0.09
Sinusitis	0.18	0.14
HEALTH BEHAVIORS:		
Current drinker	0.47	0.62
Ever drinker	0.69	0.76
Never drinker	0.29	0.22
Current smoker	0.4	0.21
Former smoker	0.15	0.22
Never smoker	0.44	0.56
MEDICAL CARE LAST YEAR:		
Flu shot	0.23	0.28
Hospital overnight	0.19	0.07
HEALTH CONDITIONS IN LAST TWO WEEKS:		
Stomach problems	0.08	0.05
ANY OF FOOD IN LAST MONTH:		
Pizza	0.74	0.78
Nondiet soda	0.66	0.54
Salad	0.79	0.86

SOURCE: Author's calculations using NHIS data.

NOTES: Table reports means for adults (age eighteen and older) reporting SNAP last year (column 1) and for adults reporting no SNAP last year (column 2). All differences between columns 1 and 2 are significant at the 1 percent level except the following: (1) significant at the 5 percent level for one to seven bed-disability days and having had hay fever last year. Food stamp recipients are less likely to be drinkers but more likely to be smokers. Food stamp recipients are less likely to have had a pizza last month, more likely to have had nondiet soda, and less likely to have had a salad last month. Statistics weighted with person or sample adult weight as relevant and variances for tests of equality allow for stratification and clustering within PSU in the original sample with the public use NHIS stratum and PSU variables.

TABLE 5.5
Health conditions for children on and off SNAP

	SNAP	No SNAP
Age	7.6	8.6
Under five	0.33	0.27
Family number of children	2.5	2.9
DAYS OF SCHOOL LOST LAST YEAR IF SCHOOL AGE:		
None	0.18	0.2
One to five	0.32	0.4
Six to thirty	0.15	0.11
Thirty-one to 240	0.01	0.003
Not in school	0.008	0.007
DIAGNOSED WITH/HAS HEALTH CONDITION:		
ADD ever	0.1	0.06
Learning disability	0.13	0.07
Mental retardation	0.01	0.004
Other developmental delay	0.05	0.02
Asthma ever	0.19	0.12
Asthma still	0.11	0.06
Vision problem	0.04	0.02
Blind	0.002	0.001
HEALTH CONDITIONS IN LAST YEAR:		
Anemia	0.03	0.01
Frequent diarrhea	0.03	0.01
More than three ear infections	0.09	0.06
Food allergy	0.04	0.04
Respiratory allergy	0.12	0.11
Skin allergy	0.11	0.09
Hay fever	0.08	0.1
Sinusitis	0.07	0.07
PREVENTIVE CARE:		
Flu shot last year	0.27	0.23
HEALTH CONDITIONS IN LAST TWO WEEKS:		
Stomach problems	0.08	0.06

SOURCE: Author's calculations using NHIS data.

NOTES: Table reports means for children (age seventeen and younger) reporting SNAP last year (column 2) and for children reporting no SNAP last year (column 3). All differences between columns 2 and 3 are significant at the 1 percent level except the following: (1) no significant differences for child didn't attend school (if age five and older), days of school missed not reported, child was blind; (2) significant at the 5 percent level for respiratory allergy. Hay fever is the only health condition or negative outcome that is more common for non–food stamp recipient children than food stamp recipient children, and having a flu shot last year is the only other outcome where food stamp recipient children are more advantaged. Statistics weighted with person or sample child weight as relevant and variances for tests of equality allow for stratification and clustering within PSU in the original sample with the public use NHIS stratum and PSU variables.

food-related outcomes for adults. Adults on SNAP are shorter and heavier than are non-SNAP adults. They are more likely to have had at least one bed disability day in the previous year. They are also much more likely than are non-SNAP recipients to have ever been diagnosed with the following conditions: ADD, asthma, a vision problem even with glasses, blindness, diabetes, a heart attack, a stroke, or an ulcer. They are also more likely to have recent back problems or frequent migraines. All of these differences between SNAP recipients and nonrecipients are highly statistically significant.

Regarding health behaviors, adult SNAP recipients are less likely to report current or ever drinking but are more likely to report smoking than are nonrecipients. They have spent more time in the hospital in the last year but are less likely to have had a flu shot. Finally, as measured by the three questions on food consumption—having in the last month had a pizza, a nondiet soda, or a salad—the SNAP recipients had less healthful diets than did nonrecipients.

Table 5.5 reports health conditions for children on and off SNAP. Children on SNAP were much more likely to have missed school and to have been diagnosed with a learning disability, ADD, mental retardation, or another developmental delay. They were also more likely to have ever been diagnosed with asthma, to still suffer from asthma, or to have a severe vision problem or be blind. Using more current measures of health, the SNAP child recipients also look worse off, with higher rates of anemia, recent illnesses, allergies, and stomach problems. They are, however, more likely than nonrecipients to have had a flu shot in the last year.

Differences between SNAP Recipients and Nonrecipients in the NHANES

Tables 5.6 through 5.8 present results from analysis of the NHANES for 2007 to 2008. In addition to knowing food stamp authorization in the last year in NHANES, one also knows whether someone was ever authorized for food stamps. One downside of the NHANES is that the public use NHANES do not report any geographic data; thus, analysis will simply look at different time periods, pooling the two years within this wave.

I compare objective measures of height and weight for SNAP recipients and nonrecipients. A measure of anemia can also be constructed from having low hemoglobin and hematocrit based on blood examination data. The NHANES also contains information on dietary intake; analyzes total calories, total carbohydrates, and total fat consumed; and looks at indicators for low intake of calcium, fiber, iron, magnesium, protein, and zinc, and high intake of sodium, based mostly on the RDA recommendations. There are indicators that have been used in the past when analyzing the effects of food assistance programs (for example, Bhattacharya, Currie, and Haider 2006). The current analyses are not intended to assess program impacts but rather to illustrate the range of differences between groups.

TABLE 5.6
Summary statistics for NHANES 2007–2008, full sample

	Full sample	SNAP last year	No SNAP last year
Male	0.49	0.46	0.5
Age	36	27	38
Family head is high school dropout	0.2	0.44	0.16
Family of seven or more	0.05	0.12	0.04
Child age zero to five	0.08	0.16	0.07
High school dropout/child in school	0.32	0.53	0.29
High school or GED	0.2	0.17	0.44
More than high school	0.4	0.14	0.44
Hispanic	0.15	0.25	0.14
White	0.66	0.44	0.7
Black	0.12	0.27	0.1
Other race (non-Hispanic)	0.06	0.05	0.06
Citizen	0.93	0.92	0.93
Income under 200 percent of poverty level	0.36	0.86	0.28
SNAP RECEIPT:			
Ever	0.21	1	0.08
Last year	0.14	1	0
SNAP don't know or refused to answer	0.01	0	0
N	10,149	2,188	7,873

SOURCE: Author's calculations using National Health and Nutrition Examination Survey (NHANES) data.

NOTES: Table reports means for full sample (column 1), for those reporting SNAP last year (column 2), and those reporting no SNAP last year (column 3). Statistics weighted with person weight.

Existing work by Cole and Fox (2008) examines many of these outcomes, comparing SNAP participants to two groups of nonparticipants, income-eligible nonparticipants and those whose income is high enough to make them ineligible for SNAP. Cole and Fox found that food stamp recipients have worse diets than do either comparison group. Food stamp recipients were less likely to get the appropriate amount of vitamins and minerals than were the higher-income group of ineligibles. Adults on SNAP were found to get a larger share of energy from solid fats, alcohol, and added sugars than other adults. Female adults on food stamps were heavier than members of both comparison groups. Finally, they looked at the Healthy Eating Index (HEI) 2005, which measures food choices relative to the guidelines in the 2005 Dietary Guidelines for Americans and the 2005 My Pyramid, which was a food guidance system that "translates the dietary guidelines into a total diet meeting nutrients" while limiting intake of certain foods typically overconsumed. Food stamp recipients had lower scores on the HEI than did the comparison group. Note, however, that IOM and NRC (2013) discusses the challenges with associating indicators like the HEI 2005 with diet quality as well as with associating diet quality in a causal fashion with chronic disease.

TABLE 5.7
Means for SNAP and non-SNAP recipients, adults

	SNAP last year	No SNAP last year
DIETARY OUTCOMES; TWENTY-FOUR-HOUR RECALL; ADULTS		
Total calories	2,052	2,132
Protein (grams)	76	82
Protein less than recommended daily allowance	0.29	0.19
Carbohydrates	257	257
Fiber (grams)	13	16
Fiber less than RDA	0.94	0.88
Cholesterol (milligrams)	293	292
Cholesterol less than daily guidelines (DG)	0.34	0.34
Fat (grams)	77	81
Outside Acceptable macronutrient distribution range (AMDR) fat limits	0.49	0.51
Calcium (milligrams)	809	951
Below RDA for calcium	0.74	0.68
Zinc (milligrams)	14	12
Below RDA for zinc	0.5	0.41
Iron (milligrams)	14	15
Below RDA for iron	0.5	0.33
Magnesium	246	299
Below RDA for magnesium	0.83	0.74
EXAMINATION WEIGHT, HEIGHT, AND BODY-MASS INDEX (BMI):		
Weight (kilograms)	83	81
Height (centimeters)	167	169
BMI	30	28
Underweight (BMI less than 18.5)	0.04	0.02
Obese (BMI greater than 30)	0.4	0.32

SOURCE: Author's calculations using 2007–2008 NHANES data.

NOTES: Table reports SNAP and no SNAP means in outcome for adults (age eighteen and older). Statistics weighted with person diary or exam weight as relevant.

Table 5.6 presents the individual characteristics of the NHANES adult sample. Table 5.7 shows our dietary and nutritional differences for adults and Table 5.8 for children by "SNAP last year/no SNAP last year" status. First, based on the RDA and other recommendations, we look at whether children and adults are meeting nutritional recommendations from the USDA and the IOM (and others). We also look at levels of these nutritional measures consumed. Tables 5.7 and 5.8 show that, on a number of dimensions, SNAP recipients have worse nutritional outcomes than do nonrecipients, and this is true for both children and adults. Differences in Table 5.7 for adults that are statistically significant indicate SNAP adult recipients consume less protein, less fiber, less calcium, less iron, less zinc, and less magnesium than do other adults, as measured in levels or by having consumed less than the 2010 recommended daily allowance (RDA) or other standards (not shown in tables). SNAP recipient adults are also statistically significantly

TABLE 5.8
Means for SNAP and non-SNAP recipients, children

	SNAP last year	No SNAP last year
DIETARY OUTCOMES: TWENTY-FOUR HOUR RECALL, CHILDREN/PROXY:		
Total calories	1,778	1,820
Protein (grams)	60	65
Protein less than recommended daily allowance (RDA)	0.11	0.09
Carbohydrates	242	242
Fiber (grams)	12	12
Fiber less than RDA	0.88	0.9
Cholesterol (milligrams)	196	216
Cholesterol at daily guidelines (DG) or above	0.19	0.22
Fat (grams)	65	68
Outside acceptable macronutrient distribution range (AMDR) fat limits	0.55	0.53
Calcium (milligrams)	956	985
Below RDA for calcium	0.62	0.65
Zinc (milligrams)	10	10
Below RDA for zinc	0.26	0.28
Iron (milligrams)	13	13
Below RDA for iron	0.33	0.37
Magnesium	201	218
Below RDA for magnesium	0.42	0.46
EXAMINATION WEIGHT, HEIGHT, BODY MASS INDEX (BMI):		
Weight (kilograms)	35	39
Height (centimeters)	134	140
WEIGHT RELATIVE TO WORLD HEALTH ORGANIZATION (WHO) STANDARDS FOR CHILDREN AGE ZERO TO TEN:		
Weight at or below 5th percentile	0.02	0.02
Weight at or below 10th percentile	0.06	0.05
Weight at or above 90th percentile	0.25	0.2
HEIGHT BELOW VARIOUS WHO STANDARDS FOR CHILDREN TWO TO TEN:		
Height at or below 5th percentile	0.06	0.04
Height at or below 10th percentile	0.11	0.07

SOURCE: Author's calculations using in 2007–2008 NHANES data.

NOTES: Table reports SNAP and no SNAP means in outcome for children (age seventeen and younger). Statistics weighted with person diary or exam weight as relevant.

more likely to be underweight or obese as measured by BMI being above and below thresholds (not shown in the tables). This is also true if we control for demographics (gender, age, race/ethnicity), family head's education, day of interview, and no food stamp receipt reported (not shown).

Table 5.8 shows the outcomes for children. Again, children on SNAP are less likely to get the RDA of fiber but are also less likely to consume more than the recommended amount of cholesterol. SNAP recipient children are also less likely with or without regression adjustment (adjustment not shown) to have not obtained enough iron. SNAP recipient children are statistically more likely to have weight above the 90th percentile of the World Health Organization (WHO) standards for healthy growth and are also more likely to have height below the 10th percentile of the WHO standards.

All in all, the NHANES results suggest that adults on SNAP have worse nutrition on many dimensions, although SNAP children's nutritional outcomes are not as different from the rest of the population. It is also perhaps worth noting given perceptions about eating habits of those on SNAP that neither adults nor children on SNAP consume significantly more fat or cholesterol than do nonrecipients. In fact, the children on SNAP consume less cholesterol than do other children.

Overall, this descriptive analysis using the NHIS and NHANES has confirmed what we already knew from other settings. SNAP recipients are less healthy than is the general population, and this is true whether we focus on measures of health that are stock variables and likely to have been unchanged for quite some time and may predate use of the program or whether we focus on health measures that can adjust more quickly. SNAP recipients also have worse diets based on various micronutrients and also based on some macronutrients. Of course, ideally, we would be able to control for selection in some way to see whether SNAP recipients are less healthy to start, but this is not feasible in the public use NHIS and NHANES, where state identifiers are unavailable. Research opportunities await those who gain access to the restricted use data and combine that with policy variation. But the takeaway message is clear: SNAP recipients are less healthy than are others, and this is likely in part for reasons that have little or nothing to do with SNAP use.

Next we turn to a review of existing knowledge of the causal health and nutrition effects of SNAP.

CHALLENGES TO EVALUATION OF SNAP

Obtaining causal estimates of the effects of national food assistance programs like SNAP is challenging. Comparisons of SNAP recipients to the full population of nonrecipients is sure to be somewhat misleading due to selection in who takes up these programs (a selection we have already documented). Given that SNAP eligibility is tied to having low income and asset holdings, comparisons of health outcomes for program recipients to those of the general population are unlikely to yield the true causal effects of the program on health. Even among those eligible for the SNAP program, recipients may be positively or negatively selected compared to eligible nonparticipants due to the fact that participation is an individual choice, and existing evidence suggests that this might be the case for SNAP (for example, Wilde, Troy, and Rogers 2009). When recipients are healthier, more motivated, or more knowledgeable about the program than are nonparticipants, comparisons may suggest the program has a more positive effect than it actually does. Alternatively, if participants are more disadvantaged than are eligible nonparticipants, comparisons of these two groups could lead to underestimates of the effects of the program. With SNAP, most research suggests participants are more disadvantaged than eligible nonparticipants (for example, Gundersen, Jolliffe, and Tiehen 2009). And, in fact, we have already seen that, compared to the general population, SNAP recipients are less healthy when measured using adult height or the presence of other conditions such as having been diagnosed with a learning disability that SNAP likely did not affect. Finally, an additional challenge to such evaluation is tied to under-reporting of program benefits in most large survey data sets (for example, Marquis and Moore 1990; Bitler, Currie, and Scholz 2003; Meyer, Mok, and Sullivan 2009). This means that SNAP receipt is underreported, and the reported SNAP recipients may be those with more attachment to SNAP or may otherwise be different from nonreporters (for example, Bollinger and David 1997). Abreveya, Hausman, and Scott-Morton (1998) discuss issues with estimation with this type of misreporting.

There are several approaches that researchers have taken to avoid selection bias (see the review articles by Gundersen, Kreider, and Pepper 2011 and by Meyerhoefer and Yang 2011). One approach compares outcomes among individuals in geographic areas with different program rules, using panel data on individuals or pooled cross-sections of individuals, typically with controls for geographic entities and time. This approach relies on individuals with similar incomes and other characteristics being comparable across states or counties with different income thresholds for eligibility for the program or different rules about how individuals stay eligible for programs or have different access to the program. This approach is particularly problematic for SNAP because until recently this program was national with common rules across states. For example, until recently, SNAP or Food Stamps allowed little leeway for states to set program rules. Examples of this approach for SNAP using more recently introduced state rule variation include Currie and Grogger (2002), Kabbani and Wilde (2003), Yen and colleagues (2008), and Ratcliffe, McKernan, and Zhang (2011); Ganong and Liebman (2013) document that, even more recently, wider state experimentation has led to increases in use of SNAP, as does Ziliak (Chapter One in this volume).

When there is no geographic variation in federal rules, another common approach is to limit the analysis to more comparable treatment and control groups. Another approach when program rules do not vary across areas is to look at the effects of the introduction of programs in an event study, comparing otherwise similar individuals in places before and after programs are introduced. Another approach to studying the effects of programs is to use random assignment. If program administrators are able to randomly assign an offer of program participation to otherwise identical eligible individuals, then comparisons of those assigned to be eligible for the program with those denied the option to participate can yield unbiased estimates of the effects of the program. In the case of food stamps, there have been several demonstration projects funded by the USDA that have yielded evidence about the effects of cashing out food stamp benefits on food spending (for example, Fraker, Martini, and Ohls 1995). More recently, a pilot program has evaluated the use of financial incentives to consume more fruits and vegetables (the Healthy Incentives Pilot, Bartlett et al. 2013).

WHAT DO WE KNOW NOW?

In this section, we review in more detail the existing causal evidence about SNAP and nutrition and health.

Does SNAP Improve Nutrition Outcomes?

Much of the evidence about the effects of SNAP on nutrition is based on cross-sectional studies comparing SNAP recipients and eligible nonrecipients and thus is potentially biased for the reasons already discussed, even when observable differences are controlled for. This cross-sectional evidence is summarized in various places, including IOM and NRC (2013) and Currie (1995, 2008). There is evidence suggesting SNAP recipients spend more on food than do other similar families and that they have higher nutrient availability than these others. An example of this literature, which does deal in part with selection, is Devaney and Moffitt (1991), which finds that food stamp benefits had larger dietary effects than cash income does, using data from 1979 to 1980.

The lack of good causal evidence about the effects of SNAP on nutrition is in part due to the many challenges with evaluating what was for most of its life a national program with consistent rules across places, making it impossible to use the most common quasi-experimental estimators: difference-in-differences, or DD. Fox, Hamilton, and Lin (2004) review the older literature for USDA in a technical report, summarizing it as finding no important impacts of SNAP or food stamps on dietary intake despite the fact that food stamp recipients had higher spending on food and higher availability of nutrients. Gleason, Rangarajan, and Olson (2000) and Currie (1995) point out additional challenges with measuring nutrition. One is related to different dietary needs for different types of people (that is, children need less food than do most adults). Another challenge is the difficulty of measuring diet quality with even a two-day record of dietary intake, due to day-to-day variation in intake. There are also challenges with creating overall summary measures of diet that actually measure dietary quality. Finally, there is the challenge that any of these comparisons of recipients and nonrecipients in standard data sets suffer from misclassification, as SNAP use is underreported, and some of the reported nonrecipients are actually getting SNAP (for example, Bollinger and David 1997).

Evidence already discussed about the introduction of the program as part of the War on Poverty, however, does find that introduction of SNAP in one's county increases spending on food and decreases spending on food away from home but does not look at specific nutrients due to data constraints (Hoynes and Schanzenbach 2009). An additional advantage to this work beyond superior identification (like other work using policy variation in lieu of self-selected participation) is that underreporting of participation does not affect it.

Another natural experiment was part of the American Recovery and Reinvestment Act of 2009, which increased SNAP benefits by 15 percent on average. A recent paper using the Consumer Expenditure Survey (Beatty and Tuttle 2012) finds evidence that this substantial increase in SNAP benefits in ARRA did increase food expenditures at home.

Finally, the USDA has been using randomized control trials to evaluate new changes to SNAP, which introduce incentives to purchase fruits, vegetables, or other healthful foods. Bartlett and colleagues (2013) report the impact of an experiment in Hampden County, Massachusetts, in 2011 and 2012. SNAP recipients were randomly assigned to a treatment group, who got the incentive, or to a control group, who faced the usual SNAP rules. In the treatment group, SNAP recipients receive an additional $0.30 for each dollar of SNAP benefits spent on fruits and vegetables. Surveys of the participants show that the treatment group consumed more targeted fruits and vegetables per day than did the control group, an increase of 25 percent over control group consumption. Take-up of at least some incentive payments was about two-thirds in the treatment group, with about $12 a month spent on the targeted fruits and vegetables. This additional spending was fairly evenly split between fruits and vegetables. This type of experiment is very useful for learning about ways to increase purchase and consumption of healthful foods. A final report not yet complete will analyze shopping patterns, incentive earnings, and presumably provide a cost-benefit analysis of the experiment.

How Does SNAP Affect Health?

Turning now to health, all of the same challenges arise in finding causal estimates of the effect of SNAP on health as did with looking at effects on nutrition, and there are some new ones.[3] Descriptively, in the preceding pages, I showed that SNAP recipients look less healthy even on dimensions where at least current SNAP receipt is likely happening long after the health event in question (for example, height, having ever been diagnosed with asthma). An additional challenge with evaluating effects on health is that health itself is primarily a stock variable, which evolves slowly.

Again, important work here relies on variation in the introduction of the Food Stamp Program. Hoynes and Schanzenbach (2009) find that introduction of the Food Stamp Program led to increases in food consumption. Almond, Hoynes, and Schanzenbach (2011) find that the introduction of food stamps led to increases in birth weight, as do Currie and Moretti (2008). Hoynes, Schanzenbach, and Almond (2012) look at the long-run impacts of being exposed to the Food Stamp Program while age zero to five on adult obesity, high blood pressure, and diabetes, finding positive effects on health.

There can be, however, important challenges with using evidence about program introduction to inform current debate. First, program rules may change in important ways over time, potentially raising questions about the ongoing validity of historical estimates for evaluating programs today. Second, the counterfactual in the absence of the program can be different than those at the time of program introduction.

In a series of papers, Brent Kreider and Craig Gundersen and their coauthors have addressed the issues discussed in the preceding paragraphs with misreporting of SNAP and how it affects estimates of SNAP's effects. Their most recent work also deals with selection. Kreider and colleagues (2012) use techniques on bounding to deal with these two issues simultaneously. They find that with strong assumptions about the level of endogeneity and misreporting, SNAP is favorable for children's health, whereas weaker assumptions leave even the sign of the causal effect unidentified.[4]

CONCLUSION

In this chapter, I have shown that selection into SNAP is likely negative, with SNAP recipients having worse health in ways that are not plausibly due to use of SNAP. SNAP recipients also have some worse nutritional outcomes, with lower levels of some micro- and macronutrients. Interestingly, however, SNAP recipients do not consume significantly higher amounts of calories or fat. This selection into who uses SNAP highlights why comparisons of outcomes for recipients and nonrecipients are unlikely to tell us about causal effects of SNAP.

I have also reviewed the literature on SNAP and health and nutrition, highlighting the more compelling work. That said, a richer understanding of the effects of SNAP on health and nutrition awaits one of two innovations. First, there is room for work using policy variation at the state level. Ganong and Liebman (2013) have documented that this policy variation has had a modest effect on use of SNAP as has Ziliak (Chapter One in this volume). Work looking at impacts on nutrition and health is the next step. Second, it would be useful to have further experimentation into either more carrots (following on the HIP pilots) with subsidies for more purchases of fruits and vegetables or more testing of what nutrition education is effective. Finally, it seems as though there is room for the insights of behavioral economics to be brought to bear.

APPENDIX

The National Health Interview Survey (NHIS) underreports SNAP use compared to the administrative totals, but the two lines track one another closely.[5] (This is shown in Figure 5.A.1.) Of course, this comparison is imperfect. First, NHIS doesn't track the full population, and, to the extent the persons not in scope are SNAP participants, the NHIS total should be smaller. Second, NHIS asks about use in the last year. To the extent that short

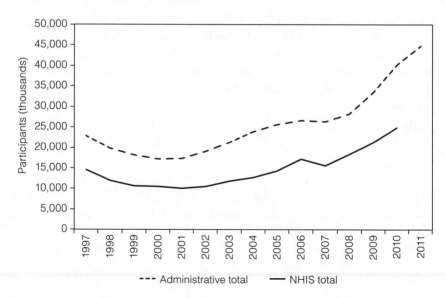

Figure 5.A.1.   Administrative and NHIS-generated total SNAP participants by year.
NOTES: This figure shows total administrative persons on average on SNAP per month by fiscal year and the total weighted number of persons on SNAP in the previous year by NHIS survey year.
SOURCE: Author's calculations using NHIS data and USDA Food and Nutrition Service SNAP Program Data.

spells are common, NHIS totals should be relatively bigger. This level of misreporting is a bit better than what Meyer, Mok, and Sullivan (2009) report for the Current Population Survey-Annual Social and Economic Supplement (CPS-ASEC). Finally, NHIS assigns receipt to members of the family, but SNAP benefits are intended for household members who share resources, which could be a larger unit. A comparison of household-level SNAP receipt with the number of households as reported in Table 12 of Meyer, Mok, and Sullivan (2009) shows NHIS captures 76 percent of the administrative recipiency unit receipt for 2007. And this suggests that the NHIS is no worse than many other commonly used cross-sectional data sets.

NOTES

I thank Kosali Simon, Colleen Heflin, Hilary Hoynes, Diane Schanzenbach, Jim Ziliak, Craig Gundersen, Judi Bartfeld, Tim Smeeding, and audience participants at APPAM as well as an anonymous referee for helpful feedback. This paper made use of Integrated Health Interview Survey extracts, and I thank the MPC and SHADAC for making these available. I gratefully acknowledge financial support from the University of Kentucky's Center for Poverty Research and the University of Wisconsin's Institute for Research on Poverty.

1. Appendix Figure 5.A.1 shows the administrative average participation levels by fiscal year as well as the NHIS total reported SNAP participation levels, and the differences in the concepts of SNAP measured and the totals and underreporting are discussed further there.

2. Note that in the NHIS this variable measures participation in a state or county cash assistance program and respondents are prompted not to report SSI/SNAP/LIHEAP or Medicaid or state medical assistance.

3. Note that other chapters in this volume address food insecurity; thus, I do not discuss the findings for food insecurity.

4. One possible issue with their analysis is that they use NHANES, which has very little information on income and nothing about assets. Arguably this is less an issue for a sample of children than it might be for adults, but they are likely to be missing eligibles with gross income above 130 percent of poverty in states with generous broad-based categorical eligibility.

5. Meyer, Mok, and Sullivan (2009) document this underreporting in the CPS, SIPP, and PSID. For FY2008 to FY2010, I compared total reported use of SNAP in the last year to the average number of participants. Between 62 percent and 65 percent of the administrative total number of participants from USDA administrative totals report SNAP in the NHIS.

REFERENCES

Abreveya, J., J. Hausman, and F. Scott-Morton. 1998. "Misclassification of the Dependent Variable in a Discrete-Response Setting." *Journal of Econometrics* 87: 239–269.

Almond, D., H. Hoynes, and D. Schanzenbach. 2011. "Inside the War on Poverty: The Impact of Food Stamps on Birth Outcomes." *Review of Economics and Statistics* 93(2): 387–403.

Bartlett, S., J. Klerman, P. Wilde, L. Olsho, M. Blocklin, C. Logan, and A. Enver. 2013. "Healthy Incentives Pilot Interim Report." Washington, DC: USDA FNS Office of Research and Analysis.

Beatty, T., and C. Tuttle. 2012. "Expenditure Response to Increases in In-Kind Transfers: Evidence from the Supplemental Nutrition Assistance Program." Working paper, University of Minnesota.

Bhattacharya, J., J. Currie, and S. Haider. 2006. "Breakfast of Champions? The Effects of the School Breakfast Program on the Nutrition of Children and Their Families." *Journal of Human Resources* 41(3): 445–466.

Bitler, M., J. Currie, and J. K. Scholz. 2003. "WIC Eligibility and Participation." *Journal of Human Resources* 38(s): 1139–1179.

Bollinger, C., and M. David. 1997. "Modeling Discrete Choice with Response Error: Food Stamp Participation." *Journal of the American Statistical Association* 92(439): 827–835.

Cole, N., and M. K. Fox. 2008, "Diet Quality of Americans by Food Stamp Participation Status: Data from the National Health and Nutrition Examination Survey, 1999–2004." Washington, DC: USDA Food and Nutrition Service ORNA.

Currie, J. 1995. *Welfare and the Well-Being of Children*. Chur, Switzerland: Harwood Academic Publishers.

———. 2008. *The Invisible Safety Net: Protecting the Nation's Poor Children and Families*. Princeton, NJ: Princeton University Press.

Currie, J., and F. Gahvari. 2008. "Transfers in Cash and In-Kind: Theory Meets the Data." *Journal of Economic Literature* 46(2): 333–383.

Currie, J., and J. Grogger. 2002. "Medicaid Expansions and Welfare Contractions: Offsetting Effects on Maternal Behavior and Infant Health." *Journal of Health Economics* 21(2): 313–335.

Currie, J., and E. Moretti. 2008. "Did the Introduction of Food Stamps Affect Birth Outcomes in California?" In R. Schoeni, J. House, G. Kaplan, and H. Pollack, eds., *Making Americans Healthier: Social and Economic Policy as Health Policy*, 122–142. New York: Russell Sage Foundation.

Devaney, B. and R. Moffitt. 1991. "Dietary Effects of the Food Stamp Program." *American Journal of Agricultural Economics* 73(1): 202–211.

Fox, M. K., Hamilton, W. and Lin, B.-H. 2004. *Effects of Food Assistance and Nutrition Programs on Nutrition and Health: Volume 3 Literature Review*. Washington, DC: USDA ERS FANRP 19-3.

Fraker, T., A. Martini, and J. Ohls. 1995. "The Effect of Food Stamp Cashout on Food Expenditures: An Assessment of the Findings from Four Demonstrations." *Journal of Human Resources* 30(4): 633–649.

Ganong, P., and J. Liebman. 2013. "The Decline, Rebound, and Further Rise in SNAP Enrollment: Disentangling Business Cycle Fluctuations and Policy Changes." NBER Working Paper 19363.

Gleason, P., A. Rangarajan, and C. Olson. 2000. *Dietary Intake and Dietary Attitudes among Food Stamp Participants and Other Low-Income Individuals.* Princeton, NJ: Mathematical Policy Research report for USDA.

Grossman, M. 1972. "On the Concept of Health Capital and the Demand for Health." *Journal of Political Economy* 80(2): 223–255.

Gundersen, C., D. Jolliffe, and L. Tiehen. 2009, "The Challenge of Program Evaluation: When Increasing Program Participation Decreases the Relative Well-Being of Participants." *Food Policy* 34(4): 367–376.

Gundersen, C., B. Kreider, and J. Pepper. 2011. "The Economics of Food Insecurity in the United States." *Applied Economic Perspectives and Policy* 33(3): 281–303.

Hoynes, H. W., and D. Schanzenbach. 2009. "Consumption Responses to In-Kind Transfers: Evidence from the Introduction of the Food Stamp Program." *American Economic Journal: Applied Economics* 1: 109–139.

Hoynes, H. W., D. Schanzenbach, and D. Almond. 2012. "Long Run Impacts of Childhood Access to the Safety Net." NBER Working Paper 18535. Cambridge, MA: National Bureau of Economic Research.

IOM and NRC. 2013. *Supplemental Nutrition Assistance Program: Examining the Evidence to Define Benefit Adequacy.* Washington, DC: The National Academies Press.

Kabbani, N., and P. Wilde. 2003. "Short Recertification Periods in the US Food Stamp Program." *Journal of Human Resources* 38(S): 1112–1138.

Kreider, B., J. Pepper, C. Gundersen, and D. Jolliffe. 2012. "Identifying the Effects of SNAP on Child Health Outcomes when Participation Is Endogenous and Misreported." *Journal of the American Statistical Association* 107(499): 958–974.

Lowe, C., G. Forbes, S. Garn, G. Owens, N. Smith, W. Weil Jr., and L. Filer Jr. 1973. "The Ten-State Nutrition Survey: A Pediatric Perspective." *Pediatrics* 41: 1095–1099.

Marquis, K. and J. Moore. (1990). *Measurement Errors in SIPP Program Reports in Proceedings of the Bureau of the Census Annual Research Conference.* Washington, DC: Bureau of the Census, 721–745.

Meyer, B., W. Mok, and J. Sullivan. 2009. "The Under-Reporting of Transfers in Household Surveys: Its Nature and Consequences." NBER Working Paper 15181. Washington, DC: The National Academies Press.

Meyerhoefer, C. and M. Yang. 2011. "The Relationship between Food Assistance and Health: A Review of the Literature and Empirical Strategies for Identifying Program Effects." *Applied Economic Perspectives and Policy*: 1–41.

Ratcliffe, C., S. McKernan, and S. Zhang. 2011. "How Much Does the Supplemental Nutrition Assistance Program Reduce Food Insecurity?" *American Journal of Agricultural Economics* 93: 1082–1098.

Rose, D. 2007. "Food Stamps, the Thrifty Food Plan, and Meal Preparation: The Importance of the Time Dimension for US Nutrition Policy." *Journal of Nutrition Education and Behavior* 39(4): 226–232.

Wilde, P., L. Troy, and B. Rogers. 2009. "Food Stamps and Food Spending: An Engel Function Approach." *American Journal of Agricultural Economics* 91(2): 416–430.

Yen, S., M. Andrews, Z. Chen, and D. Eastwood. 2008. "Food Stamp Program Participation and Food Insecurity: An Instrumental Variables Approach." *American Journal of Agricultural Economics* 90(1): 117–132.

CHAPTER SIX

SNAP and Obesity

Craig Gundersen

Hunger and its accordant consequences were serious problems in the United States fifty years ago. In response, the U.S. government established the Supplemental Nutrition Assistance Program (SNAP, then known as the Food Stamp Program). Over time, the program expanded extensively such that in 2012 it served approximately 47 million people, with total benefits of almost $74 billion. In the aggregate, the program is large; in addition, the benefits received by individuals can be quite large. For example, the maximum benefit level was $668 for a family of four in 2012. Due to its total size and importance to individual households, SNAP has become a central component of the social safety net and the subject of much discussion in the United States.

The central goal of SNAP is to alleviate hunger and, as part of this, SNAP is designed to increase the food expenditures of low-income Americans. A body of research has examined whether SNAP has achieved these goals. Early work demonstrated that the receipt of SNAP in the United States leads to increases in food consumption (in comparison to equivalent amounts of cash), and nutrient intakes of SNAP recipients were higher than those of eligible nonrecipients.[1] After the advent of various measures of food insecurity, research further demonstrated that SNAP recipients are less likely to be food insecure than eligible nonrecipients and, as found in some studies, substantially less likely to be food insecure.[2] Along with these direct impacts on food intakes, SNAP has also been found to improve well-being over other dimensions, including reductions in poverty, as shown in Chapter Two in this volume by Laura Tiehen, Dean Jolliffe, and Timothy Smeeding (see also Bishop, Formby, and Zeager 1996; and Tiehen, Jolliffe, and Gundersen 2012); improvements in birth outcomes (Almond, Hoynes, and Schanzenbach 2011); lower mortality (Krueger et al. 2004); and better general health (Kreider et al. 2012). Moreover, by reducing food insecurity, the negative impacts of food insecurity on various health outcomes are diminished.[3] See Chapters Three, Four, and Five of this volume, as well as this one, for a discussion of various health effects of SNAP.

It is perhaps relatively noncontroversial to state that SNAP has been successful at improving the well-being of low-income Americans. In recent years, though, there have been some proposals that have sought to change the structure of SNAP such that it becomes, at least in part, an "antiobesity" program. These proposals have emerged due to a perception that SNAP leads recipients to have higher weights than nonrecipients. They are also part of a wide array of other proposals to change or implement policies to reduce obesity in the United States. These are in part in response to obesity rates that, while leveling off recently, increased from 1960 to 2000 (Burkhauser, Cawley, and Schmeiser 2009).

In this chapter, I begin with a theoretical consideration of whether SNAP benefits lead to increases in food consumption that could lead to increases in weight status. Theoretically, the effect of SNAP is ambiguous. On the one hand, receiving more resources to make food purchases has the potential to allow for healthier food choices and free up income for other healthier activities—both of which could lead to declines in weight status. On the other hand, more resources could lead to purchases of more calories, which may not be healthy; for example, the income freed up could be spent on leisure activities that are not conducive to an active lifestyle. Both of these factors could lead to a higher weight status.

Insofar as SNAP is a near-cash program, I next consider whether, empirically, higher incomes are associated with higher rates of obesity. This is done for both children and for adults. I show, consistent with previous work, that income is, in general, inversely related to rates of obesity.

Given the inverse relationship between income and obesity, one would anticipate that SNAP receipt would lead to reductions in obesity. A series of recent papers has considered whether, in fact, SNAP does lead to reductions in obesity. I next review the results of these papers. The evidence there is mixed—two have shown slightly elevated probabilities of obesity for at least a subset of recipients, whereas most have shown no impact or reductions in the probability of obesity.

Despite the lack of convincing evidence that SNAP leads to increases in obesity, several proposals have emerged to restrict what SNAP participants can purchase with their benefits. I review these proposals. I then conclude with a discussion of some of the potential consequences of these restrictions for the well-being of low-income households.

THEORETICAL CONSIDERATION OF THE IMPACT
OF SNAP BENEFITS ON OBESITY

A household eligible for SNAP must make a decision about whether to receive benefits. The two primary costs associated with participating in SNAP are stigma and transaction costs. The stigma associated with receiving SNAP can arise due to a person's own distaste for receiving SNAP, the fear of disapproval from others when redeeming SNAP, and/or the possible negative reaction of caseworkers.[4] Second, transaction costs can diminish the attractiveness of participation, including travel time to and time spent in a SNAP office; the burden of transporting children to the office or paying for childcare services; and the direct costs of paying for transportation. A household faces these costs on a repeated basis because it must recertify its eligibility.[5] The amount of SNAP benefits a household receives is decreasing in income and increasing in family size. If the benefits exceed the costs, a household will decide to enter the program.

The solid line in Figure 6.1 displays the budget constraint for a household prior to receiving SNAP.[6] This is expressed in terms of the

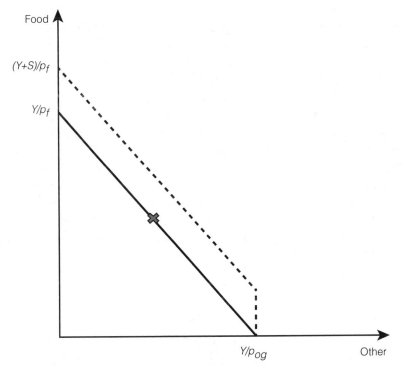

Figure 6.1. Consumption choices available to a household due to SNAP receipt.

choices available to a household between food and other goods. The asterisk on the line represents the choice made by a household. The dashed line represents the choices available to a household due to the receipt of SNAP (denoted as *S* in the figure).[7] Although, technically, a household could reduce its expenditures on food, there is no empirical evidence of a negative marginal propensity to consume food out of SNAP benefits. So, we would anticipate that, due to receiving SNAP, households would increase their food expenditures (that is, move toward the upper left on the figure). One should note that this is akin to a similar increase in income—if a household saw an increase in income due to, say, an increase in wages for a household member, one would see an increase in food expenditures.

This shift out in the budget constraint could lead to an increase in calories, which could lead to an increase in weight for individuals in the household. In addition, a household could purchase goods that would lead to an increase in sedentary activities, which, again, could lead to an increase in weight. So, in theory, receiving SNAP, just as with any increase in income, could lead to an increase in weight. The converse could also hold. Considering other goods in isolation, an increase in income could enable a household to engage in activities that would lead to less sedentary activities (for example, the purchase of a membership at a YMCA).

At least implicitly, the central argument used by those who believe SNAP leads to increases in obesity is that recipients will choose to purchase more products that lead to weight gain. Suppose households allocate consumption to a combination of at-home purchases of "healthy food" and "unhealthy food."[8] As in Figure 6.1, in Figure 6.2 the household's pre-SNAP choices are represented by a solid line (and the choice of food types by the asterisk), and the post-SNAP choices are represented by a dashed line. Without more information about the preferences of the household, it is not clear what will happen to the consumption of "healthy" and "unhealthy" foods. If "unhealthy foods" ("healthy foods") are an inferior good, then the total consumption of "unhealthy foods" ("healthy foods") would fall resulting in a proportional increase in "healthy foods" ("unhealthy foods"). If both "unhealthy foods" and "healthy foods" are normal goods, then consumption of both would increase. In any case, the combined influence of increased income due to SNAP receipt is theoretically ambiguous.[9]

EMPIRICAL CONSIDERATION OF THE IMPACT OF INCOME ON OBESITY

I now consider some empirical evidence regarding rates of obesity at various income levels.[10] If there are differences in obesity rates at different levels of

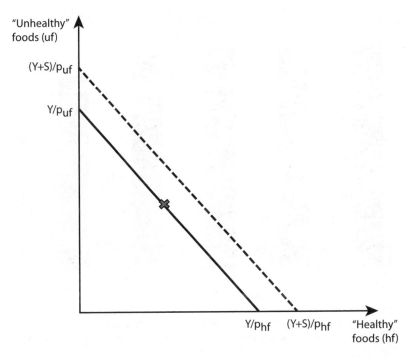

Figure 6.2. Food consumption choices available to a household due to SNAP receipt.

income, this would provide some empirical evidence regarding the theoretically ambiguous effect of SNAP discussed in the preceding pages.

To examine the relationship between income and obesity, I use data from the 2001 to 2010 waves of the National Health and Nutrition Examination Survey (NHANES). The NHANES, conducted by the National Center for Health Statistics, Centers for Disease Control (NCHS/CDC), is a program of surveys designed to collect information about the health and nutritional status of adults and children in the United States through interviews and direct physical examinations. The survey currently includes a national sample of about 5,000 persons each year, about half of whom are children. Vulnerable groups, including Hispanics and African Americans, are oversampled.

Given the problems associated with self-reports of heights and weights in surveys (see Connor Gorber et al. 2007 for a review), a key advantage of the NHANES is that heights and weights were measured with an automated data-collection system by a trained technician in the NHANES mobile examination center. With these heights and weights, one can calculate the BMI (kg/m^2). For adults I consider two categories: obese (BMI above 30) and, as a subset of obese, those who are severely or very severely obese (BMI

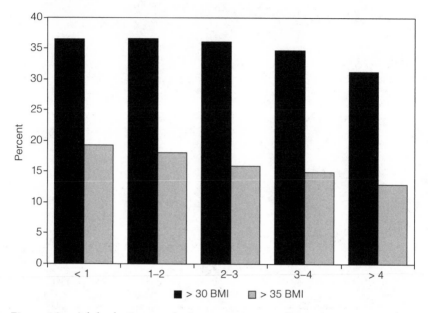

Figure 6.3.   Adult obesity rates by income-to-poverty-line ratio.
SOURCE: Author's calculations using 2001–2010 National Health and Nutrition Examination Survey (NHANES) data.

above 35).[11] For children, these heights and weights are mapped into a percentile by using age- and gender-specific reference values of the CDC growth charts for the United States (Ogden et al. 2002). To somewhat mimic the categories for adults, I consider two BMI percentile cutoffs: at or above the 95th percentile and at or above the 99th percentile.

In each of the following figures we show the proportion of persons who are obese, broken down by income categories defined with respect to the poverty line (less than the poverty line, between 100 percent and 200 percent of the poverty line, between 200 percent and 300 percent of the poverty line, between 300 percent and 400 percent of the poverty line, above 400 percent of the poverty line). In Figure 6.3 I begin with a comparison for all adults (that is, those age eighteen and over) in the sample.[12] As seen there, obesity rates fall from the lowest income category to the highest income category— from 36.3 percent for the highest income category to 31.3 percent for the lowest. For the above 35 BMI category, there is a secular decline with respect to income with a similar absolute decline from the highest to the lowest income categories (19.1 percent to 13.0 percent).

In Figure 6.4, the relationship between income and obesity is broken down by gender. For males, the proportion of those in the obese category is actually higher for those with incomes above 400 percent of the poverty line in comparison to those with incomes below the poverty line. When the

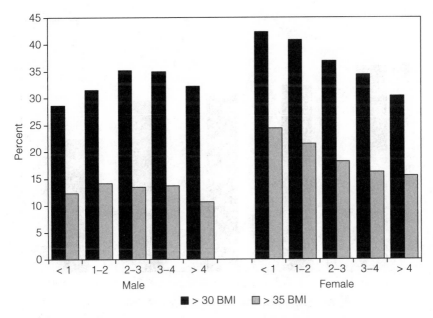

Figure 6.4.   Adult obesity rates by income-to-poverty-line ratio and gender.
SOURCE: Author's calculations using 2001–2010 NHANES data.

breakdown is for over 35 BMI, the two lowest levels are in the ends of the income distribution. For females, the story is markedly different. There is a steady decline in the proportion of those who are obese and severely or very severely obese as income increases. A comparison between the highest and lowest income categories for both obesity categories demonstrates a very large decline: from 42.3 percent to 30.4 percent and from 24.4 percent to 15.5 percent. Based on these gender comparisons, one can state that the inverse relationship between income and the probability of obesity among adults is primarily due to the relationship for women. Why the relationship between income and obesity differs between men and women is not clear and, to the best of my knowledge, has not been addressed in other work. Although this question is beyond the scope of this chapter, future research may wish to pursue it.

Figure 6.5 is for all children between the ages of three and seventeen.[13] There is a steady decline in probabilities of obesity as income increases when all children are included. For example, from the lowest to the highest income spectrum there is a decline in the probability of being in the 95th percentile or higher from 20.4 percent to 13.2 percent, and for being in the 99th percentile or higher from 6.1 percent to 2.6 percent. Unlike those for adults, these results are similar in terms of increasing income being associated with lower probabilities of obesity for both boys and girls (see Figure 6.6).

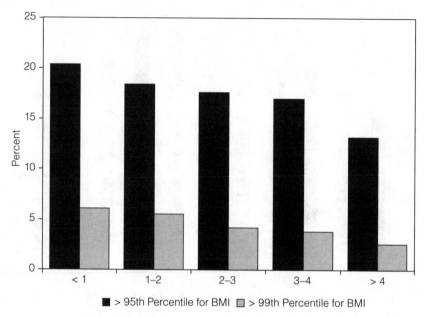

Figure 6.5. Child obesity rates by income-to-poverty-line ratio.
SOURCE: Author's calculations using 2001–2010 NHANES data.

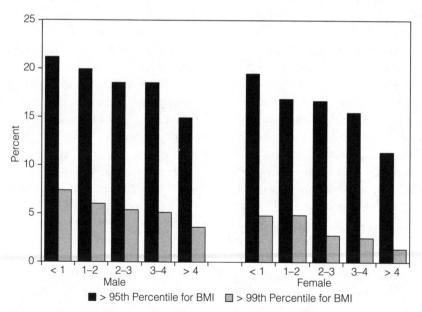

Figure 6.6. Child obesity rates by income-to-poverty-line ratio and gender.
SOURCE: Author's calculations using 2001–2010 NHANES data.

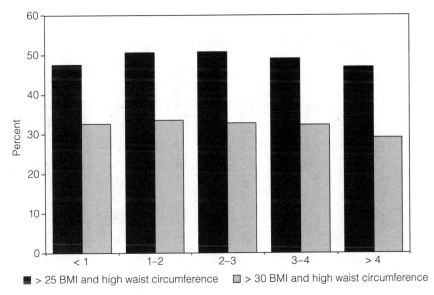

Figure 6.7.   Adult BMI and waist circumference status by income-to-poverty-line ratio.

NOTE: BMI = body mass index.

SOURCE: Author's calculations using 2001–2010 NHANES data.

Along with BMI, there are other measures of obesity that can be examined when considering the relationship between income and obesity.[14] For adults I consider waist circumference combined with BMI as a measure of obesity. Based on the criterion from www.nhlbi.nih.gov/health/public/heart/obesity/lose_wt/bmi_dis.htm, persons with BMIs above 25 and waist circumferences above 102 cm (men) or 88 cm (women) are considered at a similar level of risk for negative health outcomes as those with BMIs above 30 but without waist circumferences above those critical values. A similar story holds for persons with BMIs above 30 and waist circumferences above the critical values listed here—they are considered at a similar level of risk as those with BMIs above 30 but without a waist circumference above those critical values. As seen in Figure 6.7, there is not the decline in obesity as incomes increase one sees when just BMI is used. Although those with incomes above 400 percent of the poverty line have lower rates of obesity under either measure than those with incomes below the poverty line, the intermediate income categories, in the main, have higher rates of obesity than those found among the poor. In Figure 6.8, breakdowns by gender over these measures are displayed. Two things are worth emphasizing. First, for men, the extent of obesity is actually higher for those with incomes over 400 percent of the poverty line in comparison to those with incomes under the

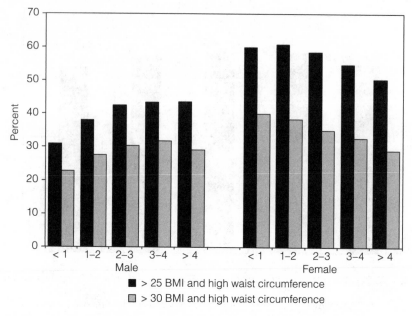

Figure 6.8. Adult BMI and waist circumference status by income-to-poverty-line ratio and gender.

SOURCE: Author's calculations using 2001–2010 NHANES data.

poverty line. This is similar to the result found for the over 30 BMI measure found in Figure 6.4. In contrast, for women, there is a secular decline as income increases, similar to Figure 6.4. Second, although the proportions of men found to be obese in Figure 6.8 are slightly higher than in Figure 6.4, the proportions of women found to be obese in Figure 6.8 are substantially higher than in Figure 6.4.

Turning to children, tricep skinfold and subscapular skinfold are two ways of measuring obesity in children. Here we use the 95th percentile thresholds established in Addo and Himes (2010). In Figure 6.9 the results are displayed in a manner akin to Figure 6.5. The patterns are similar in the two figures insofar as increased incomes are associated with lower levels of obesity whether measured by BMI, tricep skinfold, or subscapular skinfold. In Figure 6.10 the results are broken down by gender. For girls, the patterns with both skinfold measures are similar to those with BMI—a steady decline in obesity as income increases. For boys, the pattern is slightly different between Figures 6.6 and 6.10—there is a slight increase in obesity rates for skinfold measures as income increases (in contrast to BMI), and the drop is especially marked in Figure 6.10 for children in households with incomes between three and four times the poverty line to those with incomes above four times the poverty line.

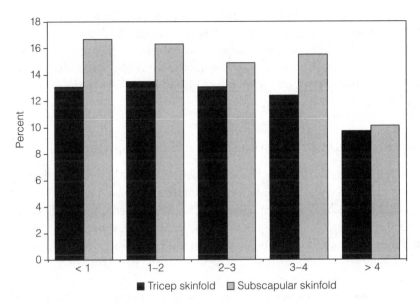

Figure 6.9. Skinfold measures of child obesity by income-to-poverty-line ratio.
SOURCE: Author's calculations using 2001–2010 NHANES data.

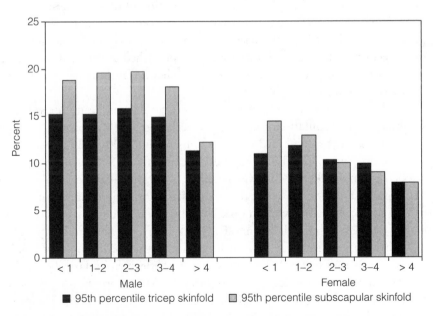

Figure 6.10. Skinfold measures of child obesity by income-to-poverty-line ratio and gender.
SOURCE: Author's calculations using 2001–2010 NHANES data.

In general, empirical evidence points to higher incomes being associated with lower probabilities of obesity and severe obesity. And, this, in general, holds with alternative measures of obesity. As a consequence, one's prior, with the exception of adult men, is that mechanisms like SNAP that would increase the ability to purchase food would lead to declines in the probability of being obese.

FINDINGS REGARDING THE EFFECT OF SNAP ON OBESITY

Given the empirical evidence already presented, it may be unlikely that receiving more money to purchase food will lead to increased probabilities of obesity. As such, we would anticipate that SNAP recipients are less likely to be obese than eligible nonrecipients. It may be the case, though, that SNAP recipients are more likely to be obese than nonrecipients. This could occur if, for example, households that choose to enter the program are those that are more prone toward higher weights. A third possibility is that SNAP has no impact on the probability of obesity of SNAP participants. This could occur if, for example, the extra money received by participating in SNAP is not enough to change outcomes.

The literature looking at SNAP and obesity has found evidence of each of these three possibilities. I now turn to a selection of these studies. Insofar as SNAP participants are unlikely to be similar to eligible SNAP nonparticipants over unobserved characteristics, I limit myself to studies that address this selection issue and to studies that were published in refereed journals. In discussing each of these, I concentrate on what the authors perceive to be the central findings from their work.

Two studies have found positive effects of SNAP on obesity for at least a subset of the population. The first, Meyerhoefer and Pylypchuk (2008), used data from the combined cross sections of the 2000 to 2003 Medical Expenditure Survey (MEPS). They find that female SNAP participants are 5.9 percent more likely to be overweight or obese than eligible female nonparticipants. For men, however, there is no statistically significant impact of SNAP participation on weight status. The second study to find a positive impact of SNAP on obesity is Baum (2011). Like Meyerhoefer and Pylypchuk, he finds a positive impact for women but not for men. Although the result is statistically significant, Baum notes that the "effects are relatively small."

The majority of studies have found that SNAP has no effect on obesity for any subset of the population. Using longitudinal data from the National Longitudinal Study of Youth (NLSY) 1979 restricted to adult women, Fan (2010) finds no evidence of a relationship between SNAP participation and obesity. This result is for both short-term and long-term participation and after performing several robustness checks. Baum (2012) considers whether

SNAP promotes excessive weight gain during pregnancy with data from the NLSY 1979. He finds that although SNAP does decrease the probability of gaining too little weight during pregnancy, SNAP participation does not lead to increases in the probability of gaining too much weight. Some have argued that the pattern of higher rates of obesity among low-income households is due to SNAP participation. If this were the case, then the gap between low-income Americans and non–low-income Americans would persist over time. Ver Ploeg and colleagues (2007), using a series of cross sections from the NHANES, find that this gap has not persisted and, in fact, has narrowed over time. Also using the NHANES, Kreider and colleagues (2012) find that SNAP participants are between 3.3 percentage points and 47.4 percentage points less likely to be food insecure than SNAP nonparticipants, but the result is not statistically significantly different from zero.

A third set of studies finds that SNAP participation leads to reductions in the probability of obesity. In a sample of boys and girls between the ages of five and eighteen from the NLSY 1979, Schmeiser (2012) finds that boys and girls between the ages of five and eleven and boys between the ages of twelve and eighteen who participate in SNAP have lower probabilities of overweight and obesity than eligible nonparticipants. Among girls between the ages of twelve and eighteen, SNAP participation has no statistically significant effect on obesity or overweight. Other studies have examined the contemporaneous impact of SNAP participation, but Hoynes, Schanzenbach, and Almond (2012) use data from the Panel Study of Income Dynamics and information on the rollout of Food Stamps from 1961 to 1975 to consider the effect of participation in SNAP in childhood on adult obesity. They find that participation in SNAP in childhood leads to reductions in the probability of obesity in adulthood. Burgstahler, Gundersen, and Garasky (2012) use a data set composed of households with children in counties with poverty rates over 20 percent from three states—Illinois, Iowa, and Michigan. They find that children in SNAP-participating households are less likely to be overweight than children in nonparticipating eligible households. This effect is strong—for each 10 percent increase in SNAP participation rates, there would be a 5.7 percent decrease in overweight rates. These three studies demonstrate that, even though SNAP is not designed to reduce someone's probability of obesity, there is evidence that this is occurring as one of the indirect effects of SNAP.

POTENTIAL CONSEQUENCES OF PROPOSALS TO LIMIT PURCHASES WITH SNAP

The preceding discussion provides some context about the role SNAP may play, in its current configuration, in addressing the issue of obesity in the

United States. There have been several recent proposals that have sought to fundamentally change the structure of SNAP with the stated goal of reducing obesity among low-income Americans. I now cover these proposals. Following that, I consider the potential consequences of these proposals.

Proposals to Limit SNAP Purchases

Over the past fifty years, there have been multiple attempts to restrict purchases of certain food items. These attempts arise from desires to "improve the nutrient intake of recipients," prohibit recipients from purchasing "luxury items," or stigmatize certain food products.[15] The most recent proposals have generally concentrated on restricting specific categories of foods deemed as "unhealthy foods" or "junk foods."

The most highly publicized and discussed effort to restrict SNAP purchases was contained in a waiver request to the USDA by the New York Department of Health and Mental Hygiene and Human Resources Administration (2010). This waiver request, which was turned down by the USDA, would have banned SNAP recipients from using SNAP benefits to purchase almost any beverage with more than 10 calories per 8-ounce serving. This ban would have included things such as sports drinks (such as Gatorade, Powerade), soda (such as Coca-Cola, Mountain Dew), vegetable drinks (such as V8), and iced tea drinks. Other products with more than 10 calories per 8-ounce serving would still have been allowed, though, including milk, milk substitutes, and 100 percent fruit juices.

There have been other state-level efforts. In Maine, a proposal by Governor LePage (LD 1411) would not allow SNAP benefits to be used to purchase any product that is subject to the state sales tax (Stone 2013).[16] This would primarily rule out the purchase of certain beverages and snack items with SNAP benefits. In Wisconsin, a proposal by Representative Dean Kaufert would not restrict the purchase of any individual items but would instead impose limits on the proportion of SNAP purchases that could be made (Clark 2013). A SNAP recipient would have to use two-thirds of his or her SNAP benefits to purchase "healthy foods," where this list is taken from a list of foods approved for purchases with WIC benefits and then some other foods are added.[17] The other one-third of SNAP benefits could then be used to purchase whatever foods a recipient chooses. This proposal differs from the other proposals already covered as eligible purchases would be defined by (a) a list of approved items (rather than restricted items), and (b) what has already been purchased by a recipient. How exactly this would be implemented was never articulated in the proposal but it was approved by the Wisconsin State Assembly (Marley and Stein 2013). Governor Haley in South Carolina has also proposed making restrictions on what can be purchased (Holleman 2013).

These proposals for restrictions mirror previous state proposals. For example, in 2004, Minnesota requested a waiver from the USDA to prevent SNAP recipients from using SNAP benefits to purchase certain food items. These items generally fell under the category of "candy," but some items commonly thought of as "candy" were exempted from these restrictions if they contained flour. For example, Kit Kat bars were exempt from this restriction, whereas Hershey bars were not. Like other waiver requests, this was not approved by the USDA (Holden 2004).

National-level proposals have surfaced as well. One from Senator Coburn (OK), in "Coburn Amendment number 421"[18] to the Senate Budget, proposed that no junk foods be allowed for purchase with SNAP benefits. A later proposal by Senator Coburn, "Coburn Amendment number 1000,"[19] was added to the Farm Bill.

Potential Consequences of Imposing Restrictions

The stated goal underlying each of the proposals to restrict SNAP purchases is that these restrictions will lead to reductions in obesity among low-income Americans. As with many new policies, it is unclear whether this goal will be achieved.[20] The goal may be achieved if households do decide to substitute consumption of "unhealthy foods" for "healthy foods" and, as a further step, this substitution leads to reductions in weight. In theory, there is no guarantee this will hold insofar as virtually all SNAP recipients are inframarginal (see, for example, Breunig and Dasgupta 2005), and, therefore, recipients may just reallocate the distribution of food purchases out of SNAP and out of cash. Even if there was a total reallocation of purchases of "healthy foods," for reasons discussed in the following pages, it is not clear whether this policy would lead to reductions in obesity. An indirect way that these restrictions may lead to reductions in obesity is via the decline in the number of SNAP recipients. Although, as already covered, there is no clear evidence that SNAP leads to increases in obesity, some in favor of restrictions on purchases implicitly believe that there is evidence of this.[21] For reasons discussed in what follows, the imposition of SNAP restrictions will lead to a decline in the number of participants—according to those who believe that SNAP is associated with increases in obesity, even if there is no net change in "healthy" and "unhealthy" foods, the decline in SNAP participation will lead to reductions in obesity.

The restrictions on SNAP purchases may also lead to an increase in obesity in the United States. Most of the evidence shows that SNAP (as currently constructed) leads to reductions in obesity or, at the very least, no change in obesity. As a consequence, making changes to SNAP that lead to declines in participation (see the following discussion) could lead to increases in obesity. Or, to put it a different way, this will lead to reductions in income, which, as seen in Figures 6.3 through 6.6, generally lead to increases in obesity.

Although the potential effect of restrictions on SNAP purchases on obesity in the United States is ambiguous, the effect of these restrictions on the overall well-being of low-income Americans is relatively clear. I now turn to the negative impact these restrictions would have on low-income Americans.

As already covered, SNAP participants have been shown, among other things, to have lower probabilities of food insecurity, poverty, and low birth weights and higher levels of food expenditures and nutrient intakes. If the participation rate among SNAP-eligible households was to decline, in the aggregate, the well-being of low-income Americans would decline. These restrictions would lead to declines in participation insofar as they would lead to increases in stigma and transactions costs. I now turn to each.

Increases in Stigma

Restrictions on SNAP benefits would increase the stigma associated with SNAP, as participants would feel singled out as being irresponsible and incapable of making well-informed food purchases. Participants also would be worried when making purchases that some of what they have purchased is not eligible for SNAP. This information, which can be stigmatizing, would then be revealed to others in the check-out line either through a request by the cashier to provide cash or other funds to make the purchase of those items or by having to make a request of the cashier to remove the items from the purchase. SNAP restrictions also send a negative message about the program in general, by implicitly assuming that SNAP recipients have worse diets and are more likely to be obese.

That restrictions would lead to increases in stigma has also been recognized by the USDA. To use their words, in response to a request for restrictions by Minnesota, "Such a program change could add confusion and embarrassment at the point of sale when program recipients attempt to purchase food items once allowable but now deemed ineligible. Moreover, implementation of this waiver would perpetuate the myth that FSP participants do not make wise food purchasing decisions" (Holden 2004).

Increases in Transaction Costs

In deciding whether to receive SNAP, there are several costs that recipients need to incur. Restrictions on SNAP purchases would further increase these transaction costs over two main dimensions.

First, SNAP recipients will need to spend more time figuring out which food items are eligible for purchase with SNAP benefits and which are not. In stores where "SNAP eligible" or "SNAP ineligible" is clearly and correctly displayed, ascertaining which are eligible would be straightforward on arriving at the food retailer. But, in stores without such displays, SNAP recipients would need to ascertain this information on their own (that is, the opportunity cost of shopping with SNAP is higher).

Second, the number of stores accepting SNAP benefits would likely decline if restrictions were put into place. This is due to the higher costs to stores associated with implementing these restrictions; in response, many stores will simply choose not to accept SNAP benefits rather than incur those higher costs. This would raise the transaction costs to SNAP recipients because they would have to go farther to use their SNAP benefits.

CONCLUSION

SNAP has proven to be one of the most successful safety net programs since its implementation fifty years ago. This program has often come under attack throughout its history for many perceived problems (for example, that it discourages labor force participation). Most recently, SNAP has come under attack for being perceived as one of the causes of the current rates of obesity found in the United States. One response that has gained some traction is to restrict what can and cannot be purchased with SNAP.

As covered here, there is very little evidence that SNAP is associated with higher probabilities of obesity among participants in comparison to eligible nonparticipants. In contrast, there is clear evidence that (a) SNAP improves the well-being of recipients over numerous dimensions and (b) imposing restrictions would lead to declines in participation. In light of this evidence, policy makers and program administrators should be reluctant to make fundamental changes to a program as successful as SNAP.

NOTES

1. Examples of this work includes Salathe (1980); Johnson, Burt, and Morgan (1981); Chavas and Yeung (1982); Basiotis, Brown, and Johnson (1983); Smallwood and Blaylock (1985); Senauer and Young (1986); Basiotis, Johnson, and Morgan (1987); Hama and Chern (1988); Devaney and Fraker (1989); Devaney and Moffitt (1991); and Levedahl (1995). More recent work on this topic includes Hoynes and Schanzenbach (2009).

2. Recent work includes DePolt, Moffitt, and Ribar (2009); Nord and Golla (2009); Mykerezi and Mills (2010); Ratcliffe, McKernan, and Zhang (2011); and Kreider et al. (2012).

3. Among children, the effects of food insecurity includes higher risks of some birth defects (Carmichael et al. 2007), anemia (Skalicky et al. 2006 and Eicher-Miller et al. 2009), lower nutrient intakes (Cook et al. 2004), greater cognitive problems (Howard 2011), higher levels of aggression and anxiety (Whitaker,

Phillips, and Orzol 2006), higher probabilities of being hospitalized (Cook et al. 2006), poorer general health (Cook et al. 2006 and Gundersen and Kreider 2009), higher probabilities of asthma (Kirkpatrick, McIntyre, and Potestio 2010), higher probabilities of behavioral problems (Huang, Oshima, and Kim 2010), and more instances of oral health problems (Muirhead et al. 2009). Among adults, consequences include lower nutrient intakes (McIntyre et al. 2003 and Kirkpatrick and Tarasuk 2007), mental health problems (Heflin, Corcoran, and Siefert 2007), physical health problems (Tarasuk 2001), depression (Whitaker, Phillips, and Orzol 2006), diabetes (Seligman et al. 2007), higher levels of chronic disease (Seligman et al. 2009), and worse outcomes on health exams (Stuff et al. 2004). Food-insecure seniors have lower nutrient intakes (Lee and Frongillo 2001 and Ziliak, Gundersen, and Haist 2008), are more likely to be in poor or fair health (Lee and Frongillo 2001 and Ziliak, Gundersen, and Haist 2008), and are more likely to have limitations in activities of daily living (ADL) (Ziliak, Gundersen, and Haist 2008).

4. For a discussion of stigma associated with participation in assistance programs see, for example, Rainwater (1982); Moffitt (1983); Ranney and Kushman (1987); Stuber and Kronebusch (2004); Stuber and Schlesinger (2006); and Wu and Eamon (2010).

5. See, for example, Ponza et al. (1999) for evidence of the impact of transactions costs from household surveys and, for example, Ziliak, Gundersen, and Figlio (2003) for evidence of the impact of transactions costs from data on state caseloads. Although transactions costs can play an effective targeting role by discouraging those in less need from applying for a program, in the United States it often appears that transactions costs are often actually discouraging those most in need. In SNAP, this can occur when the application process is too difficult for those with limited education levels and those with limited education levels who also have lower incomes. For more on this, see Currie and Gahvari (2008).

6. In this figure, p_f denotes the price of food, p_{og} denotes the price of other goods, Y denotes income, and S denotes SNAP benefits.

7. Because SNAP can be spent only on food purchased from approved retail food outlets, it differs from the shift out that would occur if a household received the same amount in income.

8. These terms are in quotes because virtually no food is completely healthy, and no food is completely unhealthy. In terms of the connection to obesity, the consumption of more "unhealthy foods" is generally seen as associated with increases in the probability of obesity, but there are obviously many other factors that influence a person's weight status. Of course, due to the receipt of SNAP (or any other increase in income), households will do other things in terms of food consumption including, for example, purchasing food that has been prepared by others. I concentrate on the "healthy" and "unhealthy" foods because this seems to be the main potential consequence for those who believe SNAP participation leads to increases in obesity.

9. Along with influencing food choices, SNAP can have other effects on obesity. One key area is with respect to stress. The stress experienced by households has been associated with higher probabilities of obesity, especially among children. (See Gundersen et al. 2011 for a review.) If receiving SNAP reduces stress, this could be an indirect avenue through which SNAP participation can lead to reductions in obesity.

10. This is intended as purely a descriptive exercise. As such, I'm overlooking numerous issues including, for example, the potential effect of weight status on wages (see Kline and Tobias 2008 for more on this issue).

11. Recent studies have demonstrated that although those with BMIs above 35 have higher mortality risks than those who are "normal weight" (BMIs between 20 and 25), there is less evidence that those who have BMIs above 30 (but below 35) have higher mortality risks (Gronninger 2006; Mehta and Chang 2009; Flegal et al. 2013). Nevertheless, because the obesity category is often invoked in research on weight status and, in particular, on studies examining the impact of SNAP, it is included here.

12. Those who are pregnant are not included in the adult or child analyses.

13. Children under the age of three are not included in the sample because there is no commonly accepted way to establish body mass index (BMI) percentiles for children this young.

14. There have been several other studies that have examined the relationship between obesity and income including, for adults, for example, Wardle, Waller, and Jarvis (2002); Zhang and Wang (2004); Chang and Lauderdale (2005); Mclaren (2007); Reynolds and Himes (2007); Garcia Vilar and Quintana-Domeque (2009); and Jolliffe (2011); and, for children, for example, Phipps et al. (2006); Shrewsbury and Wardle (2008); and Margerison-Zilko and Cubbin (2013). To the best of my knowledge, this is the first time the relationship between income and non-BMI measures of obesity has been examined.

15. Some have also argued that, irrespective of the impact purchases of certain products may have on recipients, the government should not be involved in promoting certain food items.

16. In Maine, unless otherwise taxed, there is no sales tax for food items.

17. Some foods that are often considered healthy—for example, organic foods—would generally be banned for purchase under the "two-thirds of healthy foods rule" because most organic foods cannot be purchased with WIC benefits.

18. The full text of this amendment is available on Congress.gov at www .congress.gov/amendment/113th-congress/senate-amendment/421/text, posted as submitted on March 3, 2013.

19. The full text of this amendment is available on Congress.gov at www .congress.gov/amendment/113th-congress/senate-amendment/1000/, posted as submitted on May 21, 2013.

20. Even if some believe that SNAP leads to increases in the probability of obesity, the reasons for why government policy should be directed toward changing people's weight status are not altogether clear. One reason that is sometimes given is that there are negative externalities associated with obesity. However, there is no clear evidence of these negative externalities. For more discussion about why government should or should not be involved in this realm, see Bhattacharya and Sood (2011) and Lusk (2013).

21. Other proponents of imposing restrictions may acknowledge that research demonstrates SNAP does not lead to increases in obesity but, nevertheless, think that SNAP can do more in efforts to reduce obesity in the United States. Irrespective of the reasons for wanting to change the structure of SNAP, the consequences due to restrictions discussed in this section remain the same.

REFERENCES

Addo, O., and J. Himes. 2010. "Reference Curves for Triceps and Subscapular Skinfold Thicknesses in US Children and Adolescents." *American Journal of Clinical Nutrition* 91: 635–642.

Almond, D., H. Hoynes, and D. Schanzenbach. 2011. "Inside the War on Poverty: The Impact of Food Stamps on Birth Outcomes." *The Review of Economics and Statistics* 93(2): 387–403.

Basiotis, P., M. Brown, and S. Johnson. 1983. "Nutrient Availability, Food Costs, and Food Stamps." *American Journal of Agricultural Economics* 65: 685–693.

Basiotis, P., S. Johnson, and K. Morgan. 1987. "Food Stamps, Food Costs, Nutrient Availability and Nutrient Intake." *Journal of Policy Modeling* 9: 383–404.

Baum, C. 2011. "The Effects of Food Stamps on Obesity." *Southern Economic Journal* 77(3): 623–651.

———. 2012. "The Effects of Food Stamp Receipt on Weight Gained by Expectant Mothers." *Journal of Population Economics* 25(4): 1307–1340.

Bhattacharya, J., and N. Sood. 2011. "Who Pays for Obesity?" *Journal of Economic Perspectives* 25(1): 139–158.

Bishop, J., J. Formby, and L. Zeager. 1996. "The Impact of Food Stamps on U.S. Poverty in the 1980s: A Marginal Dominance Analysis." *Economica* 63: S141–S162.

Breunig, R., and I. Dasgupta. 2005. "Food Stamp Cash-Out Puzzle." *American Journal of Agricultural Economics* 87(3): 552–568.

Burgstahler, R., C. Gundersen, and S. Garasky. 2012. "The Supplemental Nutrition Assistance Program, Financial Stress, and Childhood Obesity." *Agricultural and Resource Economics Review* 41(1): 29–42.

Burkhauser, R., J. Cawley, and M. Schmeiser. 2009. "The Timing of the Rise in U.S. Obesity Varies with Measure of Fatness." *Economics and Human Biology* 7: 307–318.

Carmichael, S., W. Yang, A. Herring, B. Abrams, and G. Shaw. 2007. "Maternal Food Insecurity Is Associated with Increased Risk of Certain Birth Defects." *Journal of Nutrition* 137: 2087–2092.

Chang, V., and D. Lauderdale. 2005. "Income disparities in body mass index and obesity in the United States, 1971–2002." *Archives of Internal Medicine* 165: 2122–2128.

Chavas, J., and M. Yeung. 1982. "Effects of the Food Stamp Program on Food Consumption in the Southern United States." *Southern Journal of Agricultural Economics* 14(1): 131–139.

Clark, F. 2013. "Wisconsin Bill to Limit Use of Food Stamps for Junk Food Would Restrict Organic Foods, Democratic Lawmaker Says." *Milwaukee Journal Sentinel*, May 7.

Connor Gorber, S., M. Tremblay, D. Moher, and B. Gorber. 2007. "A Comparison of Direct vs. Self-Report Measures for Assessing Height, Weight and Body Mass Index: A Systematic Review." *Obesity Reviews* 8(4): 307–326.

Cook, J., D. Frank, C. Berkowitz, M. Black, P. Casey, D. Cutts, et al. 2004. "Food Insecurity Is Associated with Adverse Health Outcomes among Human Infants and Toddlers." *Journal of Nutrition* 134: 1348–1432.

Cook, J., D. Frank, S. Levenson, N. Neault, T. Heeren, M. Black, et al. 2006. "Child Food Insecurity Increases Risks Posed by Household Food Insecurity to Young Children's Health." *Journal of Nutrition* 136: 1073–1076.

Currie, J., and F. Gahvari. 2008. "Transfers in Cash and In-Kind: Theory Meets the Data." *Journal of Economic Literature* 46(2): 333–383.

DePolt, R., R. Moffitt, and D. Ribar. 2009. "Food Stamps, Temporary Assistance for Needy Families and Food Hardships in Three American Cities." *Pacific Economic Review* 14: 445–473.

Devaney, B., and T. Fraker. 1989. "The Effect of Food Stamps on Food Expenditures: An Assessment of Findings from the Nationwide Food Consumption Survey." *American Journal of Agricultural Economics* 71(1): 99–104.

Devaney, B., and R. Moffitt. 1991. "Dietary Effects of the Food Stamp Program." *American Journal of Agricultural Economics* 73(1): 202–211.

Eicher-Miller, H., A. Mason, C. Weaver, G. McCabe, and C. Boushey. 2009. "Food Insecurity Is Associated with Iron Deficiency Anemia in U.S. Adolescents." *American Journal of Clinical Nutrition* 90: 1358–1371.

Fan, M. 2010. "Do Food Stamp Contribute to Obesity in Low-Income Women? Evidence from the National Longitudinal Survey of Youth 1979." *American Journal of Agricultural Economics* 92(4): 1165–1180.

Flegal, K., B. Kit, H. Orpana, and B. Graubard. 2013. "Association of All-Cause Mortality with Overweight and Obesity Using Standard Body Mass Index Categories: A Systematic Review and Meta-Analysis." *Journal of the American Medical Association* 309(1): 71–82.

Garcia Vilar, J., and C. Quintana-Domeque. 2009. "Income and Body Mass Index in Europe." *Economics and Human Biology* 7:73–83.

Gronninger, J. 2006. "A Semiparametric Analysis of the Relationship of Body Mass Index to Mortality." *American Journal of Public Health* 96: 173–178.

Gundersen, C., and B. Kreider. 2009. "Bounding the Effects of Food Insecurity on Children's Health Outcomes." *Journal of Health Economics* 28: 971–983.

Gundersen, C., D. Mahatamaya, S. Garasky, and B. Lohman. 2011. "Linking Environmental and Psychosocial Stressors and Childhood Obesity." *Obesity Reviews* 12(501): e54–e63.

Hama, M., and W. Chern. 1988. "Food Expenditure and Nutrient Availability in Elderly Households." *Journal of Consumer Affairs* 22(1): 3–19.

Heflin, C., M. Corcoran, and K. Siefert. 2007. "Work Trajectories, Income Changes, and Food Insufficiency in a Michigan Welfare Population." *Social Service Review* 81(1): 3–25.

Holden, O. 2004. "Letter to M. Gomez in Response to Request for Waiver from State of Minnesota." May 4. Available at www.heartland.org/policy-documents/state-minnesotas-response-request-waiver-definition-eligible-foods.

Holleman, J. 2013. "SC Food Stamp Restrictions Face Tall Hurdles." *The State*, March 2.

Howard, L. 2011. "Does Food Insecurity at Home Affect Non-Cognitive Performance at School? A Longitudinal Analysis of Elementary Student Classroom Behavior." *Economics of Education Review* 30: 157–176.

Hoynes, H., and D. Schanzenbach. 2009. "Consumption Responses to In-Kind Transfers: Evidence from the Introduction of the Food Stamp Program." *American Economic Journal: Applied Economics* 1(4): 109–139.

Hoynes, H., D. Schanzenbach, and D. Almond. 2012. "Long Run Impacts of Childhood Access to the Safety Net." NBER Working Paper 18535. Cambridge, MA: National Bureau of Economic Research.

Huang, J., K. Matta Oshima, and Y. Kim. 2010. "Does Food Insecurity Affect Parental Characteristics and Child Behavior? Testing Mediation Effects." *Social Service Review* 84: 381–401.

Johnson, S., J. Burt, and K. Morgan. 1981. "The Food Stamp Program: Participation, Food Cost, and Diet Quality of Low-Income Households." *Food Technology* 35(10): 58–70.

Jolliffe, D. 2011. "Overweight and Poor? On the Relationship between Income and the Body Mass Index." *Economics and Human Biology* 9: 342–355.

Kirkpatrick, S., L. McIntyre, and M. Potestio. 2010. "Child Hunger and Long-Term Adverse Consequences for Health." *Archives of Pediatric and Adolescent Medicine* 164(8): 754–762.

Kirkpatrick, S., and V. Tarasuk. 2007. "Food Insecurity Is Associated with Nutrient Intakes among Canadian Adults and Adolescents." *Journal of Nutrition* 138: 604–612.

Kline, B., and J. Tobias. 2008. "The Wages of BMI: Bayesian Analysis of a Skewed Treatment-Response Model with Nonparametric Endogeneity." *Journal of Applied Econometrics* 23(6): 767–793.

Kreider, B., J. Pepper, C. Gundersen, and D. Jolliffe. 2012. "Identifying the Effects of SNAP (Food Stamps) on Child Health Outcomes when Participation is Endogenous and Misreported." *Journal of the American Statistical Association* 107(499): 958–975.

Krueger, P., R. Rogers, C. Ridao-Cano, and R. Hummer. 2004. "To Help or to Harm? Food Stamp Receipt and Mortality Risk Prior to the 1996 Welfare Reform Act." *Social Forces* 82(4): 1573–1599.

Lee, J., and E. Frongillo. 2001. "Nutritional and Health Consequences Are Associated with Food Insecurity among Elderly Persons." *Journal of Nutrition* 131: 1503–1509.

Levedahl, J. 1995. "A Theoretical and Empirical Evaluation of the Functional Forms Used to Estimate the Food Expenditure Equation of Food Stamp Recipients." *American Journal of Agricultural Economics* 77: 960–968.

Lusk, J. 2013. "The Thin Logic of Fat Taxes." In *The Food Police: A Well-Fed Manifesto about the Politics of Your Plate*, chapter 8. New York: Random House.

Margerison-Zilko, C., and C. Cubbin. 2013. "Dynamic Poverty Experiences and Development of Overweight in a Prospective Cohort of U.S. Children Aged 4–14 years." *Obesity* 21(7): 1438–1445.

Marley, P., and J. Stein. 2013. "Assembly Passes Bill Requiring That Most Food Stamp Benefits Go to Purchasing Healthy Foods." *Milwaukee Journal Sentinel*, May 7.

McIntyre, L., T. Glanville, K. Raine, J. Dayle, B. Anderson, and N. Battaglia. 2003. "Do Low-Income Lone Mothers Compromise Their Nutrition to Feed Their Children?" *Canadian Medical Association Journal* 198: 686–691.

Mclaren, L. 2007. "Socioeconomic Status and Obesity." *Epidemiologic Reviews* 29: 29–48.

Mehta, N., and V. Chang. 2009. "Mortality Attributable to Obesity among Middle-Aged Adults in the United States. *Demography* 46(4): 851–872.

Meyerhoefer, C., and Y. Pylypchuk. 2008. "Does Participation in the Food Stamp Program Increase the Prevalence of Obesity and Health Care Spending?" *American Journal of Agricultural Economics* 90(2): 287–305.

Moffitt, R. 1983. "An Economic Model of Welfare Stigma." *American Economic Review* 73: 1023–1035.

Muirhead, V., C. Quiñonez, R. Figueiredo, and D. Locker. 2009. "Oral Health Disparities and Food Insecurity in Working Poor Canadians." *Community Dentistry and Oral Epidemiology* 37: 294–304.

Mykerezi, E., and B. Mills. 2010. "The Impact of Food Stamp Program Participations on Household Food Insecurity." *American Journal of Agricultural Economics* 92(5): 1376–1391.

New York Department of Health and Mental Hygiene and Human Resources Administration. 2010. *Removing SNAP Subsidy for Sugar-Sweetened Beverages: How New York City's Proposed Demonstration Project Would Work, and Why the City is Proposing It*. New York: Author.

Nord, M., and A. Golla. 2009. *Does SNAP Decrease Food Insecurity? Untangling the Self-Selection Effect*. Washington, DC: USDA, Economic Research Service. Economic Research Report No. 85.

Ogden, C., R. Kuczmarski, K. Flegal, et al. 2002. "Centers for Disease Control and Prevention 2000 Growth Charts for the United States: Improvements to the 1977 National Center for Health Statistics Version." *Pediatrics* 109(1): 45–60.

Phipps, S., P. Burton, L. Osberg, and L. Lethbridge. 2006. "Poverty and the Extent of Child Obesity in Canada, Norway, and the United States." *Obesity Reviews* 7: 5–12.

Ponza, M., J. Ohls, L. Moreno, A. Zambrowski, and R. Cohen. 1999. *Customer Service in the Food Stamp Program*. Princeton, NJ: Mathematica Policy Research.

Rainwater, L. 1982. "Stigma in Income-Tested Programs." In I. Garfinkel, ed., *Income Tested Programs: For and Against*, 19–46. New York: Academic Press.

Ranney, C., and J. Kushman. 1987. "Cash Equivalence, Welfare Stigma, and Food Stamps." *Southern Economic Journal* 53: 1011–1027.

Ratcliffe, C., S. McKernan, and S. Zhang. 2011. "How Much Does the Supplemental Nutrition Assistance Program Reduce Food Insecurity?" *American Journal of Agricultural Economics* 93(4): 1082–1098.

Reynolds, S., and C. Himes. 2007. "Cohort Differences in Adult Obesity in the U.S.: 1982–1996." *Journal of Aging and Health* 19: 831–850.

Salathe, L. 1980. "The Food Stamp Program and Low-Income Households' Food Purchases." *Agricultural Economic Research* 32(4): 33–41.

Schmeiser, M. 2012. "The Impact of Long-Term Participation in the Supplemental Nutrition Assistance Program of Child Obesity." *Health Economics* 21: 386–404.

Seligman, H., A. Bindman, E. Vittinghoff, A. Kanaya, and M. Kushel. 2007. "Food Insecurity Is Associated with Diabetes Mellitus: Results from the National Health Examination and Nutritional Examination Survey 1999–2002." *Journal of General Internal Medicine* 22: 1018–1023.

Seligman, H., B. Laraia, and M. Kushel. 2009. "Food Insecurity Is Associated with Chronic Disease among Low-Income NHANES Participants." *Journal of Nutrition* 140: 304–310.

Senauer, B., and N. Young. 1986. "The Impact of Food Stamps on Food Expenditures: Rejection of the Traditional Model." *American Journal of Agricultural Economics* 68(1): 37–43.

Shrewsbury, V., and J. Wardle. 2008. "Socioeconomic Status and Adiposity in Childhood: A Systematic Review of Cross-Sectional Studies 1990–2005." *Obesity* 16: 275–284.

Skalicky, A., A. Meyers, W. Adams, Z. Yang, J. Cook, and D. Frank. 2006. "Child Food Insecurity and Iron Deficiency Anemia in Low-Income Infants and Toddlers in the United States." *Maternal and Child Health Journal* 10(2): 177–185.

Smallwood, D., and J. Blaylock. 1985. "Analysis of Food Stamp Program Participation and Food Expenditures." *Western Journal of Agricultural Economics* 10(1): 41–54.

Stone, M. 2013. "LePage Proposal Would Bar Food Stamp Use on Junk Food." *Bangor Daily News*, July 7.

Stuber, J., and K. Kronebusch. 2004. "Stigma and Other Determinants in TANF and Medicaid." *Journal of Policy Analysis and Management* 23(3): 509–530.

Stuber, J., and M. Schlesinger. 2006. "Sources of Stigma for Means-Tested Government Programs." *Social Science and Medicine* 63(4): 933–945.

Stuff, J., P. Casey, K. Szeto, J. Gossett, J. Robbins, and P. Simpson, et al. 2004. "Household Food Insecurity Is Associated with Adult Health Status." *Journal of Nutrition* 134: 2330–2335.

Tarasuk, V. 2001. "Household Food Insecurity with Hunger Is Associated with Woman's Food Intakes, Health and Household Circumstances." *Journal of Nutrition* 131: 2670–2676.

Tiehen, L., D. Jolliffe, and C. Gundersen. 2012. *Alleviating Poverty in the United States: The Critical Role of SNAP Benefits*. Washington, DC: USDA, Economic Research Service. ERR 132.

Ver Ploeg, M., L. Mancino, B. Lin, and C. Wang. 2007. "The Vanishing Weight Gap: Trends in Obesity among Adult Food Stamp Participants (US) (1976–2002)." *Economics and Human Biology* 5: 20–36.

Wardle, J., J. Waller, and M. Jarvis. 2002. "Sex Differences in the Association of Socioeconomic Status with Obesity." *American Journal of Public Health* 92: 1299–1304.

Whitaker, R., S. Phillips, and S. Orzol. 2006. "Food Insecurity and the Risks of Depression and Anxiety in Mothers and Behavior Problems in Their Preschool-Aged Children." *Pediatrics* 118: e859–e868.

Wu, C., and M. Eamon. 2010. "Need for and Barriers to Accessing Public Benefits among Low-Income Families with Children." *Children and Youth Services Review* 32(1): 58–66.

Zhang, Q., and Y. Wang. "Socioeconomic Inequality of Obesity in the United States: Do Gender, Age and Ethnicity Matter?" *Social Science and Medicine* 58: 1171–1180.

Ziliak, J., C. Gundersen, and D. Figlio. 2003. "Food Stamp Caseloads over the Business Cycle." *Southern Economic Journal* 69(4): 903–919.

Ziliak, J., C. Gundersen, and M. Haist. 2008. *The Causes, Consequences, and Future of Senior Hunger in America*. Lexington: Special Report by the University of Kentucky Center for Poverty Research for the Meals on Wheels Association of America Foundation.

CHAPTER SEVEN

SNAP and the School Meal Programs

Judith Bartfeld

The Great Recession and its immediate aftermath have brought increasing attention both to food insecurity among children and to the associated food safety net. After a decade of largely stable food insecurity rates, the share of children living in food-insecure households jumped by one-third between 2007 and 2008 and has remained stubbornly high since then. As of 2013, 21.4 percent of all children lived in food-insecure households (Coleman-Jensen, Gregory, and Singh 2014). The scope and reach of the food safety net for children has likewise grown—a response to rising need, efforts to reduce administrative and logistical barriers to participation, and expansions in eligibility.

This chapter examines how SNAP functions as a component of the broader food assistance safety net for school-age children, focusing on connections between SNAP and the school meal programs at a policy level and patterns in children's participation across programs. The chapter has two components: In Part I, I provide an overview of the programs, highlighting both geographic variability in each of the programs and structural features that create explicit, in addition to potentially unintended, linkages between them. My focus is on exploring the mechanisms by which variation in access to SNAP—whether from current cross-state variation or from broader policy changes—can have spillover effects on school meal programs. I argue that, although the food safety net for children is national in design, in practice it varies considerably across states and furthermore that geographic and temporal variation in SNAP policy has important ramifications for children's access to school meals due to policy linkages between the programs at both household and institutional levels. In Part II, I use recent national data to formally explore the role of the combined food assistance safety net for school-age children during and immediately after the Great Recession—a period in which the demands placed on food assistance programs for children reached historic highs. I demonstrate that there is considerable variation in the way that children access and package programs, both cross-sectionally and over time; that children tend to transition into use of food assistance programs sequentially rather than adding multiple programs at once; that low-income children in food-insecure households are much more likely than their food-secure counterparts to transition into food assistance programs; and that food assistance programs constitute a substantial share of household resources for those families who receive them. I conclude by discussing implications of both the programmatic linkages and the empirical patterns of participation for policy and research and argue that understanding the impacts of food assistance programs requires greater effort to consider them in tandem versus in isolation.

PART I: THE FOOD ASSISTANCE SAFETY NET
FOR SCHOOL-AGE CHILDREN

The primary components of the federally funded food safety net for school-age children include SNAP, the National School Lunch Program (NSLP), and the School Breakfast Program (SBP). These programs play a large and growing role in helping children meet their food needs. In a typical month in 2011, over 13 million school-age children—over 24 percent of all children between the ages of five and seventeen—participated in SNAP (Strayer, Eslami, and Leftin 2012). Likewise, the USDA estimates that over 21 million children received a free or reduced-price lunch from the NSLP each month, and over 10 million received a free or reduced-price breakfast from the SBP—corresponding to 39 percent and 19 percent, respectively, of all school-age children.[1]

Current participation rates reflect substantial growth, particularly over the past decade. Between 2000 and 2011, the share of children participating in SNAP more than doubled (Strayer, Eslami, and Leftin 2012); the share receiving a free or reduced-price lunch in a typical month increased by 35 percent, roughly tracking the growth in the child poverty rate over the same period; and the share eating free or reduced-price breakfast increased by 69 percent (Food and Nutrition Service 2013).

Collectively, the programs present a substantial but far from perfect bulwark against childhood food insecurity. Indeed, the food insecurity rate among households with children, which jumped sharply in 2008 in tandem with increases in unemployment and child poverty, stabilized (albeit at high levels) even as child poverty and food assistance caseloads continued to climb, with some evidence that SNAP benefit increases may have played a stabilizing role (Nord and Prell 2011). At the same time, food insecurity among children—including and especially among program participants—remains high (Coleman-Jensen, Gregory, and Singh 2014).

In the remainder of this section, I provide an overview of SNAP, the NSLP, and the SBP, with an eye toward understanding how policy decisions in SNAP—whether related to state flexibility or national policy—have the potential to influence school meals.

The Supplemental Nutrition Assistance Program (SNAP)

SNAP is the cornerstone of the nation's food assistance safety net. To review, the program provides monthly benefits, delivered via electronic benefit card, which can be used to purchase food at authorized food outlets. The core SNAP features are the same nationwide (see the introduction to this volume for details about federal rules regarding eligibility and benefits).

Although there are overarching federal rules, states have some flexibility with regard to certain aspects of the program—flexibility that has become more available and more widely used in recent years—such that, in practice, the program operates differently from state to state (see Ziliak, Chapter One in this volume, for discussion of state policy options). State discretionary rules affect both the eligibility criteria for many households with children and the nature and extent of logistical burdens associated with participation. This variation has implications not only for potential SNAP recipients but, as discussed in the next section, for the school meal programs as well due to explicit and implicit linkages between the programs.

The most important differences in eligibility stem from variation in the use of broad-based categorical eligibility, an option that allows states to effectively use more generous income limits and/or to remove liquid asset tests governing SNAP eligibility in conjunction with the provision of TANF-funded services. As of 2012, varying use of broad-based categorical eligibility resulted in households with children facing gross income limits that ranged between the standard limit of 130 percent of the poverty line to limits up to 200 percent of the poverty line, and liquid asset tests that ranged from the standard limit of $2,000 to removal of all asset limits. Variation in eligibility across this range is not trivial in terms of SNAP's ability to reach vulnerable children, as over 30 percent of households with children in the 130 to 185 percent of poverty range were food insecure in 2013 (Coleman-Jensen, Gregory, and Singh 2014). Eligibility also varies across states due to differing treatment of how vehicles affect eligibility, although all states have opted for some form of liberalization over the federally established vehicle limit of $4,650, and the vast majority have waived such limits altogether (SNAP Policy Database 2013).

In addition to eligibility differences, states differ in a range of policy choices that affect the ease of access for potential participants. State decisions with regard to the frequency and manner of periodic recertification requirements, the nature of ongoing reporting requirements, and requirements for fingerprinting of applicants have all been found, with varying degrees of consistency across studies, to affect the likelihood of participation (see Ziliak, Chapter One in this volume, and, for example, Klerman and Danielson 2011; Hanratty 2006; Ratcliffe, McKernan, and Finegold 2008; and Mabli, Martin, and Castner 2009).

Finally, although absolute benefit levels are the same across states (with the exception of Alaska and Hawaii), the purchasing power of those benefits varies widely. This stems from geographic differences in food costs that affect not only the purchasing power of SNAP (Leibtag 2007; Nord and Hopwood 2007; Todd, Leibtag, and Penberthy 2011), but also the risk of child food insecurity (Gregory and Coleman-Jensen 2012).

In short, although SNAP is a national program, there are substantial differences in the extent to which it is available to at-risk children, the likelihood that eligible households participate, and the adequacy of benefits with regard to the cost of meeting food needs. Although the implications of these differences for children are not entirely clear, we do know that the estimated share of eligibles who participate in SNAP varies dramatically among states, that the antipoverty effectiveness of SNAP varies considerably across states, and that there is at least some evidence that state policy choices affect its antipoverty effectiveness (for more information about the effect of SNAP on poverty, see Tiehen, Jolliffe, and Gundersen 2012; Cunnyngham, Sukasih, and Castner 2013; and Tiehen, Jolliffe, and Smeeding, Chapter Two in this volume). As I discuss in the next section, there are a number of ways in which variation could likewise have spillover effects on children via impacts on the school meal programs.

The National School Lunch Program and the School Breakfast Program

The NSLP and SBP provide financial assistance to participating schools to support the provision of subsidized meals to students. The amount of reimbursement to the school—and thus the amount of federal funds provided to run the program—depends on the share of participants who have been certified to receive free meals, reduced-price meals, or "full-price" meals.

The programs share common eligibility criteria that determine whether students qualify for either free or reduced-price meals. Students can qualify for such meals by having household income below 130 percent of the federal poverty line for free meals or from 131 to 185 percent of the poverty line for reduced-price meals. The free-meal threshold therefore coincides with the federal SNAP limit, whereas the reduced-price threshold is near the high end of the broad-based categorical eligibility limit—though it is currently below that limit in thirteen states. There are no other restrictions on eligibility, and noncitizens, regardless of status, may participate if they meet income criteria. Once eligible, students retain eligibility for the rest of the school year and thirty days into the subsequent year (Hanson and Oliveira 2012). Incomes are self-reported and not routinely verified, although schools are required to verify eligibility for a random sample of applicants each year (Child Nutrition Programs 2013). Students can also be deemed categorically eligible by virtue of participation of the child or a household member in either SNAP, TANF, or the Food Distribution Program on Indian Reservations (FDPIR). The link to SNAP thus provides a formal linkage between policies and practices that affect SNAP eligibility and uptake and subsequent school meal eligibility and certification.

Since 1989 districts have been encouraged to use direct certification— that is, automatic administrative data-matching procedures—to identify children who qualify for free meals via categorical eligibility, thus eliminating the need for such students to complete a paper application; since 2008 to 2009, all districts have been required to have such procedures in place (Hanson and Oliveira 2012). Direct certification appears to increase the share of children certified for free meals relative to using only paper applications (Jackson et al. 2000; Hanson and Oliveira 2012) and presumably increases the likelihood that changes in SNAP participation—whether due to changes in eligibility or uptake—translate into concurrent changes in school meal certification and potentially participation. However, it also—at least in the earlier period of adaptation when it was not yet mandatory—appeared to certify students who, as a group, had lower propensity to actually participate in school meals even when certified, relative to those who qualified through traditional paper applications (Jackson et al. 2000). As of 2003, one in four students who were certified for free meals and in districts that used direct certification had been certified via direct certification rather than a paper application (Gleason et al. 2003).

Although the programs operate in accordance with federal rules, there are in practice geographic differences in low-income children's access to school meals. This is primarily true for the SBP: although both programs are optional for schools, almost all public schools offer the NSLP, whereas 91 percent offer the SBP, with substantial state-to-state variation—ranging from 65 percent to 100 percent, with availability most common in the South and least common in the Midwest and Northeast (Bartfeld and Kim 2010; Food Research and Action Center 2013). This variation has important ramifications for at-risk children, in that availability of school breakfast appears to reduce the risk of marginal food security as well as breakfast skipping among low-income elementary schoolchildren (Bartfeld and Ahn 2011; Bartfeld and Ryu 2011). Advocacy groups and some policy makers have made the expansion of school breakfast a high priority, and, although availability still falls well below school lunch, it has expanded considerably over the past decade (Food Research and Action Center 2013). One factor in this growth has been state mandates obligating some or all schools to offer the program, typically based on the school exceeding a threshold of students who qualify for free or reduced-price meals. As of the 2011 to 2012 school year, twenty-seven states had such a mandate (Food Research and Action Center 2013). Linking the requirement that schools offer breakfast to the share of certified students represents yet another mechanism by which SNAP eligibility and participation have the potential to also influence children's access to school meals.

An important and evolving aspect of the school meal programs is the increasing availability and use of provisions that allow, in high-poverty schools and districts, all students to receive free meals through the school meal infrastructure, even as federal payments for free meals remain limited to the actual or estimated share of participants who qualify under prevailing regulations. These legal structures are geared toward schools with large shares of students who are certified for free or reduced-price meals, with the idea that the savings in administrative costs to the school from foregoing annual certification efforts, coupled with the larger number of certified students who are induced to participate under universal programs, can generate sufficient additional funds to cover the costs of providing free meals to more students—sometimes in conjunction with nonfederal sources such as state and local contributions, private-sector partners, or profits from sale of competitive foods.

There are both established and newer frameworks that support the provision of universal free meals. Long-standing legal structures referred to as "Provisions 2 and 3" allow schools that offer universal free meals to fix their federal reimbursement percentages for several years to the ratio of free, reduced, and full-pay meals certified in a base year. Although it is difficult to ascertain how many additional students receive free meals by virtue of these provisions, the program is fairly substantial in scope: In the 2012 to 2013 school year, there were approximately 4,500 institutions with aggregate enrollments of slightly over 2 million students that were serving free meals to all students under Provisions 2/3.[2] A newer provision—the Community Eligibility Option (CEO), introduced into law in the Healthy, Hunger-Free Kids Act of 2010 and actively promoted by the anti-hunger community—eliminates eligibility paperwork altogether and ties a participating school's reimbursement ratio for four years to a multiplier of the share of students who are directly certified via program match in the initial year. Community Eligibility is available to schools or groups of schools with direct certification rates (that is, the share of students certified as eligible via data match) over 40 percent; it was phased in over several years, and as of the 2014 to 2015 school year was available as an option to eligible schools nationwide.[3] Early studies show substantial increases in both breakfast and lunch participation in CEO schools (Food Research and Action Center 2013). Because both the eligibility of a school to use the CEO and the economic feasibility of doing so (it requires a sufficiently large share of certified students in the base year to be economically viable) are linked to the share of students directly certified—most commonly on the basis of SNAP—the potential impact of this option is closely linked to national as well as state policy and practice with regard to SNAP eligibility and enrollment.

Neither free and reduced-price school lunch nor breakfast are uniformly used by eligible children, with participation in breakfast trailing well behind lunch. Comparing estimates across studies is challenging as participation rates are not treated consistently in the research and may variously describe the share of qualifying children who have been certified to receive free or reduced-price meals (regardless of participation); the share of all children who eat school meals without regard to certification status; or the share of qualifying children who report eating free or reduced-price meals. The latter approach shows an increase in participation of eligible children in free or reduced-price lunch from 63.9 percent to 71.8 percent from 1993 to 1994 to 2003 to 2004 and an increase in the breakfast participation rate from 27.9 percent to 48.7 percent over the same period (Dahl and Scholz 2011), rates which are presumably higher now in the advent of fully implemented direct certification requirements. Participation in free and reduced-price breakfast continues to trail lunch considerably, with half as many students participating in breakfast as lunch on a typical day in 2012 (Food Research and Action Center 2013). Community Eligibility is being viewed as a way to increase breakfast participation, because universal free meals allow schools to implement creative delivery models, such as breakfast in the classroom, that have been linked to increased participation.

Summary

Two main conclusions emerge from this discussion. First, whereas the nutritional safety net targeting school-aged children is national in design and scope, flexibilities granted to states and local educational authorities have provided substantial opportunities for both formal and de facto differences in program access across locations—variation that is linked to real differences in the effectiveness of the safety net in reaching at-risk children and potentially reducing food hardships. More importantly, perhaps, SNAP and the school meal programs have become increasingly interconnected over the past decade, by virtue of formal linkages that tie SNAP eligibility rules and participation patterns to school meal access at both the individual and potentially the institutional level. The implication is that changes in SNAP policy, whether at the state or national level, have the potential for spillover effects onto school meals that may magnify the impact of SNAP changes in ways not fully intended or anticipated.

At the individual level, the potential impacts of SNAP changes on school meal access stem from categorical eligibility linked to SNAP, whereby access to free meals extends to students at higher income levels than the 130 percent of poverty for free meals and 185 percent of poverty for reduced-price meals established by traditional eligibility rules; potential impacts likewise stem from the increasing prominence of direct certification as the means of free meal certification. Policy changes that constrain SNAP eligibility may well lead to reductions in free meal certification even among those still eligible, by virtue of the loss of a routinized certification process—much as happened when food stamp enrollments declined in tandem with declines in TANF caseloads, at rates that exceeded what could be explained by changes in eligibility.

At the institutional level, the potential impacts that could arise from SNAP changes are twofold: first, they stem from the link between school-level free and reduced-price meal certification rates and state mandates that obligate schools with certification rates above a specified threshold to offer the School Breakfast Program. Indeed, the growing number of children certified in recent years appears to have contributed to the number of schools offering breakfast as their certification rates crossed relevant state thresholds (Food Research and Action Center 2013); to the extent that SNAP changes result in lower certification rates, more schools will fall out of mandate range. There are also potentially far-ranging institutional impacts of SNAP policy due to the new Community Eligibility Option, which ties both a school's eligibility to offer universal free meals under the CEO and the economic viability of doing so to its direct certification rate. Because Community Eligibility became available nationwide only in 2014 to 2015, the potential ramifications are unclear, but the early indication is that CEO is a popular option for eligible schools and has led to significant increases in school meal participation rates (Food Research and Action Center 2013). As such, the potential impact of either state-level variation or cross-cutting changes in SNAP policy on this option is of considerable importance and remains largely unknown.

PART II: EMPIRICAL EVIDENCE ON THE ROLE OF FOOD
ASSISTANCE DURING AND IMMEDIATELY AFTER THE
GREAT RECESSION

I turn now from an examination of potential policy linkages between programs to an empirical examination of how children and their households used the various food assistance programs in the very recent economic and policy context. I provide a descriptive analysis of patterns of food assistance program participation during 2008 through early 2012, drawing on a nationally representative sample of children age five to seventeen. My focus is on cross-sectional and longitudinal patterns of participation in SNAP, the NSLP, and the SBP, and the contribution of these programs to children's overall household resource packages.[4]

This work builds on earlier work by Todd, Newman, and Ver Ploeg (2010) and Newman, Todd, and Ver Ploeg (2011), which explored trends in patterns and determinants of multiple food assistance program participation among children since the early 1990s, highlighting the substantial changes in program packaging and the determinants of multiple program receipt over this period. My analysis expands on past work by focusing on participation in the period during and immediately after the Great Recession; looking exclusively at school-age children; treating the NSLP and the SBP as distinct programs, in light of differences in availability and uptake; and looking at patterns of separate and combined program participation from both a cross-sectional and longitudinal perspective.

Data and Analytic Issues

Data Overview   Data are from the first eleven waves of the 2008 panel of the Survey of Income and Program Participation (SIPP), which collectively span the period of May 2008 through March 2012. I note here several analytic decisions central to the interpretation of the results. First, because my interest is in understanding the extent to which children benefit from each of the programs, rather than in the measurement of formal participation rates, I measure participation in a program based on whether anybody in the child's household was a participant—under the assumption this would benefit the child either directly or indirectly, and consistent with how others have measured food assistance benefit packaging (for example, Todd, Newman, and Ver Ploeg 2010; Newman, Todd, and Ver Ploeg 2011).[5] Second, I measure participation in four-month intervals corresponding to survey waves, where participation indicates at least one month of benefit receipt; concurrent participation thus refers to participation in multiple programs during the same four-month interval. This approach reflects that school meal participation is assessed only at the wave level in the underlying data, unlike SNAP participation, which is measured monthly (though subject to seam bias in the reporting of transitions). Third, my measures of participation in school meal programs specifically pertain to receipt of free or reduced-price meals and not meals purchased at full cost. My primary sample includes children age five to seventeen, and for most analyses I use a sample consisting of child waves (that is, where each child contributes up to eleven records, limited to waves when the child's age is in range).

A Note on Accuracy of Reported Program Participation Data   The SIPP is subject to underreporting of SNAP participation, though at considerably lower rates than other national data sets (Meyer, Mok, and Sullivan 2009). Across fiscal years 2009 to 2011, my estimates yield a weighted monthly average number of child participants age zero to seventeen that is 81.5 percent of the administratively reported number of child recipients over the same period (Strayer, Eslami, and Leftin 2012), an underreporting rate in line with estimates for earlier SIPP panels (Meyer, Mok, and Sullivan 2009).[6]

Reporting accuracy for school meals is more difficult to assess. Official participant counts from administrative data are derived from monthly numbers of meals served, with the assumption that the same children are eating the meals on a near-daily basis over the course of a given month (Food and Nutrition Service 2013). If this is not accurate—that is, if aggregate meal numbers actually reflect more children participating but with less day-to-day consistency—then absent any underreporting, we would expect more parents to report that their child "usually" eats the school meal than the official number of participants estimated in the administrative count (Dahl and Scholz 2011). Indeed, analyses of survey data in Wisconsin suggest that, particularly in the case of school breakfast, children who eat school meals the majority of days in a week do not necessarily do so on all days.[7] A second issue is that an undetermined number of children receive free meals at school (more commonly breakfast than lunch) that are not included in the administrative counts, as the latter do not account for children who, although not themselves certified for free meals, nonetheless receive free meals through various universal free meal structures.[8] In short, parents may accurately report receipt of a free meal, even as that meal is not counted as free by the federal funder. Linked survey and administrative data have also shown that parents overreport their children's school meal participation—particularly breakfast and particularly for older children (Moore, Hulsey, and Ponza 2009). Weighted counts of recipients of free and reduced-price breakfast and lunch during the 2008 to 2009, 2009 to 2010, and 2010 to 2011 school years are consistent with these potential confounders. My SIPP estimates of free and reduced price lunches are 89.6 percent, 100 percent, and 102 percent, respectively, of the official counts, and for breakfast the estimates are 135 percent, 156 percent, and 158 percent, respectively, which are broadly consistent with reporting ratios reported elsewhere for the SIPP (Dahl and Scholz 2011).

In sum, the reported SNAP participation data are subject to a known and moderate amount of underreporting, whereas the reporting accuracy of the school meals data cannot be formally assessed—but there are a variety of plausible reasons why parents would, legitimately, report more free meals than are captured in the administrative records. I do not attempt to adjust for either under- or overreporting in my analyses, as there is little guidance in the data for what adjustments would be appropriate in the case of school meals.

Results

How Common Is Food Assistance among School-Aged Children? Food assistance programs were a mainstay of children's overall household resources during and immediately after the Great Recession. During a typical four-month period, 44 percent of school-age children were in households that participated in at least one—and typically more than one—of the three primary programs (Table 7.1). This includes 22 percent of children

TABLE 7.1

Participation in SNAP, the National School Lunch Program, and the School Breakfast Program among school-age children, 2008–2012

| | Percent of children participating in program(s) during average four-month period | | | | | | |
| | Program: | | | | Number of programs: | | |
	SNAP	SBP	NSLP	Any	1 Prog.	2 Progs.	3 Progs.
ALL CHILDREN	21.6	30. 1	40.8	43.8	10.6	17.4	15.7
PARTICIPANTS IN:							
SNAP	100.0	73.0	88.5	100.0	9.9	17.3	72.1
School breakfast	52.6	100.0	97.3	100.0	2.0	46.0	52.0
School lunch	47.1	71.8	100.0	100.0	19.4	42.2	38.4
Any program	50.0	69.0	93.0	100.0	24.3	39.7	35.6
SNAP and lunch	100.0	81.4	100.0	100.0	0.0	18.6	81.4
SNAP and breakfast	100.0	100.0	98.7	100.0	0.0	1.3	98.7
Lunch and breakfast	46.6	100.0	100.0	100.0	0.0	53.4	46.6

SOURCE: Author's weighted estimates using the 2008 panel of the Survey of Income and Program Participation (SIPP).

NOTES: Sample includes children during each wave in which they are age five through seventeen at the start of the wave. Participation is based on household participation in a program at any time during the wave. N = 178,797 child waves.

who participated in SNAP, 41 percent who participated in free or reduced-price school lunch, and 30 percent who benefited from free or reduced-price breakfast.

Of note is that the relative prevalence of program receipt differs from that suggested by the aggregate participation numbers cited earlier—by which the NSLP was the most common, followed by SNAP, with participation in the SBP the lowest. This discrepancy likely reflects to some degree the moderate underreporting of SNAP in the SIPP, but the largest factor is the substantially higher rates of school breakfast reported here than suggested by the estimates from the administrative data. As per the earlier discussion, my assumption is that this reflects some combination of actual participation patterns whereby more children eat breakfast some of the time, though on average less frequently than every day; that some parents accurately report free meals that were received via universal free breakfast programs, even as those meals were not part of the federally funded count; and that some parents unknowingly overestimate their child's breakfast participation such that the participation numbers may reflect a combination of parents' intentions for their children's meals and the children's actual eating patterns.

The separate programs function to a large degree as components of a food assistance package, with most children who benefited from any of the programs benefiting from more than one—albeit in various combinations. Table 7.1 shows that school-aged children who benefited from SNAP usually benefited from school meals as well (90 percent of SNAP recipients), most commonly both lunch and breakfast (72 percent of SNAP recipients). Children who benefited from school breakfast almost always benefited from school lunch as well (97 percent), and slightly over half of breakfast participants were concurrent participants in all three programs. Lunch participants were the most variable in their benefits packaging, with close to half participating in SNAP, 72 percent participating in school breakfast, and 38 percent participating concurrently in all three programs.

Overall, these patterns are consistent with differences in eligibility among programs (in that SNAP participants almost always participate in lunch, whereas the converse is not true), but also with differences in relative preferences or differential program availability (in that a substantial minority of students who participate in lunch do not participate in breakfast, despite the programs having identical eligibility criteria). Students who participate in both lunch and SNAP are considerably less likely to forego school breakfast than are students who participate only in lunch—suggesting that children who receive SNAP may have stronger relative preferences, needs, and/or access to school breakfast. Nonetheless, more than one-quarter of school-age SNAP participants did not participate in at least one and sometimes both of the school meal programs from which they could presumably benefit.

Beneficiary Profiles   Among all school-age children who receive some form of food assistance, three forms of benefit packaging are by far the most common and together make up 85 percent of all participants: concurrent participation in all three programs (36 percent of participants), school lunch and school breakfast (31 percent of participants), and school lunch only (18 percent of participants). Less common packages are SNAP and school lunch (without breakfast) (8 percent) and SNAP only (5 percent).

Profiles differ substantially among beneficiary groups (Table 7.2). Consistent with the lower eligibility threshold, children in benefit groups that

TABLE 7.2
Characteristics of school-age children participating in various food assistance programs, 2008–2012

	Beneficiary groups:						
	SNAP	NSLP/ SNAP	All	NSLP/ SBP	NSLP	Any food assistance	None
PERCENT OF ALL FOOD ASSISTANCE PARTICIPANTS IN GROUP	(5%)	(8%)	(36%)	(31%)	(18%)	(100%)	(0%)
MEDIAN INCOME: POVERTY RATIO	1.20	0.93	0.80	1.52	1.89	1.22	3.52
MEAN INCOME: POVERTY RATIO	1.71	1.14	0.94	1.71	2.27	1.49	4.28
EMPLOYED HOUSEHOLD HEAD (PERCENTAGE):							
No	36.2	40.6	46.3	24.2	19.5	33.2	15.2
Yes	63.8	59.4	53.7	75.8	80.5	66.8	84.8
EDUCATION OF HOUSEHOLD HEAD (PERCENTAGE):							
Less than high school	14.4	19.1	32.3	26.6	15.3	25.2	4.4
High school	29.7	33.1	30.4	28.7	28.1	29.6	16.6
Some college	42.0	40.0	34.0	35.4	40.5	36.6	36.9
College or higher	13.9	7.9	3.3	9.3	16.1	8.6	42.1
RACE/ETHNICITY OF CHILD (PERCENTAGE):							
White	47.3	43.5	27.4	29.3	45.7	33.7	73.1
Black	20.5	19.4	31.0	17.9	14.2	22.3	7.3
Hispanic	22.0	28.1	35.5	45.3	31.2	36.5	11.0
HOUSEHOLD TYPE (PERCENTAGE):							
Family, married head	46.9	37.2	35.7	63.6	67.4	51.2	81.2
Family, single head	51.7	61.6	63.4	35.5	31.6	47.8	18.2
CHILD IS U.S. CITIZEN (PERCENTAGE):							
No	3.1	2.9	3.3	7.5	5.4	5.0	1.9
Yes	96.9	97.1	96.7	92.5	94.6	95.0	98.1

SOURCE: Author's weighted estimates using the 2008 panel of the SIPP.

NOTES: Sample includes children during each wave in which they are age five through seventeen at the start of the wave. Participation group is based on household participation in a program at any time during the wave. N = 178,797 child waves.

include SNAP (columns 1–3) are more disadvantaged on a number of dimensions than children who participate only in school meals (columns 4–5); and children who participate in all three programs (column 3) are more disadvantaged than those who participate in fewer.

Children in the SNAP-only group (column 1) have substantially higher needs-adjusted incomes than either of the other SNAP subgroups (columns 2–3). They differ in other ways as well: They are more likely to live with a married household head than are the groups that combine SNAP with school meals, and they live in households with higher levels of education and higher rates of current employment, particularly compared to those who combine SNAP with both meal programs.[9] Among the two larger groups of SNAP recipients, those children who participate in SNAP and both school meals (column 3) are worse off economically than are those who combine SNAP only with school lunch (column 2). The sharpest distinctions between the groups are in race and education: The full-participation group includes substantially larger shares of both black and Hispanic children and disproportionately are in households headed by persons with lower education levels than the children who forego school breakfast. Note that eligibility differences do not explain these different program profiles, in that breakfast and lunch share eligibility criteria, although differences in availability of breakfast could play a role.

Both of the remaining groups—the breakfast-lunch and lunch-only groups—are better off economically than any of the SNAP beneficiary groups. They also have a much higher share of married households and a much larger share of noncitizen children. Children in the lunch-only group have a substantially different profile and are in many respects better off than the other groups. They differ considerably from their counterparts who also participate in school breakfast, in terms of higher incomes, much higher household education levels, and a much smaller minority representation.[10]

Which Children Use Food Assistance Programs? The preceding profiles of recipient groups suggest that economic and demographic characteristics are differentially associated with participation in the various food assistance programs. Table 7.3 shows participation in the three programs limited to a sample of low-income children, with children included for each wave in which they have at least one month with household income below 185 percent of the poverty line. This criterion captures the vast majority of children whose households fall within the income ranges targeted by food assistance programs. Note that reference to participation rates here refers to the share of all low-income children who benefit from a program, where that may be influenced by eligibility, availability (in the case of school breakfast), and/or preferences—although the eligibility rules for school meals are

TABLE 7.3

Participation in food assistance programs among low-income school-age children during average four-month period, 2008–2012

| | Percent participating in program | | | | |
	SNAP	SBP	NSLP	All	Any
ALL LOW-INCOME CHILDREN	44.3	55.5	71.3	33.0	76.0
LOWEST INCOME: POVERTY IN WAVE					
Less than 0.5	61.7	62.3	75.3	48.1	80.5
0.5–1.3	49.3	60.3	75.6	36.6	80.7
1.3–1.85	20.1	41.6	60.4	13.3	64.0
EMPLOYED HOUSEHOLD HEAD:					
No	58.3	62.9	77.5	45.0	82.7
Yes	36.7	51.6	67.9	26.6	72.3
EDUCATION:					
Less than high school	53.9	72.6	84.9	45.0	88.7
High school	47.4	57.5	74.9	34.8	79.8
Some college	42.9	51.9	69.0	30.5	74.2
College or higher	17.9	23.2	38.0	9.3	42.1
RACE:					
White	34.3	37.3	55.1	22.1	59.9
Black	63.8	71.9	83.8	52.1	89.2
Hispanic	45.3	69.1	84.0	36.1	88.0
HOUSEHOLD HEAD:					
Married	29.8	48.6	64.1	21.9	68.0
Single	60.3	63.3	79.3	45.5	84.8
NUMBER OF CHILDREN:					
One	34.5	39.8	58.4	19.5	65.4
Two	38.6	49.0	66.2	27.1	71.0
Three or more	50.8	64.5	78.5	40.9	82.4
CITIZENSHIP					
No	30.2	62.2	79.1	22.6	83.5
Yes	45.0	55.2	70.9	33.5	75.6

SOURCE: Author's weighted estimates from the 2008 panel of the SIPP.

NOTES: Sample includes children during each wave in which they are age five through seventeen at the start of the wave and have at least one month in the wave with household income below 185 percent of the federal poverty line. Participation is based on household participation in a program at any time during the wave. $N = 80,422$ child waves.

straightforward enough that all children with any months of income below 185 percent of the poverty line would presumably qualify.

Participation patterns among low-income children vary in fairly predictable fashion across a variety of demographic characteristics. The ordering of program use is consistent across virtually all subgroups: Participation in free and reduced price lunch is most common, followed by school breakfast, with SNAP the least common. Across programs, participation is higher among children in households that are traditionally more disadvantaged and presumably have greater need—those with lower income, less-educated household heads, nonemployed household heads, more children, and unmarried household heads. There are sizable differences by race and ethnicity, with participation higher among black and Hispanic children as compared to white children, potentially reflecting differences in norms among groups. The differential pattern for citizen and noncitizen children is notable: Noncitizens have higher participation rates in both the school meal programs, though substantially lower participation in SNAP, compared to children who are U.S. citizens, consistent with school meal programs having fewer real or perceived participation barriers for noncitizens. As already noted, these differences in participation are not intended to speak to differential gaps in program uptake among eligibles but, rather, simply to highlight the differences among demographic groups in the centrality of the various programs as sources of support—where those differences may arise for reasons ranging from eligibility to access to awareness to norms and preferences.

How Do Children Use Food Assistance over Time?   Food assistance use isn't static—and in particular, the ways in which children access and combine programs over time is not static. Cross-sectional benefit packages are informative with regards to understanding how children combine assistance across programs at a point in time—but programs can potentially be accessed either simultaneously or sequentially, reflecting changes in eligibility as well as changes in the relative perceived costs and benefits of participating. Table 7.4 shows an analysis of children's transitions into programs over the 2008 to 2012 period. Each transition can be viewed as either a first-tier, second-tier, or third-tier transition, depending on whether it represents the start of a new food assistance spell, the second program added to an existing spell, or the third program added to an existing spell. The columns represent transitions into a particular program or programs; rows indicate what program(s) children were already receiving, if any, prior to transitioning on to a particular program.

The three food assistance programs play very different roles, in ways that are not apparent from a cross-sectional perspective. Free or reduced-price lunch is most commonly used as a first-tier program: Almost three-quarters of children who start using school lunch do so at the beginning of a spell of food assistance. Most of the remainder use it as a second-tier program, with 17 percent adding it after already being on SNAP—a pattern that is consistent with direct certification, whereby SNAP participants are identified by schools and certified as eligible for free meals—and 6 percent begin participating in lunch after only previously participating in breakfast; only

TABLE 7.4

School-age children's transitions onto food assistance programs, 2008–2012

Transition type:	Program(s) before transition:	Program added: NSLP	SBP	SNAP	Programs after transition ALL (percentage of column)
		(percentage of column)			
FIRST TIER (NEW FOOD ASSISTANCE SPELL)	No programs	73	33	23	5
SECOND TIER (ALREADY ON ONE PROGRAM)	Any one program	23	43	21	21
	Lunch only	0	33	19	6
	Breakfast only	6	0	2	1
	SNAP only	17	10	0	14
THIRD TIER (ALREADY ON TWO PROGRAMS)	Any two programs	4	24	56	74
	Lunch and breakfast	0	0	56	36
	Lunch and SNAP	0	24	0	34
	Breakfast and SNAP	4	0	0	4

SOURCE: Author's weighted estimates from the 2008 panel of the SIPP.

NOTES: Sample includes children during each wave in which they are age five through seventeen at the start of the wave and experience a transition onto a new program or programs. Values are the percent of all transfers *into* a given program(s) that have transitioned from a particular program status. Boldfaced type is used to distinguish upper-level values with subvalues.

4 percent add it as a third-tier program after already receiving both SNAP and breakfast. School breakfast, on the other hand, is much less likely to be a first-tier program: Only one-third of entrants are at the start of a food assistance spell—and almost all who start a food assistance spell with school breakfast begin participating in lunch at the same time (concurrent initial participation is not shown on the table). More commonly, it is a second-tier program, with 33 percent of breakfast entrants previously receiving only lunch and 10 percent only SNAP; for one-quarter of entrants it serves as a third-tier program for children already receiving both SNAP and school lunch. Finally, SNAP is least likely to be a first-tier program and most likely to be a third-tier program. Fewer than one-quarter of new users are at the start of a food assistance spell, 21 percent use SNAP as a second-tier program (almost always following participation in school lunch), and the majority (56 percent) were already participating in both breakfast and lunch.

The last column shows transitions into full participation. This indicates any changes in food assistance receipt that resulted in full program participation, where children may have added one, two, or three programs to become full participants. Notably, almost all the full participants added programs sequentially rather than at once. Only 5 percent of them began using all three programs simultaneously, shown here as first-tier transitions, and only 21 percent started full-program use as a second-tier transition; the most common paths were to transition to full participation by adding SNAP to ongoing receipt of breakfast and lunch (36 percent) or to add breakfast to ongoing receipt of lunch and SNAP (34 percent). A relatively small share (14 percent) became full participants by adding both breakfast and lunch to ongoing SNAP receipt.

Overall, these patterns suggest that families use food assistance as part of a managed process for addressing food needs—adding programs over time in ways that often don't appear linked to changes in eligibility (as in, for instance, adding school breakfast later than school lunch despite equivalent eligibility standards, or adding one or occasionally both school meals after SNAP despite the latter having stricter eligibility criteria). The variety in program sequencing—particularly the relative ordering of SNAP and school breakfast—further suggests that there are differences across families in the relative trade-offs inherent in different programs.

Food Security and Program Transitions   With regard to program transitions, I also assess the extent to which low-income food insecure children are differentially likely to access the various food assistance programs, relative to their food-secure counterparts. To address this, I focus on the subset of transitions that occur immediately following the two waves in which food security is measured in the SIPP panel—waves 6 and 9.[11] I compare the rate at which low-income food-insecure and food-secure children who are not participating in a given program when food security is measured are observed to transition to the program in the next wave.

Nonparticipating low-income children in food-insecure households are significantly and substantively more likely to transition onto each of the food assistance programs than are low-income children in food-secure households (Table 7.5), with differences larger in percentage terms in the case of SNAP, though larger in absolute terms for the school meal programs. Among low-income children not participating in SNAP at the time of food security measurement, 10.9 percent of those who were in food-insecure households transitioned onto the program in the next wave—twice the transition rate for children in food-secure households. In the case of the NSLP, more than one-third of low-income nonparticipants in food-insecure households transitioned onto the program in the next wave (37.5 percent), as compared to 20.7 percent of low-income food-secure nonparticipants. Among those not initially participating in the SBP, the transition rates were 25.1 percent and 15.8 percent for the food insecure and food secure, respectively.

TABLE 7.5

Percentage of low-income nonparticipants transitioning onto food assistance programs, by food security status

Program	N	Percent transitioning onto program in wave following food security measurement	
		Food insecure	Food secure
SNAP	7,620	10.9**	5.4
NSLP	4,214	37.5**	20.7
SBP	5,103	25.1**	15.8

SOURCE: Author's weighted estimates from the 2008 panel of the SIPP.

NOTES: Sample includes children age five through seventeen with income-to-poverty ratio below 185 percent. N's are number of low-income nonparticipants in each program in wave of food security measurement. All differences in transition rates between food-insecure and food-secure households are statistically significant, $p < .01$.

Note that this analysis does not attempt to control for differences among children other than limiting the analysis to those who are low income in the wave during which food insecurity is measured; it merely illustrates that, across programs, experiencing an episode of food insecurity is associated with a substantially increased likelihood of program engagement. Results are consistent with food assistance programs being used differentially in response to perceived inability to meet food needs—evidence of a target efficiency that policy makers would presumably support, though also highlighting the inherent challenge in using food insecurity status of participants to assess program impact (see, for example, Gregory, Rabbitt, and Ribar in Chapter Three of this volume).

How Does Food Assistance Contribute to Overall Household Resources? The relative importance of food assistance across demographic groups depends not just on differential rates of receipt but also on the magnitude of its contribution to overall household resources. To assess the importance of food assistance as part of children's overall resource packages, I impute dollar values to SNAP and school meals. I value SNAP benefits at face value and, consistent with past work in this area (Todd, Newman, and Ver Ploeg 2010), I value school meals at the federal reimbursement rate paid to schools in the relevant year and assume that recipients—identified in the data on the basis of "usually" participating—do so on all school days.[12] To the extent that households receive WIC benefits on behalf of pregnant women and younger children also in the household, I also add in the face value of those benefits to the total food resource package, although such benefits are not a specific focus of this analysis. I add the value of food assistance to the household's total income to obtain a measure of total food and nonfood resources and assess the role of food assistance and its components relative to the households' total monthly resource packages. This is basically a cash plus food assistance measure of household resources; I do not impute EITC, as that is not relevant to monthly income flows. Whereas school meals are not typically treated as income in measures of household resources, I do so here for purposes of illustrating the magnitude of food assistance as a cohesive package, both overall and relative to other available resources. Note that I likely underestimate the value of SNAP (the SIPP historically has captured roughly 90 percent of SNAP dollars; Meyer et al. 2009) and overestimate the value of school meals (in that children who usually participate may not necessarily do so on all days, nor in all months of a wave). Finally, note that I do not capture the role of summer feeding programs, nor do I capture emergency or private forms of food assistance.

Across all low-income school-age children in a typical four-month period, food assistance averages 17.8 percent of total household resources, with a slightly larger share from SNAP than from school meals (10.4 percent versus 6.9 percent) for an average child and including 10 percent of children for whom food assistance comprises more than half of household resources (Table 7.6).[13] The contribution of food assistance varies considerably across groups—from an average of 51.9 percent of household resources for children below 50 percent of the poverty line to 7 percent for those between 130 and 185 percent of the poverty line. Other low-income groups for whom food assistance plays a particularly large role include households without an employed head (averaging 26.6 percent of resources), households with high school or less education (18.4 to 23.6 percent of resources), and households headed by a single parent (25.1 percent of resources).

The relative contribution of SNAP and school meals also varies among groups, consistent with the different participation patterns discussed earlier. Broadly speaking, SNAP tends to constitute a larger share of household resources than school meals, but in some groups the programs play roughly equivalent roles (households with a college-educated head, Hispanics), and, in the case of noncitizens, school meals are a larger income component than SNAP. Not surprisingly, food assistance plays the greatest role among children who participate in all three programs: Food assistance makes up an average of 35.4 percent of their household resources, with roughly two-thirds coming from SNAP and one-third from school meals; for almost one-quarter of these children, food assistance makes up more than half of their total household resources. In contrast, food assistance makes up an average of 23.4 percent of resources for children who participate only in SNAP and a much smaller 7.3 percent for those who participate only in school lunch.

TABLE 7.6
Role of food assistance programs in household resource packages among low-income school-age children during average four-month period, 2008–2012

	Average percentage of total household resources from program			Share of group with food assistance in stated range	
	All food assistance	SNAP	School meals	> 25%	> 50%
ALL LOW-INCOME CHILDREN	19.3	10.4	8.5	17.9	10.6
INCOME–TO-POVERTY RATIO:					
Less than 50%	55.9	33.8	20.7	86.9	57.9
50–130%	22.6	12.2	9.8	35.7	8.5
130–185%	7.6	3.1	4.3	8.6	4.3
EMPLOYED HOUSEHOLD HEAD:					
No	29.2	16.8	11.7	43.0	21.3
Yes	14.0	6.9	6.7	19.8	4.8
EDUCATION:					
Less than high school	24.8	13.0	10.9	37.7	14.8
High school	20.3	11.2	8.5	28.5	10.6
Some college	17.9	9.6	7.9	25.4	9.4
College or higher	8.7	4.1	4.4	11.6	4.5
RACE:					
White	14.9	8.4	6.2	19.7	8.1
Black	27.5	16.2	10.7	43.0	16.7
Hispanic	20.4	9.6	10.0	28.5	10.6
HOUSEHOLD HEAD:					
Married	13.1	5.9	6.7	16.7	5.2
Single	26.1	15.2	10.4	40.4	16.5
CITIZENSHIP					
No	15.2	5.4	9.0	18.3	5.2
Yes	19.5	10.6	8.4	28.4	10.8

SOURCE: Author's weighted estimates from the 2008 panel of the SIPP.

NOTES: Sample includes children during each wave in which they are age five through seventeen at the start of the wave and have at least one month in the wave with household income below 185 percent of the federal poverty line. Participation is based on household participation in a program at any time during the wave. N = 80,422 child waves.

CONCLUSIONS

This chapter has addressed the connections between SNAP and school meal programs—both from a policy standpoint and from the standpoint of participation patterns. With regard to the former, I argue that SNAP and the school meal programs have become increasingly interconnected over the past decade, such that changes in SNAP policy—whether due to state decisions about expanding or contracting their use of policy options or to federal decisions that could have more far-reaching effects—may have ripple effects that expand to school meals. That a relatively small share of children certified for free meals could lose eligibility for those meals altogether in the absence of broad-based categorical eligibility has certainly been widely discussed. But the potential implications are much broader, both due to the likelihood of reduced certification among eligible children should fewer eligible children be identifiable through the direct certification process, and to the ramifications of lower direct certifications on the viability of implementing universal free meal programs—and such programs have been well-regarded among participating schools and an important priority in the antihunger community.

In terms of separate and combined participation patterns, results confirm that food assistance programs are a mainstay of children's overall household resources. Nearly half of children used at least one—often more—during any four-month period; and for an average low-income child, food assistance made up almost one-fifth of total household food and nonfood resources—a figure that rises to 35 percent of resources among children who participate in all three programs. Although there is a substantial degree of overlap among programs, there is nonetheless considerable variation in the ways children access and package programs, both cross-sectionally and over time. In particular, the sequencing of programs is consistent with use of food assistance as part of a managed process for dealing with food needs—in that children are far likelier to add programs sequentially than all at once, in orders that are not always consistent simply with changes in eligibility over time. Across all programs, I find substantially greater likelihood that food-insecure as compared to food-secure low-income nonparticipants will transition into program use shortly after I observe their food security status—suggesting that the programs are, indeed, differentially targeting the subset of low-income households with difficulty meeting food needs.

The food assistance participation patterns documented here raise a number of questions and point toward some potentially fruitful lines of research. Although an extensive body of research has examined impacts of food assistance programs on a wide range of outcomes—from food security, to nutrition, to health, to educational outcomes—there has been exceedingly little attention to how the programs might operate in tandem to affect outcomes of interest (a notable exception is Roy, Millimet, and Tchernis 2012). Yet the findings discussed here—both in terms of policy synergies between programs, as well as considerable overlap in program participation—suggest that studying programs in isolation might not be the optimal strategy. Research examining how programs work together to affect food security or other outcomes would be of particular interest and value. One could imagine, for instance, that the impact of SNAP would be different when used as the sole form of food assistance than when used in combination with school meals or that the magnitude of overall assistance could potentially matter more than the specifics of its components.[14] Other questions of interest involve the extent to which programs serve as complements or substitutes and, more generally, how participation in one program affects participation in another and how the sequencing of programs differs according to factors such as need, expected benefit, stigma and norms, and access to program information. Likewise, there are important questions about how cross-state and temporal variation in policies—such as discussed in Part I of this chapter—translate into different patterns of use.

NOTES

I am grateful to Fei Men for outstanding research assistance and to Alison Jacknowitz for helpful comments. The opinions expressed are solely those of the author and do not necessarily reflect the views of any sponsoring agency.

1. The USDA estimates the number of school meal participants by dividing the average daily participation by an attendance factor of approximately 0.93, an approach that assumes the same children are generally eating meals over the course of a given month (Food and Nutrition Service 2013). If participation was more variable among children, the number of unique participants in a month would be higher. During July of the same year, about 2.8 million children—or 5.2 percent of school-age children—ate free meals through one of the two federally funded summer feeding programs. Although those programs play a vital role, I do not discuss them in this chapter due to their much more limited scope.

2. Personal communication with John Endahl, Senior Program Analyst, Office of Policy Support, FNS/USDA, August 2013; the true number is higher, because the numbers do not include schools operating in a base year, that is, the first year of the four-year authorization period.

3. USDA guidance for schools on Community Eligibility, July 25, 2014, available at www.fns.usda.gov/sites/default/files/cn/SP21-2014oscover.pdf.

4. I do not consider summer feeding programs in these analyses, as information is not available in the Survey of Income and Program Participation (SIPP) data. As noted earlier (see note 2), those programs are substantially smaller in scope than SNAP or either of the school meal programs—although certainly a vital part of the food safety net.

5. Defining participation at the individual versus household level has only minimal impact on the results, reducing SNAP participation by roughly 2 percentage points, breakfast participation by 1.6 percentage points, and lunch by 1 percentage point.

6. Whereas my primary analyses use a household-level measure of participation, I use individual SNAP participation to construct reporting ratios.

7. Author's analysis of data from the Wisconsin Schools Food Security Survey. The WSFSS asks parents how many days in a typical five-day school week that their child eats the breakfast and lunch served by the school.

8. Personal communication with John Endahl, Senior Program Analyst, Office of Policy Support, FNS/USDA, August 2013.

9. Children in households receiving SNAP are categorically eligible for free school meals. As such, their lack of participation is not due to ineligibility. Potential explanations for nonparticipation range from lower perceived need (consistent with their relatively higher income-to-poverty ratios); perceived stigma associated with school meals; or lack of availability (although almost all schools do offer at least the NSLP, even if not the SBP). In analyses not shown, I also find that children spend fewer months in the SNAP-only category, relative to other categories, tending to either add programs or to exit from SNAP.

10. The lunch-only participants have a mean per wave income that exceeds the normal eligibility standard of 185 percent of the poverty line. Although I do not attempt to formally assess the share who appear to be income eligible, I note that the lunch-only children are substantially more likely to have one or more below 185 percent poverty months over the past year than are nonparticipants; children are required to become certified only once per year and may retain their status for the remainder of the school year. In a more formal assessment of over-certification using the SIPP, Dahl and Scholz (2011) likewise found that assessing eligibility just prior to the start of the school year substantially reduced the share of seeming higher-income lunch recipients.

11. The SIPP uses an abbreviated five-item food security scale, which has been found to have reasonable reliability and validity (Nord 2006).

12. I assume twenty-two school days per month during September through May, with half that number in June and August and no school days during July. It is necessary to adjust for summer months because school meal participation is reported on a per-wave versus a per-month basis. Although I define participation at the household level, I construct benefit contributions based on the number of individual children in the household who are reported to have usually eaten school meals, among households in which one or more children received free or reduced-price meals.

13. Note that the income shares are averages calculated at the microlevel, rather than aggregate income shares. The former are higher than the latter because of food assistance being concentrated among lower-income households.

14. Indeed, recent research on the nonfood safety net found that the overall level of benefits—regardless of from which program(s)—is significantly linked to food insecurity (Schmidt, Shore-Sheppard, and Watson 2012).

REFERENCES

Bartfeld, J., and H-M. Ahn. 2011. "The School Breakfast Program Strengthens Household Food Security among Low-Income Households with Elementary School Children." *Journal of Nutrition* 141: 470–475.

Bartfeld, J., and M. Kim. 2010. "Participation in the School Breakfast Program: New Evidence from the ECLS-K." *Social Service Review* 84(4): 541–562.

Bartfeld, J., and J-H. Ryu. 2011. "The Impact of the School Breakfast Program on Breakfast-Skipping among Elementary School Children in Wisconsin." *Social Service Review* 85(4): 619–634.

Child Nutrition Programs. 2013. *Eligibility Manual for School Meals: Determining and Verifying Eligibility.* Washington, DC: U.S. Department of Agriculture, Food and Nutrition Service.

Coleman-Jensen, A., C. Gregory, and A. Singh. 2014 (September). *Household Food Security in the United States in 2013.* Washington, DC: U.S. Department of Agriculture, Economic Research Service, ERR-173.

Cunnyngham, K., A. Sukasih, and L. Castner. 2013. *Empirical Bayes Shrinkage Estimates of State Supplemental Nutrition Assistance Program Participation Rates in 2008–2010 for All Eligible People and the Working Poor.* Final Report. Princeton, NJ: Mathematica Policy Research.

Dahl, M., and J. K. Scholz. 2011. "The National School Lunch Program and School Breakfast Program: Evidence on Participation and Noncompliance." Unpublished manuscript. Available at www.econ.wisc.edu/~scholz/Research/Lunch.pdf.

Food and Nutrition Service, U.S. Department of Agriculture. 2013. Program Data. Available at www.fns.usda.gov/pd/.

Food Research and Action Center. 2013. *School Breakfast Scorecard: School Year 2011–2012.* Washington, DC: FRAC.

Gleason, P., T. Tasse, K. Jackson, P. Nemeth, and L. M. Ghelfi. 2003. *Direct Certification in the National School Lunch Program—Impacts on Program Access and Integrity: Final Report.* Available at www.ers.usda.gov/publications/efan03009.

Gregory, C., and A. Coleman-Jensen. 2012. "Do Food Prices Affect Food Security for SNAP Households? Evidence from the CPS Matched to the Quarterly Food-At-Home Price Database." Available at SSRN: http://ssrn.com/abstract=1850545.

Hanratty, M. 2006. "Has the Food Stamp Program Become More Accessible? Impacts of Recent Changes in Reporting Requirements and Asset Eligibility Limits." *Journal of Policy Analysis and Management* 25(3): 603–621.

Hanson, K., and V. Oliveira. 2012. *How Economic Conditions Affect Participation in USDA Nutrition Assistance Programs.* Economic Information Bulletin No. 100. Washington, DC: U.S. Department of Agriculture, Economic Research Service.

Jackson, K., P. Gleason, J. Hall, and R. Strauss. 2000. *Study of Direct Certification in the NSLP.* CN-00-DC. Washington, DC: U.S. Department of Agriculture.

Klerman, J., and C. Danielson. 2011. "Transformation of the Supplemental Nutrition Assistance Program." *Journal of Policy Analysis and Management* 30(4): 863–888.

Leibtag, E. 2007. *Can Food Stamps Do More to Improve Food Choices? An Economic Perspective—Stretching the Food Stamp Dollar: Regional Price Differences Affect Affordability of Food.* Economic Information Bulletin No. (EIB-

29-2). Washington, DC: U.S. Department of Agriculture, Economic Research Service.

Mabli, J., E. S. Martin, and L. Castner. 2009. *Effects of Economic Conditions and Program Policy on State Food Stamp Program Caseloads, 2000–2006.* Technical Report 56. Princeton, NJ: Mathematica Policy Research.

Meyer, B. D., W. K. C. Mok, and J. X. Sullivan. 2009. "The Under-Reporting of Transfers in Household Surveys: Its Nature and Consequences," NBER Working Paper 15181. Cambridge, MA: National Bureau of Economic Research.

Moore, Q., L. Hulsey, and M. Ponza. 2009. *Factors Associated with School Meal Participation and the Relationship between Different Participation Measures.* Contractor and Cooperator Report No. 53. Washington, DC: U.S. Department of Agriculture, Economic Research Service.

Newman, C., J. E. Todd, and M. Ver Ploeg. 2011. "Children's Participation in Multiple Food Assistance Programs: Changes from 1990 to 2009." *Social Service Review*: 535–547.

Nord, M. 2006. *Survey of Income and Program Participation 2001 Wave 8 Food Security Data. File Technical Documentation and User Notes.* Washington, DC: U.S. Department of Agriculture, Economic Research Service. Available at www.ers.usda.gov/datafiles/Food_Security_in_the_United_States/Survey_of_Income_and_Program_Participation_SIPP/2001/2001.pdf.

Nord, M., and H. Hopwood. 2007. *Higher Cost of Food in Some Areas May Affect Food Stamp Households' Ability to Make Healthy Food Choices.* Economic Information Bulletin 29-3. Washington, DC: U.S. Department of Agriculture.

Nord, M., and M. Prell. 2011. *Food Security Improved Following the 2009 ARRA Increase in SNAP Benefits.* Washington, DC: U.S. Department of Agriculture, Economic Research Report ERR-116.

Ratcliffe, C., S.-M. McKernan, and K. Finegold. 2008. "Effects of Food Stamp and TANF Policies on Food Stamp Receipt." *Social Service Review* 82(2): 291–334.

Roy, M., D. Millimet, and R. Tchernis. 2012. "Federal Nutrition Programs and Childhood Obesity: Inside the Black Box." *Review of Economics of the Household* 10: 1–38.

Schmidt, L., L. Shore-Sheppard, and T. Watson. 2012. "The Effects of Safety Net Programs on Food Insecurity." University of Kentucky Center for Poverty Research Discussion Paper Series, DP2012-12.

SNAP Policy Database. 2013. Washington, DC: U.S. Department of Agriculture. Available at www.ers.usda.gov/data-products/snap-policy-database.aspx#.UjYvjD_J2E0.

Strayer, M., Eslami, E. and Leftin, J. 2012. *Characteristics of Supplemental Nutrition Assistance Program Households: Fiscal Year 2011.* Washington, DC: U.S. Department of Agriculture, Food and Nutrition Service, Office of Research and Analysis.

Tiehen, L., D. Jolliffe, and C. Gundersen. 2012. "How State Policies Influence the Efficacy of the Supplemental Nutrition Assistance Program in Reducing

Poverty." Paper presented at the Agricultural and Applied Economics Association's 2012 AAEA Annual Meeting, Seattle, WA.

Todd, J., E. Leibtag, and C. Penberthy. 2011. *Geographic Differences in the Relative Price of Healthy Foods*. Economic Information Bulletin 78. Washington, DC: U.S. Department of Agriculture, Economic Research Service.

Todd, J., C. Newman, and M. Ver Ploeg. 2010. *Changing Participation in Food Assistance Programs among Low-Income Children after Welfare Reform*. Economic Research Report No. 92. Washington, DC: U.S. Department of Agriculture, Economic Research Service.

CHAPTER EIGHT

Multiple Program Participation and the SNAP Program

Robert A. Moffitt

In fiscal year 2007, just prior to the Great Recession, the Supplemental Nutrition Assistance Program (SNAP) was the fifth largest means-tested program in the country ranked by total expenditures and the third largest ranked by the number of recipients, with over 25 million individuals receiving benefits (Moffitt 2013). In 2011, later in the Great Recession, it had climbed to second place in both expenditures and recipients, with almost 45 million individuals receiving benefits, surpassed only by Medicaid. The program is one of the most important components of the U.S. safety net, removing 3.7 million individuals from poverty in 2011, reducing the poverty rate in that year from 15.0 percent to 13.8 percent, and reducing the poverty gap by approximately 16 percent (see Tiehen, Jolliffe, and Smeeding, Chapter Two in this volume).

This chapter examines the receipt of benefits from other programs in the U.S. transfer system by SNAP recipients. Receipt of benefits from other programs is not uncommon. SNAP program administrative data from 2011 indicate that 20 percent of SNAP households received Supplemental Security Income (SSI) benefits and 22 percent received Social Security benefits (see, for example, Strayer, Eslami, and Leftin 2012). In this chapter, new evidence drawn from the Survey of Income and Program Participation (SIPP) will be used to examine multiple program receipt by SNAP recipients in more detail, showing both exactly which program benefits and which combinations of program benefits are received by SNAP participants. The new evidence covers two years in the Great Recession, an early year (2008) and a later year (2010), and also 2004 and 1993, which should establish long-run trends. The SIPP data also allow us to determine what types of SNAP families receive benefits from other programs, for such receipt varies both by the income level of the SNAP household and by its demographic type (presence of children, marital status, employment status, and so on).

The extent of multiple program receipt among SNAP households is of interest for several reasons. First, such receipt is an indirect indicator of the other needs of SNAP households, such as whether a member of the household has a disability or simply has such low income that the household needs support for other needs, such as housing, medical expenses, and general other expenses. From its inception, the Food Stamp Program was intended to be only a supplement to other forms of income received by low-income families, and it is of interest to know the extent to which it is supplementing only private income or also income from other public programs. Second, multiple program receipt is related to the issue of categorical eligibility, a subject of considerable current policy discussion because recipients of some other programs are made automatically eligible for SNAP benefits without a direct check on their income and resources for eligibility. This issue will be examined in the following pages by comparing incomes of those receiving and not receiving benefits from such other programs to determine whether SNAP families who are categorically and noncategorically eligible have differing incomes. Third, a long-standing concern of both policy analysts and researchers is that the receipt of multiple programs may have negative effects on work incentives because such receipt may result in high cumulative marginal tax rates on work effort. This issue will also be examined.

It should be noted that an additional concern with multiple program receipt among SNAP recipients is that those who receive payments from other programs may be "double-dipping" by receiving support from multiple programs for the same thing, namely, food expenditures. However, most cash benefits received by SNAP households are included in countable income and in resources both for eligibility and benefit determination, and therefore those additional income and resource items are taken into account. In-kind benefits are generally not included, however, nor are tax credits. This issue will be discussed briefly.

The first section of the chapter reviews the SNAP program rules for eligibility and benefit determination with a focus on how receipt of other benefits interacts with that determination. The next section presents new evidence on multiple program receipt from the SIPP data and discusses the implications of the findings. Trends in such receipt as well as current levels are presented. The third section analyzes the implications of multiple receipt for work incentives. A short summary at the end recapitulates the findings of the chapter.

SNAP ELIGIBILITY AND BENEFIT DETERMINATION

The SNAP program has separate eligibility rules for families classified as categorically eligible and all other families, who are classified as noncategorically eligible. For the latter, a family or group of individuals eating together must meet a gross income test, a net income test, and a resources test. The gross income test requires that the sum of all income that is "countable" be below a specified threshold, which is 130 percent of the households' poverty line income for those with no elderly or disabled member. Countable income includes most cash income but excludes in-kind income, tax credits, and income tax refunds. The net income test requires that the sum of all countable income minus a number of important deductions be below a specified threshold, which is currently equal to the household's poverty line income if it has no elderly or disabled members. The resource test requires that the sum of all countable assets be below yet a different threshold, which is currently $2,000 for nonelderly, nondisabled households. Resources include most cash assets and the market value of vehicles over certain thresholds, but states have the option of altering the vehicle rules, and most states currently exclude the value of vehicles altogether from countable assets. The Earned Income Tax Credit (EITC) and Child Tax Credit (CTC) are included in resources only if they have been unspent twelve months after receipt but were included in resources in the month of receipt prior to 2010. For households determined to be eligible on all criteria, benefits are computed by subtracting 30 percent of net income from the maximum benefit for its family size. There are minimum and maximum benefit levels as well that are imposed after computing benefits from the formula.

Categorically eligible households are eligible for SNAP if they are recipients of specified other programs. The most prominent of those are the Temporary Assistance for Needy Families (TANF) program, the Supplemental Security Income (SSI) program, and the Social Security Disability Program (SSDI).[1] Of lesser importance statistically are recipients of General Assistance (GA) benefits and certain state-level and other disability programs. Recipients of these programs do not have to meet the income and resources tests under the presumption that they have done so for the other programs and not checking them again reduces administrative costs. However, they do have their benefits calculated in the same way as for families who are noncategorically eligible. Consequently, if their incomes are sufficiently high, they will not receive a benefit and hence will not be allowed onto the program.[2]

In addition to these traditional categorical eligibility types, states now have the option to implement "broad-based" categorical eligibility, which makes additional families categorically eligible if they are recipients of certain noncash TANF benefits. Those noncash TANF benefits may include relatively modest assistance with transportation, employment assistance, child care, or even simply receipt of a pamphlet (U.S. Congressional Budget Office 2012b; Falk and Aussenberg 2013). A majority of states currently allow such broad-based categorical eligibility. However, once again, benefits for such families are determined by the same formula used for other recipients.

In FY2010, three-quarters of SNAP households were categorically eligible; of those, two-thirds were eligible under the broad-based categorical eligibility requirements, for a total of one-half of all SNAP households (U.S. Congressional Budget Office 2012b). Eliminating broad-based categorical eligibility, however, would reduce the SNAP caseload only by 4 percent because most of those households would be eligible for benefits under the standard income and resources tests. SNAP spending would fall only by 2 percent because the households rendered ineligible have benefit levels lower than those of other recipients (U.S. Congressional Budget Office 2012b).

These eligibility and benefit rules have many implications for multiple program participation among SNAP recipients. Obviously, for example, one should expect to see significant numbers of participants from the TANF, SSI, and SSDI programs, given their categorical eligibility, although the absolute numbers of such households will necessarily reflect the sizes of those programs independently. In addition, if some of those categorically eligible households have income and resources above the noncategorical limits, they will have lower benefits than noncategorical families. However, although the possibility of the "double-dipping" mentioned in the opening paragraphs of this chapter exists, the inclusion of most cash benefits from these programs in SNAP-countable income implies that food expenditure is not necessarily increased by multiple benefit receipt. If households spend 30 cents of every extra dollar on food, then an extra dollar of income from a non-SNAP program will result in a 30 cent reduction in the SNAP benefit, leaving the household's food expenditure unchanged.[3] But it is also the case that in-kind benefits (such as from housing assistance) as well as tax credits and income tax refunds are excluded from countable income, leading to a possibility that SNAP families have income that does not reduce the SNAP benefit. Although the extra support that in-kind programs like housing provides is unlikely to release much expenditure for food, tax credits like the EITC and CTC may do so, in principle. However, the literature on how EITC credits are spent suggests that they are used for debt reduction, asset-related items like down payments on a house, and short-term emergency uses like car repair (Gao, Kaushal, and Waldfogel 2009; Mendenhall et al. 2012).

NEW EVIDENCE ON MULTIPLE PROGRAM
RECEIPT FROM THE SIPP

Despite the importance of multiple program receipt, the number of studies of the topic is relatively small.[4] The new evidence provided here is gathered from the Survey of Income and Program Participation (SIPP), a set of nationally representative panels of the U.S. population. The initial results use the second wave of the 2008 panel, which covers the period from September 2008 to March 2009. These months were just at the beginning of the Great Recession but before the major national legislation that increased safety-net spending on a number of programs (comparisons to earlier and later years will be made in the following pages).

In addition to collecting socioeconomic and demographic information on the households, the interviews collected information on all forms of income receipt, including those from SNAP and other transfer programs. Here, receipt only of other "major" programs will be examined: TANF, Subsidized Housing, Special Supplemental Nutrition Program for Women, Infants, and Children (WIC), the EITC, the CTC, SSI, SSDI, Old Age Survivors Insurance (OASI), and Unemployment Insurance (UI). TANF is a cash program for low-income, mostly single-parent, families, which has shrunk in size since welfare reform in 1996. Subsidized housing programs include both Section 8 voucher programs as well as public housing. However, housing programs are not an entitlement, and there are long waiting lists for rental units. WIC provides supplemental foods, health care referrals, and nutrition education for low-income pregnant, breast-feeding, and postpartum women, and to infants and children up to age five who are found to be at nutritional risk. The EITC is a tax credit for families with earned income; although there is a small credit for childless individuals, benefits mostly accrue to families with children. The Child Tax Credit is another credit in the federal income tax, going to families with lower levels of income if they have dependent children in residence in the home. Neither the EITC nor the CTC are adequately reported in the SIPP, so here those credits are computed with the NBER TAXSIM model assuming 100 percent participation. The SSI program provides benefits to adults who are elderly, blind, or disabled and whose income and resources fall below specified levels. The SSDI program provides benefits to individuals who have a severe disability and who have worked sufficiently in the past to qualify for Social Security benefits. OASI provides benefits to retirees and survivors in families where an individual has sufficient lifetime earnings to qualify under Social Security rules. The UI program provides support to the involuntarily unemployed who have enough recent earnings and employment to be entitled to benefits while unemployed. UI benefits are limited in duration, usually twenty-six weeks in normal periods but more during recessions, including the Great Recession when Congress extended benefits.[5]

Table 8.1 shows the percentage of SNAP families receiving tax credits or benefits from other major transfer programs in late 2008 and early 2009. The most common receipt was of EITC benefits, 38 percent, reflecting the presence of families with earnings in the SNAP caseload.[6] About 28 percent

TABLE 8.1
Percent of SNAP families receiving other major tax and transfer benefits,
2008–2009

Program	Percent receiving
EITC	38
CTC	28
SSI	25
Subsidized housing	24
WIC	21
SSDI	15
OASI	15
TANF	13
UI	8
Any one of the above	91
Any one of the above, excluding EITC and CTC	76
Any one of the above or minor programs	92
Any one of the above or minor programs, excluding EITC and CTC	77

SOURCE: Author's calculations using data from the Survey of Income and Program Participation (SIPP).

NOTES: Universe = All SIPP families reporting receipt of SNAP benefits in any of the four months prior to interview. Interviews took place from January to April 2009. Transfer percentages denote the percentage of SNAP families reporting receipt of the benefit in question in any of the four months prior to interview. Tax credit percentages are calculated from NBER TAXSIM from average values of earnings, income, presence and ages of children, and other family characteristics over the four months prior to interview, assuming 100 percent participation. Minor programs are General Assistance, foster children, Workers' Compensation, Veterans Benefits, and other assistance.

of SNAP families received the other tax credit, the CTC, in this case reflecting the presence of young children and low income among SNAP families. For more traditional transfer programs, receipt of SSI or housing benefits was most common, with about a quarter (24 to 25 percent) of SNAP families receiving one of those benefits. As already noted, SSI recipients are categorically eligible for SNAP benefits, but subsidized housing recipients are not. However, subsidized housing recipients may be eligible for excess shelter deductions in the calculation of net income. Just over a fifth (21 percent) of SNAP families received WIC benefits, for SNAP families are categorically income-eligible for WIC. Turning to Social Security programs, 15 percent of SNAP families received SSDI or OASI. Again, recipients of the former are categorically eligible. Only 13 percent of SNAP families received TANF. TANF recipients are categorically eligible for SNAP benefits, so the small percentage of SNAP families receiving TANF is a reflection of the small caseload in the program subsequent to 1996 welfare reform. Finally, only 8 percent of SNAP families received UI benefits, a reflection both of the fact that the unemployment rate in late 2008 was still low and the fact that many

SNAP families, even those who work, do not have sufficient earnings and employment histories to qualify for UI when unemployed.[7]

Taking all tax credits and transfer programs together, 91 percent of SNAP families received at least one credit or benefit in late 2008 or early 2009. However, the EITC and CTC were a large part of this high rate of receipt; in fact, excluding those two credits, 76 percent of SNAP families received benefits from another traditional transfer program, down from 91 percent.

Medicare and Medicaid are excluded from these counts, but many SNAP families receive these benefits, especially Medicaid among the nonelderly (about 79 percent of SNAP families receive Medicaid). A large fraction of those are SNAP families who receive SSDI, SSI, or TANF, the receipt of which makes a family categorically eligible for Medicaid (44 percent of SNAP families receive benefits from one of those three programs). Medicaid receipt is very high among the low-income population even among non-SNAP families, so it is not surprising that it is high among SNAP families as well.

Families receiving SSDI, SSI, or TANF are categorically eligible for SNAP as well. As just noted, 44 percent of SNAP families receive one of these three benefits. Therefore, categorical eligibles constitute a large proportion of the SNAP caseload, according to the SIPP data and other data sources. Categorical eligibility would be even higher if receipt of TANF noncash benefits was included, but these benefits are not measured in the SIPP data. However, this does not mean that these families would not be eligible for SNAP anyway if their income and resources were below the eligible thresholds. Income distributions among categorical and noncategorical eligibles will be examined in the following pages.

Table 8.2 shows whether the SNAP families who receive benefits from another program typically participate only in one other program or multiple ones. Counting the two tax credits, over 28 percent of SNAP families receive only one other benefit, about 36 percent receive only two others, and about 26 percent receive three or more other benefits, a sizable percentage. But excluding the two tax credits and considering only traditional transfer programs, 41 percent of families receive only one other benefit, 27 percent receive only two others, and less than 9 percent receive three or more other programs, a much smaller fraction.

Many of the most common combinations of programs include the EITC or CTC, given the heavy participation of SNAP families in those two programs. So, for example, 8 percent of the SNAP caseload receives only those two tax credits and nothing else, and another 5 percent receives only the EITC in addition to SNAP. But when the tax credits are not treated as transfer programs, the most common form of multiple receipt is with WIC only, which over 10 percent of the SNAP families receive (and receive no third

TABLE 8.2

Percent of SNAP families receiving combinations of other major tax and transfer benefits, 2008–2009

Program	Percent Receiving		
	Including EITC/CTC		*Excluding EITC/CTC*
ONLY ONE OTHER MAJOR PROGRAM	28.5		40.6
ONLY TWO OTHER MAJOR PROGRAMS	35.9		26.5
THREE OR MORE OTHER MAJOR PROGRAMS	26.4		8.6
SEVEN LARGEST COMBINATIONS			
EITC and CTC only	8.1	WIC only	10.5
EITC only	5.2	SSI only	6.4
SSI only	4.9	Subsidized housing only	6.0
EITC, CTC, and WIC only	4.8	OASI only	5.8
OASI only	4.4	SSDI only	4.9
SSDI only	3.7	SSDI and SSI only	4.0
SSDI and SSI only	3.1	UI only	3.7

SOURCE: Author's calculations using SIPP data.

NOTES: Universe = All SIPP families reporting receipt of SNAP benefits in any of the four months prior to interview. Interviews took place from January to April 2009. Transfer percentages denote the percentage of SNAP families reporting receipt of the benefit in question in any of the four months prior to interview. Tax credit percentages are calculated from NBER TAXSIM from average values of earnings, income, presence and ages of children, and other family characteristics over the four months prior to interview, assuming 100 percent participation.

benefit). Most of the other most common forms of receipt are also receipt of just one other program, like housing assistance, SSI, SSDI, OASI, or UI. The most common form of receipt of two other programs occurs for those families who receive both SSI and SSDI, no doubt because the presence of disabled members results in participation in both. Those families constitute 4 percent of SNAP families. All other combinations of programs are rarer and occur for less than about 3 percent of the SNAP caseload.

Much of the multiple program receipt in the SNAP caseload occurs among elderly and disabled families because the former almost always receive OASI and the latter usually receive SSI and/or SSDI. In fact, because elderly and disabled families constitute 41 percent of the 2008 to 2009 caseload, and the disabled alone constitute 33 percent according to the SIPP data used here, these families have an important impact on overall patterns of multiple receipt. Table 8.3 combines the receipt categories from Tables 8.1 and 8.2 and shows them for the elderly, the disabled, and the nonelderly, nondisabled families receiving SNAP benefits. Not surprisingly, the

TABLE 8.3

Percent of SNAP families receiving other major tax and transfer programs for elderly, disabled, and non-elderly nondisabled, 2008–2009

Program	Elderly	Disabled	Nonelderly, nondisabled
EITC	10.0	17.6	52.7
CTC	7.7	10.1	40.1
SSI	45.5	75.9	0
Subsidized housing	29.0	29.3	20.8
WIC	4.4	8.9	30.1
SSDI	20.7	46.3	0
OASI	63.2	16.2	5.5
TANF	4.6	10.3	14.7
UI	1.9	2.8	10.9
Receiving at least one other program	98.7	100	85.1
Receiving at least one other program, not EITC or CTC	97.8	100	60.3
Only one other program, not EITC or CTC	39.4	34.3	41.7
Only two other programs, not EITC or CTC	45.6	45.1	15.7
Three or more other programs, not EITC or CTC	12.8	20.6	2.9
Percent of all SNAP families	15.9	32.9	59.2

SOURCE: Author's calculations using SIPP data.

NOTES: Universe = All SIPP families reporting receipt of SNAP benefits in any of the four months prior to interview. Interviews took place from January to April 2009. Transfer percentages denote the percentage of SNAP families reporting receipt of the benefit in question in any of the four months prior to interview. Tax credit percentages are calculated from NBER TAXSIM from average values of earnings, income, presence and ages of children, and other family characteristics over the four months prior to interview, assuming 100 percent participation. Elderly families and individuals are those families and unrelated individuals headed by an individual age sixty-two or older. Disabled families and individuals are those with anyone in the family who received Supplemental Security Income (SSI) or Disability Insurance (DI).

elderly and disabled are less likely to receive EITC or CTC tax credits and less likely to receive TANF, WIC, and UI but are much more likely to receive OASI, SSI, or SSDI, although the latter two are partly a matter of the definition of disability used here (see the notes to Table 8.3).[8] In addition, the last column in the table shows that, among nonelderly, nondisabled families receiving SNAP, 42 percent receive only one other benefit, 16 percent receive only two other benefits, and only 3 percent receive three or more other benefits. These patterns of multiple receipt are often considerably smaller than those for the entire caseload shown in Table 8.1. Note as well that 33 percent of the SNAP caseload is disabled, thereby constituting a major demographic group in the program.

Progressivity

An important question is how multiple receipt of SNAP and other benefits varies with position in the income distribution. Is multiple receipt progressive in the way one would expect for transfer programs, in general, with the poorest families most likely to receive other benefits and higher-income families less likely to receive other benefits? If so, this suggests that receipt of benefits other than SNAP is partly a simple result of low family income, which is also the reason for receiving SNAP. If not, it may imply that higher-income families are, for possibly categorical eligibility or other reasons, receiving more benefits than would be justified solely on an income criterion.

Table 8.4 shows how the distribution of receipt of other program benefits varies by "private" income relative to the poverty line, where private income is defined as the sum of family earned income plus nontransfer (and non–tax-credit) nonlabor income—of which there is very little in this population.[9] Overall, the distribution seems to be regressive—90 percent of SNAP families in deep (private income) poverty receive at least one benefit, but 99 percent of those in shallow (private income) poverty do so. However, this seems to be largely because of the EITC or CTC, for ignoring those programs, 83 percent of those in deep poverty receive at least one benefit, but only 65 percent of those in shallow poverty do. However, when individual programs are examined, although most of the traditional transfer programs like SSI, subsidized housing, SSDI, and TANF are progressive, many of the others are not. The EITC is regressive in the lower portion of the income distribution, but this is because earnings are necessary to receive it. The CTC is regressive because the basic credit is limited by the size of tax liability, and that liability is zero or small for those with low private income.[10] Surprisingly, the WIC program is regressive, with fewer families in deep private income poverty receiving benefits than families higher up the income distribution. The OASI and UI programs are also regressive in parts of their income ranges.

But Table 8.5 shows that many of the regressive features are eliminated when the elderly and disabled are removed from the sample. As noted previously, the elderly and disabled constitute 41 percent of the 2008 to 2009 SNAP families according to these data, and those families are disproportionately located in the deep poverty part of the income distribution and yet would typically not receive WIC or UI, for example.[11] When only the nonelderly, nondisabled SNAP recipient population is examined, WIC is roughly proportional, and UI is progressive, although UI is only mildly so, no doubt because those in deep poverty are less likely to qualify for UI payments when unemployed. For this population, too, very few SNAP families receive benefits from more than two other major programs excluding the EITC

TABLE 8.4

Percent of SNAP families receiving other major tax and transfer benefits by private family income as percent of the Federal Poverty Line, 2008–2009

Program	Percent receiving, by private family income		
	0–50%	50–100%	100–150%
EITC	24.7	89.0	64.0
CTC	5.4	71.5	65.8
SSI	32.2	11.1	13.7
Subsidized housing	31.3	17.3	10.9
WIC	18.2	28.6	26.7
SSDI	19.7	7.3	6.8
OASI	17.4	9.2	11.0
TANF	14.6	10.4	8.1
UI	6.9	9.9	6.7
Receiving at least one other program	89.7	98.7	91.9
Receiving at least one other program, not EITC or CTC	83.1	65.1	61.1
Only one other program, not EITC or CTC	39.5	41.2	41.7
Only two other programs, not EITC or CTC	31.6	20.0	16.4
Three or more other programs, not EITC or CTC	12.0	3.9	3.0
Percent of SNAP families	61.5	17.8	9.2

SOURCE: Author's calculations using SIPP data.

NOTES: Universe = All SIPP families reporting receipt of SNAP benefits in any of the four months prior to interview. Interviews took place from January to April 2009. Transfer percentages denote the percentage of SNAP families reporting receipt of the benefit in question in any of the four months prior to interview. Tax credit percentages are calculated from NBER TAXSIM from average values of earnings, income, presence and ages of children, and other family characteristics over the four months prior to interview, assuming 100 percent participation. Private income is defined as the sum of family earnings and family nonlabor, nontransfer, non–tax-credit income.

and CTC—2.9 percent for all nonelderly, nondisabled families and only 4.7 percent for those in deep poverty (1.6 percent and 0.2 percent of the higher income groups do). Thus, among traditional transfer programs, the receipt of other program benefits is indeed almost entirely progressive.

Categorical Eligibility

A question that often arises in discussing the income distribution of the SNAP caseload is whether those who are categorically eligible have higher income than those who are not so eligible. Categorically eligible families do not have to meet the income and resource tests for SNAP directly, only

TABLE 8.5
Percent of nondisabled, nonelderly, SNAP families receiving other major tax and transfer benefits by private family income as percent of the federal poverty line, 2008–2009

Program	Percent receiving, by private family income		
	0–50%	50–100%	100–150%
EITC	39.7	95.0	69.2
CTC	9.4	79.6	72.7
SSI	0	0	0
Subsidized housing	28.9	18.1	10.4
WIC	29.5	32.9	30.1
SSDI	0	0	0
OASI	6.1	3.1	4.8
TANF	19.6	9.9	8.4
UI	12.1	10.4	7.4
Receiving at least one other program	79.7	98.3	89.9
Receiving at least one other program, not EITC or CTC	66.7	56.5	51.4
Only one other program, not EITC or CTC	42.1	40.2	41.9
Only two other programs, not EITC or CTC	19.9	14.6	9.4
Three or more other programs, not EITC or CTC	4.7	1.6	.2
Percent SNAP families	30.8	14.1	7.2

SOURCE: Author's calculations using SIPP data.

NOTES: Universe = All SIPP families reporting receipt of SNAP benefits in any of the four months prior to interview. Interviews took place from January to April 2009. Transfer percentages denote the percentage of SNAP families reporting receipt of the benefit in question in any of the four months prior to interview. Tax credit percentages are calculated from NBER TAXSIM from average values of earnings, income, presence and ages of children, and other family characteristics over the four months prior to interview, assuming 100 percent participation. Elderly families and individuals are those families and unrelated individuals headed by an individual age sixty-two or older. Disabled families and individuals are those with anyone in the family who received SSI or DI.

those for the other programs in which they are enrolled. Table 8.6 answers this question for the 2008 to 2009 SIPP data, showing the private income distributions for those SNAP families also receiving SSI, SSDI, and TANF, the three categorically eligible categories measurable here. Contrary to the supposition just noted, those who are categorically eligible have lower incomes than those who are not, with 76 percent in deep poverty, for example, compared to about 51 percent of those not categorically eligible. Thus this piece of evidence does not suggest that higher income families are getting onto the SNAP caseload through categorical eligibility per se.[12]

TABLE 8.6
Private family income of SNAP families who receive other transfer benefits,
2008–2009

Program	Private family income as percent of federal poverty line		
	0–50%	50–100%	100–150%
SSI recipients	79.2	7.9	5.1
SSDI recipients	79.7	8.5	4.1
TANF recipients	71.0	14.5	5.9
SSI, SSDI, or TANF recipients	76.0	10.3	5.3
Not categorically eligible	50.9	23.3	12.1

SOURCE: Author's calculations using SIPP data.

NOTES: Universe = All SIPP families reporting receipt of SNAP benefits in any of the four months prior to interview. Interviews took place from January to April 2009. Transfer percentages denote the percentage of SNAP families reporting receipt of the benefit in question in any of the four months prior to interview. Tax credit percentages are calculated from NBER TAXSIM from average values of earnings, income, presence and ages of children, and other family characteristics over the four months prior to interview, assuming 100 percent participation.

Multiple Receipt by Family Type and Employment Status

Tables 8.7 and 8.8 show the evidence for multiple program receipt among different family types and demographic groups. Table 8.7 shows multiple program receipt, for example, for nonelderly, nondisabled, two-parent, one-parent, and childless families. Two-parent families tend to have higher private income and higher earnings than either one-parent or childless families, and this results in higher EITC and CTC receipt. Among more traditional transfer programs, single-parent families are more likely to receive subsidized housing and TANF benefits than either of the other two demographic groups. However, two-parent families are most likely to receive WIC benefits, possibly because they have higher birth rates and hence are more likely to have wives who are pregnant or who have infants or young children. Interestingly, however, overall, excluding the EITC and CTC, about the same fractions of all three family groups receive at least one other major program benefit (ranging from 50 to 67 percent) and about the same percentages receive only one other benefit (39 to 47 percent). Single-parent families are slightly more likely to be recipients of benefits from three or more other programs.[13]

Table 8.8 shows similar distributions for those with nondisabled nonelderly employed and nonemployed members. As should be expected, families with employed members are more likely to have earnings and hence more likely to receive the EITC than those with nonemployed members, and the same is true for the CTC because it is positively correlated with tax

TABLE 8.7
Percent of nonelderly, nondisabled SNAP families receiving other major tax and transfer programs, by family type, 2008–2009

| | Family type | | |
Program	Single-parent	Two-parent	Childless
EITC	58.9	71.3	31.9
CTC	42.9	78.3	10.0
SSI	0	0	0
Subsidized housing	31.9	9.0	14.7
WIC	32.1	43.5	18.2
SSDI	0	0	0
OASI	6.3	3.5	5.9
TANF	19.0	11.5	11.5
UI	8.8	13.4	11.7
Receiving at least one other program	92.2	96.9	67.7
Receiving at least one other program, not EITC or CTC	66.8	63.2	49.8
Only one other program, not EITC or CTC	40.8	47.3	38.8
Only two other programs, not EITC or CTC	21.1	14.0	9.8
Three or more other programs, not EITC or CTC	4.8	1.9	1.2
Percent of all SNAP families	25.8	14.0	20.2

SOURCE: Author's calculations using SIPP data.

NOTES: Universe = All SIPP families reporting receipt of SNAP benefits in any of the four months prior to interview. Interviews took place from January to April 2009. Transfer percentages denote the percentage of SNAP families reporting receipt of the benefit in question in any of the four months prior to interview. Tax credit percentages are calculated from NBER TAXSIM from average values of earnings, income, presence and ages of children, and other family characteristics over the four months prior to interview, assuming 100 percent participation. Single-parent families are families with children under age eighteen in the household and with one parent present. Two-parent families are families with children under age eighteen in the household and two married parents present. Childless families and individuals are those without a child under age eighteen in the household and include what Census Bureau definitions call unrelated individuals as well as families.

liability. But the nonemployed are more likely to receive subsidized housing and TANF, for example, and more likely to receive at least one other program benefit besides the EITC and CTC (68 percent versus 57 percent).

Benefits

A rather different issue surrounding multiple program receipt among SNAP families is the relative size of SNAP benefits compared to those from the other programs from which benefits are also received. As shown in Table 8.9, SNAP provides income support each month of $259, quite modest compared

TABLE 8.8
Percent of nonelderly, nondisabled SNAP families receiving other major tax and transfer programs, by employment status, 2008–2009

Program	Employed	Nonemployed
EITC	73.7	2.9
CTC	56.2	1.9
SSI	0	0
Subsidized housing	17.1	29.3
WIC	30.3	29.4
SSDI	0	0
OASI	5.1	6.4
TANF	10.9	23.8
UI	10.5	11.8
Receiving at least one other program	91.6	69.6
Receiving at least one other program, not EITC or CTC	56.9	68.0
Only one other program, not EITC or CTC	41.9	41.0
Only two other programs, not EITC or CTC	13.2	21.4
Three or more other programs, not EITC or CTC	1.8	5.6
Percent of all SNAP families	42.1	17.6

SOURCE: Author's calculations using SIPP data.

NOTES: Universe = All SIPP families reporting receipt of SNAP benefits in any of the four months prior to interview. Interviews took place from January to April 2009. Transfer percentages denote the percentage of SNAP families reporting receipt of the benefit in question in any of the four months prior to interview. Tax credit percentages are calculated from NBER TAXSIM from average values of earnings, income, presence and ages of children, and other family characteristics over the four months prior to interview, assuming 100 percent participation. Employed families are those with at least one person over age fifteen who worked in all four months prior to the interview. Nonemployed families are those without any such person.

to benefits received from other traditional transfer programs like SSI, SSDI, OASI, and even UI—which provide benefits ranging from $588 to $883 per month. Of course, this is because SNAP is intended only to support food expenditure, and the other programs are intended to provide something much closer to full support for living expenses, as high as $883 per month for SSDI.[14] Thus, from an income perspective (rather than a simple multiple-program-receipt perspective), SNAP remains the "add-on" program that it was originally intended to be for those receiving other major transfers.

TRENDS IN MULTIPLE PROGRAM RECEIPT, 1993–2010

The analysis thus far has shown the extent of multiple program receipt among SNAP families only in 2008 to 2009. But there are reasons to think that such receipt could have changed over the long term. One obvious reason is that several of the other programs have undergone significant changes in structure or size, which should be expected to affect whether SNAP families are

TABLE 8.9
Average monthly value of tax and transfer programs for SNAP recipients, 2008–2009

Program	Value (dollars)
SNAP	259
EITC	205
CTC	117
SSI	588
Subsidized housing	499
SSDI	883
OASI	851
TANF	371
UI	791

SOURCE: Author's calculations using SIPP data.

NOTES: Universe = All SIPP families reporting receipt of SNAP benefits in any of the four months prior to interview. Interviews took place from January to April 2009. Transfer percentages denote the percentage of SNAP families reporting receipt of the benefit in question in any of the four months prior to interview. Tax credit percentages are calculated from NBER TAXSIM from average values of earnings, income, presence and ages of children, and other family characteristics over the four months prior to interview, assuming 100 percent participation.

likely to receive them. A prominent example is the TANF program, which was created in 1996 from the old Aid to Families with Dependent Children (AFDC) program and which has declined in size since then. Going the other way, the SSI program grew rapidly in size in the 1990s, and the SSDI program has been growing steadily for two decades. The WIC program has also been growing over time. The two tax credits, the EITC and the CTC, have changed, for the EITC was expanded in generosity in the late 1980s and early 1990s, and the CTC was begun only in 1998 and the number of tax filers receiving it has grown. On the whole, then, aside from the TANF program, it is likely that multiple program receipt has grown over time.

Going beyond 2008, several of the programs were expanded by Great Recession legislation that relaxed eligibility requirements, temporarily increased benefit levels, or both. Programs that were affected include TANF, OASI, SSI, and the two tax credits, the EITC and CTC, which were temporarily made more generous. In addition, the major benefit duration expansions in the UI program could have affected multiple receipt of SNAP and UI as well.

Finally, there are changes in the SNAP program itself that could have affected multiple benefit receipt. The strong growth in the caseload which occurred in the 2000s resulting from changes in asset eligibility rules, less frequent redetermination, and increases in outreach could have brought in

TABLE 8.10

Percent of SNAP families receiving other major tax credit and transfer programs,
1993–2010

Program	Percent receiving by year			
	1993	2004	2008	2010
EITC	29	39	38	38
CTC	0	21	28	31
SSI	20	26	25	23
Subsidized housing	25	26	24	23
WIC	15	19	21	18
SSDI	7	14	15	15
OASI	14	14	15	17
TANF	41	17	13	9
UI	7	5	8	9
Any one of the above	89	92	91	89
Any one of the above, excluding EITC and CTC	80	77	76	72
Any one of the above or minor programs	92	92	92	90
Any one of the above or minor programs, excluding EITC and CTC	84	78	77	73
Unemployment rate	7.2	5.7	7.4	9.3

SOURCE: Author's calculations using SIPP data.

NOTES: Universe = All SIPP families reporting receipt of SNAP benefits in any of the four months prior to interview. Interviews for year 1993 took place between February and May 1993, for year 2004 between February and May 2004, for year 2008 between January and April 2009, and for year 2010 between January and April 2011. Transfer percentages denote the percentage of SNAP families reporting receipt of the benefit in question in any of the four months prior to interview. Tax credit percentages are calculated from NBER TAXSIM from average values of earnings, income, presence and ages of children, and other family characteristics over the four months prior to interview, assuming 100 percent participation. The unemployment rate is defined as the arithmetic mean over seven months covered by each wave of interviews.

families that were more likely to receive other benefits. The regulatory change in the year 2000 that established broad-based categorical eligibility could likewise have brought in additional families receiving other benefits. During the Great Recession, asset eligibility rules were further relaxed and benefits were temporarily increased, which could have brought higher-income families onto the SNAP program. The recession itself, however, brought into the program many families who were temporarily unemployed and who probably had lower levels of receipt of traditional transfer programs, although no doubt higher levels of receipt of UI both from the recession per se and from the expansions of duration that were enacted during that period.[15]

Table 8.10 shows trends in multiple income receipt from 1993 to 2010 for the same major programs shown in Table 8.1.[16] The patterns of receipt are very much in line with expectations based on the preceding thumbnail description of trends and policy reforms in those other programs. For the tax credit programs, receipt of the EITC naturally grew from 1993 to 2004 because this was the period of its greatest increase in generosity. The CTC began only in 1998 and was made more generous in the 2000s and in the Great Recession, leading to more receipt among SNAP families. Receipt of SSI benefits increased from 1993 to 2004, exactly when the SSI caseload was rising in general. The same goes for the WIC and SSDI programs, where multiple receipt expanded at the same time as the general caseloads grew. For UI, receipt naturally expands and contracts with the business cycle and reached its peak in 2010 at 9 percent of the caseload, no doubt partly the result of legislated reforms.[17] Indeed, a notable result is how small the fraction of SNAP recipients who receive UI remains even after those major expansions of the program. In all likelihood, as the UI benefit extensions expire, the fraction of SNAP recipients receiving them will fall, possibly back to its prerecession level of 5 percent.

The major exception to this trend is for the TANF program, which shrank dramatically after 1996, reducing multiple benefit receipt among SNAP families from a large 41 percent in 1993 to a small 9 percent in 2010. The TANF program was large enough in 1993 to generate a decline in the rate of overall multiple program receipt among SNAP families, for although 80 percent of those families received at least one other traditional transfer program benefit in 1993, only 72 percent did in 2010. Thus, by this definition, multiple program receipt in SNAP has fallen over time, not risen.[18]

Nevertheless, perhaps the most surprising result in Table 8.10 is the relative stability of receipt of most other program benefits from 2004 to 2010, despite the large increase in the SNAP caseload over this period and the many recession-era alterations in the other programs. Leaving aside TANF and UI, receipt of the other program benefits sometimes rose slightly and sometimes fell slightly, but there were no dramatic changes in that receipt.

CUMULATIVE TAX RATES AND WORK INCENTIVES

An important issue in multiple receipt of benefits from tax and transfer programs is that they may impose high cumulative marginal tax rates (MTRs) on earnings and hence create work disincentives that are greater than might appear from a casual inspection of each program's work disincentives alone. If a family participates in four different transfer programs, for example, and each program has a 30 percent MTR (that is, benefits in each one are reduced by 30 cents for an extra dollar of earnings), then, even though each program has a reasonably low MTR, the cumulative MTR is 120 percent. In this case, the family's income actually falls if they earn more, because the

TABLE 8.11

Cumulative marginal tax rates for single-parent and two-parent families with two children by change in earnings across U.S. states and jurisdictions, 2008 (percent)

Family type	From 0 to 50 percent of poverty line	From 50 to 100 percent of poverty line	From 100 to 150 percent of poverty line	From 0 to 100 percent of poverty line
SINGLE PARENT				
Average	2.4	17.9	50.5	10.2
Maximum	36.3	45.5	104.7	25.5
Minimum	−27.9	−1.7	26.6	−13.3
TWO PARENT				
Average	−51.2	31.8	59.2	−9.7
Maximum	−21.5	69.2	102.9	10.8
Minimum	−86.9	18.5	36.8	−34.2

SOURCE: Maag et al. (2012), Tables 1 and 3.

NOTE: Tax rates assume participation in TANF and SNAP and include all federal and state taxes, including the employee portion of the payroll tax. The average is the unweighted average across all U.S. states and jurisdictions and the maximum and minimum are those from among all the tax rates in those states and jurisdictions.

cumulative MTR exceeds 100 percent. In less severe cases, the cumulative MTR may be less than 100 percent but still high when the MTRs from each program are added together, as illustrated in Table 8.11. This concern has been expressed throughout the modern era of study of the work incentives of transfer programs, going back to the early discussions of a negative income tax in the late 1960s and early 1970s (Friedman 1969; Lampman 1975).

Before discussing the magnitude of cumulative MTRs facing SNAP families, it is useful to understand the issues with work disincentives and MTRs in general. It has been understood for many years that a high MTR does not necessarily reduce average work effort in the low-income population, and a low MTR does not necessarily increase it (for example, Moffitt 2003). This is because there are offsetting effects of a change in the MTR that go in opposite directions. An increase in the MTR, holding constant the guarantee level (that is, the benefit amount if the family has no earnings) decreases work effort for those with low hours of work or with low earnings but increases it for those working longer hours who lose eligibility. The opposite occurs when the MTR is lowered.

The issue, instead, is the distribution of MTRs over the range of earnings in the low-income population and where the MTRs are high or low. By definition, benefits in any means-tested transfer program must be phased out eventually, and the question is whether they should be phased out rapidly or slowly. If they are phased out rapidly, MTRs will be high for those on the program; but if they are phased out slowly, the MTRs will be lower but will be spread over a larger fraction of the population, which will generate more work disincentives in aggregate. Finally, holding the eligible population fixed, lowering the MTR in one range of earnings must necessarily mean that it has to be raised in another range. For example, lowering the MTR for the first dollar of earnings requires that the MTR be raised at higher levels of earnings if the size of the eligible population is held fixed.

This point is particularly important with the existence of the EITC, which is an earnings subsidy over low ranges of earnings and hence reduces MTRs or even makes them negative in that range. But having a generous earnings subsidy in low ranges of earnings means that MTRs have to necessarily be larger than they otherwise would have been (for example, than if a single average MTR had been imposed) for families higher in the earnings distribution. Therefore, the EITC should be expected to increase work incentives for those with low earnings and to decrease them for those with relatively high earnings. A question for policy makers is whether they are willing to accept that trade-off because they deem it socially desirable to put special weight on increasing work incentives for the poorest families.[19]

A less important point but one that also needs to be recognized is that, because SNAP includes almost all cash transfers in countable income, the cumulative MTR is lower than the simple sum of the MTRs in the programs in which a family participates. If t_S is the MTR in the SNAP program and t_O is the MTR in some other cash transfer program, the cumulative MTR is $(t_S + t_O - t_S t_O)$. Thus, for example, if the MTR in SNAP is 0.30 and that in TANF is 0.50, then the cumulative MTR for a SNAP family participating in both programs is not 0.80 but rather 0.65.[20]

The MTR for SNAP alone is, in addition, fairly complex, ranging over families in different circumstances and influenced by the existence of several deductions. A deduction of 20 percent of earnings by itself reduces the MTR from 30 to 24 percent. In addition, there is a standard deduction that implies that the MTR is zero in the lowest range of earnings. But these features of the benefit formula, although suggesting increased work incentives, just push the 30 percent tax rate up higher in the earnings distribution than it would be otherwise and create additional work disincentives in those higher ranges. The SNAP program also has deductions for child care expenses and some shelter expenses, and it has a maximum and minimum benefit that reduce the MTR to zero when the benefit is at those points. Taking all these factors into account, Hanson and Andrews (2009) find an average MTR in the SNAP program of 24 percent, calculated as a weighted average over families in different circumstances and with different levels of earnings, but the MTR for the first dollar of earnings is zero. Using a different methodology, Ziliak (2008) finds the effective MTR in SNAP to be about 17 percent but that it differs significantly from state to state.

These SNAP MTRs are relevant primarily for the population of SNAP families who receive no other traditional transfer program but do receive EITC and CTC credits and pay positive taxes. But this not a small fraction of the caseload, as noted previously, constituting 24 percent of the SNAP caseload overall (Table 8.1, 100 minus 76) and 40 percent of the nonelderly, nondisabled population (Table 8.4, 100 minus 60). The Congressional Budget Office (2012a) has estimated that a single mother with one child would face MTRs ranging from –34 to –49 percent from the EITC and CTC for earnings below $10,000 in 2012 dollars and rising only to 15 percent at higher earnings levels in the phase-out range of both credits (approximately $20,000 to $40,000). Thus, SNAP-only families would certainly face negative marginal tax rates at low ranges of earnings but higher MTRs at higher earnings levels, possibly up to 39 percent (24 plus 15). MTRs are even higher if state income taxes and payroll taxes are added in. In that case, while MTRs below $10,000 in annual earnings have approximately the same negative values as before, MTRs from taxes rise as high as 40 percent in the $20,000 to $40,000 range, leading to a possible 64 percent MTR when added to a 24 percent SNAP MTR.

An important question nevertheless is how many SNAP recipients are in these earnings ranges. Using the 2008 to 2009 SIPP data, 46 percent of nondisabled, nonelderly single-parent SNAP families who received no traditional transfer benefit other than SNAP have earnings below $10,000 in 2012 dollars, and only 20 percent of such families have earnings between $20,000 and $40,000 where the MTRs are higher. Thus only about a fifth of this portion of the SNAP caseload is likely to experience strong work disincentives.

Cumulative MTRs under Multiple Program Receipt

Turning to the question of the MTRs for SNAP families who participate in multiple traditional transfer programs, it must immediately be noted that the bulk of families in the SNAP caseload are unlikely to experience either seriously high MTRs or to have much labor supply responsiveness to tax rates in the first place. Among those receiving at least one other traditional transfer program benefit in addition to SNAP, 53 percent are elderly and/or disabled.[21] The elderly have very low levels of work because most are retired and work incentives are not a major issue for them, whereas the disabled have, by the evidence of most attempts to encourage them to increase their work effort by the use of financial incentives, a very low responsiveness to those incentives. Another 13 percent of the SNAP caseload receiving at least one traditional transfer program in addition to SNAP are childless, and their receipt of other programs is modest and unlikely to generate high MTRs for any but a small fraction of such families.

Work incentives among those who receive at least one traditional transfer program other than SNAP are therefore an important issue primarily only for the remaining 34 percent of such families who are nonelderly, nondisabled single-parent families or two-parent families.[22] Most of the existing literature on cumulative MTRs has, in fact, focused on such families, and more on the former than the latter. The estimates most closely aligned with the analysis here are those reported by Maag and colleagues (2012), who calculated cumulative MTRs for one-parent and two-parent families in 2008 who received TANF and SNAP, taking into account the EITC, CTC, and all other federal taxes as well as state income and payroll taxes.[23] It should be kept in mind that these single-parent families constitute only 5 percent of the SNAP caseload and these two-parent families, 1.5 percent.[24] The main results are reported in Table 8.11, which shows the average cumulative MTR across U.S. states as well as the maximum and minimum among states when earnings move across poverty levels. For single parents, those moving from nonwork to half the poverty line face only a 2.4 percent cumulative MTR, although it can be as low as –27.9 and as high as 36.3. The average MTR when moving from half poverty to the poverty line results in a 17.9 percent cumulative MTR, high but not onerous. However, the EITC and CTC phaseouts disproportionately occur when earnings go from the poverty line to 150 percent of the poverty line, resulting in an average 50.5 cumulative MTR, which is over 100 percent in one state, although most states are in the 40 percent to 60 percent range (see Maag et al. 2012 for state-by-state figures). Going from nonwork to the poverty line generates a 10.2 percent cumulative MTR.

For two-parent families, because of more generous exemption levels, the average cumulative MTR is –51.2 percent in the deep poverty range, much lower than that for single parents, but is 31.8 percent and 59.2 percent in the higher poverty ranges. Over the range from nonwork to the poverty line, the MTR remains –9.7 percent, much lower than those for single-parent families in that range.

This once again illustrates the point that a more generous earnings subsidy at low levels of earnings must generate larger MTRs at higher earnings levels, by definition, because the subsidy must be phased out. Therefore, increased work incentives at the bottom have to be balanced by greater work disincentives toward the top. For nonelderly, nondisabled single-parent families, however, the SIPP data indicate that 83 percent of those receiving both SNAP and TANF have private income in the deep poverty range, 12 percent in the shallow poverty range, and only 2 percent in the near-poverty range (100 to 150 percent of the poverty range) where the cumulative MTRs are highest. Because this category of single-parent families is only 5 percent of the SNAP caseload to begin with, this implies that only one-tenth of one percent of the SNAP caseload faces onerous work disincentives.

For two-parent families receiving both SNAP and TANF, 42 percent are in the deep private income poverty range, 34 percent in the shallow poverty range, and 10 percent are in the near-poverty range. Two-parent families typically have higher incomes than single-parent families, resulting in more of the former facing high cumulative MTRs. However, this category of families also constitutes less of the SNAP caseload (1.5 percent, as already noted), so, similar to the case for single-parent families, only slightly more than one-tenth of one percent of the SNAP caseload faces high cumulative MTRs from this source.

These estimates omit the MTRs from several other programs. The most important is Medicaid, which imposes a zero percent MTR up to the eligibility point and a greater-than-100 percent MTR at the notch where eligibility ends. The Medicaid rules are complex, covering children to income limits higher than that of adults, assuming that adults are covered at all (if not pregnant; pregnant women are also covered). The Medicaid program therefore is likely to increase the MTRs at higher income levels, sharpening the difference between those tax rates at lower and at higher levels of earnings reported here. Maag and colleagues (2012) conducted an analysis valuing Medicaid at government cost, which is an upper bound of its valuation by recipients, and find that, for single mothers with two children, average MTRs over broad ranges of earnings are, as expected, higher, but only by about 5 to 8 percentage points.

Another omitted program is subsidized housing, which has a nominal MTR in the 10 to 30 percent range. The CBO (2012a) added housing to SNAP and TANF into their calculations and find a significant increase in cumulative MTRs. However, only 8 percent of nonelderly, nondisabled single parents on SNAP received both TANF and housing subsidies in 2008, and only a fraction of those are in the range with high marginal tax rates. Other omitted programs from these MTR calculations are child care subsidies and WIC and, in the near future, the phase-out of subsidies from the Affordable Care Act. Also omitted is Unemployment Insurance, which, as argued by Mulligan (2012), increases MTRs for those who receive it (about 5 percent of SNAP families in normal times but 9 percent in the recent recession). Receipt of these programs by SNAP families would push the rates higher.

Although this analysis clearly shows that only a very small fraction of the SNAP caseload faces high cumulative MTRs, the labor supply effects for that subpopulation could be large. The ideal empirical study to measure these effects would obtain estimates only for those families in the upper earnings ranges where the MTRs are highest, and only for those families participating in at least one other program besides SNAP or, better, for different combinations of other programs. Unfortunately, these estimates are not available. Instead, the literature on the labor supply effects of SNAP has typically evaluated the work disincentives of the program as a whole. This literature usually shows modest effects of the SNAP program on work levels. The survey of the literature by Currie (2003), for example, concludes that the maximal estimate of the effect of SNAP on work effort is one hour per week. Hoynes and Schanzenbach (2012), examining the early years of the introduction of Food Stamps, find significant effects for single mothers, but estimates for the overall population are small and insignificant. There is also a larger literature on the effects of MTRs in the AFDC and TANF programs. That literature also typically shows almost no effects of lowering MTRs, although this could be because of the canceling out of large positive and negative responses (see, for example, the recent paper by Matsudaira and Blank 2014). There is also a significant literature on the effects of the EITC on labor supply, with the strongest results showing positive effects on the probability of working for single mothers (see Hotz and Scholz 2003, for a review), which is probably a result of the negative MTRs in lower earnings ranges. Eissa and Hoynes (2006), on the other hand, find small negative effects for married women, possibly because they are in the phase-out region where MTRs are the highest. Nevertheless, the literature as a whole does not suggest that work disincentives of these transfer programs are very large.

Despite the paucity of evidence on the important questions of interest, it would be surprising if very high MTRs, such as those above 75 percent or approaching or above 100 percent, did not have work disincentives. However, as has already been emphasized, these work disincentives are certain to affect only a small portion of the SNAP caseload.

SUMMARY AND CONCLUSIONS

This study of multiple program receipt among SNAP families has shown that multiple receipt is quite common but not extensive. Not counting tax credits, which are not ordinarily thought of as traditional transfer programs, 76 percent of SNAP families in 2008 to 2009 received benefits from at least one other major traditional transfer program, excluding Medicaid. However, about 40 percent received only one other program benefit, only 27 percent received benefits from two others, and less than 9 percent received benefits from three or more others. In addition, many of the SNAP families who received multiple benefits were either elderly or disabled. Among non-elderly, nondisabled families, only 16 percent received benefits from two other programs, and less than 3 percent received benefits from three or more other programs.

The most common traditional transfer programs in which SNAP families participated were subsidized housing and WIC, where a fifth to a quarter of SNAP families received benefits. About 15 percent received SSDI and SSI, only 13 percent received TANF benefits, and only 8 percent received UI.

Over the long term, since 1993, multiple benefit receipt has declined, falling from 80 percent of the SNAP caseload in that year to 72 percent in 2010, a recession year. However, this is largely because of the TANF program, which has shrunk dramatically since welfare reform in the mid-1990s, and receipt by SNAP families has fallen as well. Many other programs in the United States have instead grown over the last twenty years—such as WIC, SSI, and SSDI—and receipt of benefits from these programs has grown among SNAP families, although not enough to offset the decline in receipt of TANF benefits. Multiple program receipt also changed very little during the Great Recession. However, SNAP families, like other families in the low-income population, have also seen strong growth in the receipt of tax credits, the EITC and the CTC.

The results of the examination of high marginal tax rates indicates that those tax rates are high and a significant problem only for a small portion of the SNAP caseload. Among the 76 percent of the caseload who receive benefits from other traditional transfer programs, 53 percent are elderly and/or disabled, and another 13 percent of childless and are unlikely to face high marginal tax rates. High marginal tax rates are a potential problem only for the remaining 34 percent of multiple-program-receipt SNAP families. For that group, the vast majority have earnings so low that they face negative cumulative marginal tax rates because of the EITC and the CTC and because SNAP and other programs generally have standard deductions. High marginal tax rates occur only for those with higher levels of earnings, where benefits from multiple programs and from the EITC and CTC are being phased out. For nonelderly, nondisabled single-parent families receiving SNAP and TANF, for example, only 2 percent are in the range where cumulative marginal tax rates are high, and they constitute only one-tenth of one percent of the entire SNAP caseload. For two-parent families, those facing high marginal tax rates constitute only a bit more than one-tenth of one percent of the SNAP caseload. Thus, while cumulative marginal tax rates are high in some ranges, they are of concern only for a tiny fraction of the caseload, both because multiple receipt is not that common as well as because only a small fraction of the caseload is affected by them.

More work on multiple receipt and marginal tax rates is needed. For tax rates, the analysis here has omitted Medicaid, for example, although the higher tax rates for that program occur only at one point that is fairly high in the earnings distribution. Housing benefits and UI have also been left out of the calculations here. Although only a minority of SNAP families receive these benefits, it does imply that those families in the relevant earnings range face higher marginal tax rates than shown here. In addition, the other studies in this literature have shown that the average marginal tax rates for SNAP families also receiving TANF vary dramatically by state, and families in some states face extraordinarily high tax rates. More work on these and other issues would be desirable.

NOTES

This paper is a revised version of one presented at the conference, "Five Decades of Food Stamps" on September 22, 2013, sponsored by the University of Kentucky Center for Poverty Research and University of Wisconsin–Madison Institute for Research on Poverty. The author would like to thank the Russell Sage Foundation for financial support for this work, as well as Gary Burtless, Hilary Hoynes, Casey Mulligan, David Ribar, James Ziliak, and the other participants of the conference for comments. Gwyn Pauley provided excellent research assistance.

1. The SSDI program is often not listed as a program establishing categorical eligibility, but it is equivalent because separate rules state that individuals receiving disability payments do not have to meet income or resource tests.

2. One-person and two-person households are eligible for a small minimum benefit (currently $16 per month) regardless of net income.

3. If SNAP households treat the SNAP benefit as equivalent to income, then food expenditure will rise with an extra dollar of income from another program because some of the 70 cent net gain in income will go toward food expenditure. But this is not double-dipping as it is normally thought of.

4. A series of papers by Weinberg (1985, 1987, 1991) examined evidence on multiple program participation in the 1980s in general, not focusing only on SNAP. There has been some work conducted recently on cumulative marginal tax rates and multiple benefit receipt; these studies will be referenced in the following pages.

5. School food programs are not considered in this chapter. See Bartfeld, Chapter Seven in this volume, for a discussion of overlap in receipt between the SNAP program and the School Breakfast Program and National School Lunch Program.

6. The percentage of families with earnings in this SIPP analysis is higher than reported in SNAP administrative data. This may be because the presence of earnings in any of the four months prior to the interview is counted here, whereas the administrative data count the presence of earnings in a single month. It is also possible that the SIPP family unit is larger than the SNAP unit, a common problem in using survey data.

7. SNAP administrative data for 2008 show roughly similar participation percentages for many of these figures: 26 percent for SSI, 24 percent for Social Security (including both OASI and SSDI), 11 percent for TANF, and 2 percent for

UI (Wolkwitz and Trippe 2009, Tables A-2 and A-6). The EITC, CTC, and subsidized housing are not shown in that report. The only significant difference is for UI, which could result from a difference in time period (the administrative data are for FY2008, whereas ours are for the last few months of 2008 and the first few months of 2009), the definition of the food stamp unit from Census-defined family units, or misreporting on the SIPP.

8. Among the elderly, not all report OASI benefits (65 percent). Quite a few report receiving SSDI but note that the definition of the elderly here is that the head must be sixty-two or older, whereas transfer income receipt is defined over the entire family. Nevertheless, some families may be incorrectly classifying their programs between OASI and SSDI, or even SSI.

9. Families with private income over 150 percent of the poverty line are not shown but are available on request. Such families constitute 10 percent of the SNAP caseload according to these SIPP data.

10. Some families can receive refundable child tax credits but only if they have sufficient earnings or have paid a certain amount of taxes.

11. As will be discussed in the following pages, elderly families are those with a head aged sixty-two or over, and disabled families are those with any family member receiving SSDI or SSI. Wolkwitz and Trippe (2009) find, with administrative QC SNAP data, that 41 percent of SNAP households were elderly or disabled in FY2008, almost identical to the SIPP percentage, albeit using a different definition of disability.

12. However, as noted previously, the SIPP data do not measure receipt of noncash TANF benefits, which makes a number of families categorically eligible. However, if the SIPP data here are accurate, most of those families are receiving another benefit anyway and hence are probably low-income families.

13. A number of childless families receive benefits from the CTC, WIC, and TANF. These families have unrelated children in the family; the classification of family types in these data counts only related children.

14. But recall again that all are included in SNAP countable income, and hence those other programs are not intended to support food expenditure for SNAP families.

15. See Ziliak, Chapter One in this volume, for a more detailed summary of changes in the SNAP program over the last two decades.

16. The 1993 and 2004 years are selected because those were the years used by Ben-Shalom, Moffitt, and Scholz (2012), whose data we also use here.

17. Using SNAP administrative data, Wolkwitz and Trippe (2009) find that 2.1 percent of SNAP households received UI in 2008, and Strayer, Eslami, and Leftin (2012) find the figure to be 6.7 percent in 2011. Bitler and Hoynes (2013) report a figure of 6 percent in 2010, also using SNAP administrative data. However, Finifter and Prell (2013) find the rate to be 7.8 percent in 2005 and 14.4 percent in 2009. There are definitional differences in these calculations because the administrative data figures are for simultaneous receipt of SNAP and UI in the same month, whereas the Finifter and Prell figures are for simultaneous receipt of the two programs only in the same calendar year. The SIPP figures in this paper are for simultaneous receipt in a four-month window.

18. Bitler and Hoynes (2013), using SNAP administrative data, find TANF receipt among SNAP families to have been 23 percent in 2001 and 8 percent in 2010, roughly consistent with the figures here. They also report receipt of TANF, SSI, and

UI computed from the March CPS, finding numbers that are often in the same general range as those from the administrative data.

19. There is a theoretical literature in economics that argues that this may be the socially preferred outcome. Mirrlees (1971) argued that the MTR should be zero at the bottom of the earnings distribution, and Diamond (1980) and Saez (2002) have argued that that bottom MTR should even be negative. All these results imply that higher positive MTRs are necessary higher in the earnings distribution.

20. Other programs do not include SNAP in their countable incomes for the purpose of benefit calculation. It should be noted, however, that if families really spend 30 percent of an extra dollar of income on food, then a SNAP MTR of 0.30 is effectively a 100 percent tax rate on food expenditure.

21. This figure and the others in this paragraph are not shown in the tables but were computed separately from the 2008 to 2009 SIPP data.

22. As a percent of the entire SNAP caseload, nonelderly, nondisabled single-parent families who receive at least one other traditional transfer program benefit constitute only 17 percent of the caseload; comparable two-parent families constitute only 9 percent.

23. See also Hanson and Andrews (2009), Leguizamon (2012), and U.S. Congressional Budget Office (2012a) for other cumulative MTR calculations that are more dissimilar in definition than those discussed here. For older calculations of MTRs in the 1990s, see Dickert, Houser, and Scholz (1994) and Coe and colleagues (1998).

24. From Table 8.6, (0.258) * (0.19) = 0.049 and (0.14) * 0.115 = 0.016.

REFERENCES

Ben-Shalom, Y., R. Moffitt, and J. K. Scholz. 2012. "An Assessment of the Effect of Anti-Poverty Programs in the United States." In P. Jefferson, ed., *Oxford Handbook of the Economics of Poverty*. Oxford, UK: Oxford University Press.

Bitler, M., and H. Hoynes. 2013. "The More Things Change, the More They Stay the Same: The Safety Net, Living Arrangements, and Poverty in the Great Recession." NBER Working Paper 19449. Cambridge, MA: National Bureau of Economic Research.

Coe, N., G. Acs, R. Lerman, and K. Watson. 1998. "Does Work Pay? A Summary of the Work Incentives under TANF." Washington, DC: Urban Institute.

Currie, J. 2003. "U.S. Food and Nutrition Programs." In R. Moffitt, ed., *Means-Tested Transfer Programs in the United States*. Chicago: University of Chicago Press.

Diamond, P. 1980. "Income Taxation with Fixed Hours of Work." *Journal of Public Economics* 13 (February): 101–110.

Dickert. S., S. Houser, and J.K. Scholz. 1994. "Taxes and the Poor: A Microsimulation Study of Implicit and Explicit Taxes." *National Tax Journal* 47 (September): 621–638.

Eissa, N., and H. Hoynes. 2006. "Behavioral Responses to Taxes: Lessons from the EITC and Labor Supply." *Tax Policy and the Economy* 20: 74–110.

Falk, G., and R. Aussenberg. 2013. "The Supplemental Nutrition Assistance Program: Categorical Eligibility." Paper 7-7500. Washington, DC: Congressional Research Service.

Finifter, D., and M. Prell. 2013. *Participation in the Supplemental Nutrition Assistance (SNAP) and Unemployment Insurance: How Tight Are the Strands of the Recessionary Safety Net?* ERR-157. Washington, DC: U.S. Department of Agriculture, Economic Research Service.

Friedman, M. 1969 (November 7). Testimony on the Family Assistance Plan. In U.S. Congress, House of Representatives, Committee on Ways and Means, Social Security and Welfare Proposals, Hearings, 91st Congress, 1st Session, Part 6, 1944–1958.

Gao, Q., N. Kaushal, and J. Waldfogel. 2009. "How Have Expansions in the Earned Income Tax Credit Affected Family Expenditures?" In J. P. Ziliak, ed., *Welfare Reform and Its Long-Term Consequences for America's Poor.* Cambridge, UK: Cambridge University Press.

Hanson, K., and M. Andrews. 2009. *State Variations in the Food Stamp Benefit Reduction Rate for Earnings: Cross-Program Effects from TANF and SSI Cash Assistance.* EIB-46. Washington, DC: USDA, Economic Research Service.

Hotz, V. J., and J. K. Scholz. 2003. "The Earned Income Tax Credit." In R. Moffitt, ed., *Means-Tested Transfer Programs in the United States.* Chicago: University of Chicago Press.

Hoynes, H., and D. Schanzenbach. 2012. "Work Incentives and the Food Stamp Program." *Journal of Public Economics* 96 (February): 151–162.

Lampman, R. 1975. "Scaling Welfare Benefits to Income: An Idea That Is Being Overworked." *Policy Analysis* 1(1): 1–10.

Leguizamon, J. S. 2012. "Estimating Implicit Marginal Tax Rates of Welfare Recipients across the U.S. States." *Public Finance Review* 40: 401–430.

Maag, E., C. E. Steuerle, R. Chakravarti, and C. Quakenbush. 2012. "How Marginal Tax Rates Affect Families at Various Levels of Poverty." *National Tax Journal* 65: 759–782.

Matsudaira, J., and R. Blank. 2014. "The Impact of Earnings Disregards on the Behavior of Low Income Families." *Journal of Policy and Management* 33 (Winter): 7–35.

Mendenhall, R., K. Edin, S. Crowley, J. Sykes, L. Tach, J. Kling, and K. Kriz. 2012. "The Role of Earned Income Tax Credit in the Budgets of Low-Income Families." *Social Service Review* 86: 367–400.

Mirrlees, J. 1971. "An Exploration in the Theory of Optimum Income Taxation." *Review of Economic Studies* 38: 175–208.

Moffitt, R. 2003. "The Negative Income Tax and the Evolution of U.S. Welfare Policy." *Journal of Economic Perspectives* 17(3): 119–140.

———. 2013. "The Great Recession and the Social Safety Net." *Annals of the American Academy of Political and Social Science* 650 (November): 143–166.

Mulligan, C. 2012. "The ARRA: Some Unpleasant Welfare Arithmetic." NBER Working Paper 18591. Cambridge, MA: National Bureau of Economic Research.

Saez, E. 2002. "Optimal Income Transfer Programs: Intensive Versus Extensive Labor Supply Responses." *Quarterly Journal of Economics* 117 (August): 1039–1073.

Strayer, M., E. Eslami, and J. Leftin. 2012. *Characteristics of Supplemental Nutrition Assistance Program Households: Fiscal Year 2011.* Alexandria, VA: Food and Nutrition Service, U.S. Department of Agriculture.

U.S. Congressional Budget Office (CBO). 2012a. *Effective Marginal Tax Rates for Low- and Moderate-Income Workers.* Washington, DC: U.S. Congress.

———. 2012b. *The Supplemental Nutrition Assistance Program.* Washington, DC: U.S. Congress.

Weinberg, D. 1985. "Filling the 'Poverty Gap': Multiple Transfer Program Participation." *Journal of Human Resources* 20 (Winter): 64–89.

———. 1987. "Filling the 'Poverty Gap,' 1979–1984." *Journal of Human Resources* 22 (Fall): 563–573.

———. 1991. "Poverty Dynamics and the Poverty Gap, 1984–1986." *Journal of Human Resources* 26 (Summer): 535–544.

Wolkwitz, K., and C. Trippe. 2009. *Characteristics of Supplemental Nutrition Assistance Program Households: Fiscal Year 2008.* Alexandria, VA: Food and Nutrition Service, U.S. Department of Agriculture.

Ziliak, J. 2008. "Effective Tax Rates and Guarantees in the Food Stamp Program." Mimeo, Department of Economics, University of Kentucky.

Judith Bartfeld
Craig Gundersen
Timothy M. Smeeding
James P. Ziliak

Fifty years ago, the Food Stamp Program emerged as a relatively minor component of what was a limited social safety net in the United States. Today, SNAP is a critical pillar of a much wider social safety net. The chapters in this volume have demonstrated that SNAP has achieved many successes. However, there remains some uncertainty of effects in some domains, especially in the areas of health and nutrition, and also many important policy considerations about program size, design, and delivery. In this concluding chapter, we discuss several current policy debates surrounding SNAP that are informed by the chapters in this volume, and we highlight potential directions for further research on SNAP in the broader context of the changing safety net.

CURRENT POLICY ISSUES

A key issue going forward is whether the heightened levels of SNAP participation today are the "new normal" or if we should expect a "regression to the mean" with lower participation rates in coming years. From its primary focus on ensuring access to sufficient food, as discussed in Chapter Two, SNAP has gained prominence as a broad antipoverty program insofar as it has an antipoverty effect on the same order of magnitude as the Earned Income Tax Credit (EITC) and is dwarfed only by Social Security in this domain. Despite the formal end of the Great Recession, the labor market remains weak for many Americans, especially the working poor, and thus SNAP enrollments and outlays have remained high. There is concern that outlays will remain high for the foreseeable future, even though historical evidence presented in Chapter One suggests that SNAP outlays should fall with an expanding economy. But the economy is not expanding very rapidly for low-income and low-skill workers. The Congressional Budget Office (CBO) (2014) forecasts that SNAP spending of $83 billion in 2013 will fall only to $74 billion in 2023, reflecting the continued labor market weakness in terms of employment, wages, and hours worked. And, alongside ongoing labor market weaknesses, the food insecurity rate remains stubbornly high—ranging from 14.3 to 14.9 percent of households each year since 2008, as compared to annual rates of 10.5 to 11.9 percent during the 2000 through 2007 period (Coleman-Jensen, Gregory, and Singh 2014).

In the context of historically high caseloads, ongoing macroeconomic pressures, persistently high food insecurity, and concerns over escalating costs, SNAP in recent years has been the subject of considerable policy interest. Most recently, SNAP changes were made as part of the 2014 Farm Bill, involving a $8.55 billion cut over the next ten years stemming from a change in the benefit calculation for certain recipients who receive assistance from the Low Income Home Energy Assistance Program (Bolen, Rosenbaum, and Dean 2014). As opposed to waning as might be expected, policy attention to SNAP has only grown since the Farm Bill was passed. In the following pages, we highlight several broad types of SNAP proposals that have been prominent in recent policy discourse, noting, when relevant, the insights that the research in this volume can bring to bear.

Proposals to Change Program Funding to Block Grants

SNAP is federally funded, with a modest amount of state funds for administration, and most aspects of program design are set at the federal level. Due in part to increases in SNAP expenditures, there have been proposals to devolve SNAP to the state level as a block grant, providing states with a fixed pot of funds and increased discretion over aspects of program eligibility, benefits, and operations. This is akin to the devolution in 1996 under the Personal Responsibility and Work Opportunity Reconciliation Act, when Aid to Families with Dependent Children (AFDC) was converted to a block-grant program and renamed as Temporary Assistance for Needy Families (TANF). As part of this block-grant change, the entitlement status of AFDC disappeared. This had two main implications: Individuals were no longer automatically able to enter the program after meeting certain requirements, and, even if they were eligible to enter the program, there was not necessarily enough money available to provide assistance. Given its entitlement status, prior to the 1996 reform, AFDC was an effective antirecessionary policy tool; caseloads went up when the economy went down and down when the economy went up. Today, however, TANF is no longer an antirecession program because it is not an entitlement, and in fact TANF caseloads actually continued to fall during the Great Recession.

The current responsiveness of SNAP to macroeconomic forces, and the subsequent antipoverty and anti–food insecurity impacts of the program—documented in Chapters One, Two, and Three of this volume—raise substantial concerns about moving from an entitlement to a block grant. To be certain, the weak economy was not the only factor leading to the growth of SNAP but also changes in policy that enhanced program access and expanded eligibility. These changes occurred on the heels of welfare reform when take-up rates in food stamps among eligibles dropped over 20 percentage points to their lowest levels in the modern program era. Policy makers were rightly concerned that, in order to make the transition to a work-based safety net that was at the core of welfare reform success, families would need at least transitional assistance and potentially longer-term assistance from work-based supports including subsidized child care, the EITC, SNAP, and Medicaid. What was not expected, however, at the dawn of the twenty-first century was the flat-lining of wages even in the middle of the income distribution, weak job growth, rising disability claims, and a crushing recession that followed in the ensuing decade. In hindsight the policy reforms were prescient because they ensured that SNAP was well positioned to flexibly respond to the sequence of macroeconomic events. And as a sign of good governance, program error rates (that is, the percentage of cases with overpayment or underpayment of benefits) declined as participation rose, suggesting that the policy reforms were implemented efficiently. Our assessment is that the benefits of SNAP, including its capacity to respond to macroeconomic forces; its critical role in reducing the incidence, depth, and severity of poverty among both working and nonworking households; and its ability to reduce food insecurity would be severely jeopardized by shifting to a block grant. Such a change would fundamentally alter the central role SNAP currently plays in the safety net. Moreover, it would have spillover effects on other food assistance programs, most notably school meals, in light of the cross-program synergies discussed in Chapter Seven of this volume.

Restrictions on SNAP Purchase

Another set of proposals that would also fundamentally change the role of SNAP in the social safety net involves imposing restrictions on what can and cannot be purchased with SNAP. Currently, most food items (with the exception of alcohol and ready-to-eat prepared foods) can be purchased with SNAP benefits. This reflects, in part, the bureaucratic difficulties in deciding on what foods should or should not be eligible and the lack of foods that, say, nutritionists would declare as "completely healthful" or "completely unhealthful," as well as the logistical barriers to implementing point-of-sale restrictions.

Despite these obstacles, interest in imposing greater purchase restrictions on SNAP has grown in recent years, motivated in part by broader policy attention to obesity and the health impacts of food choices. Some proposals, as discussed in Chapter Six, would prohibit the purchase of wide classes of food products (for example, sugar-sweetened beverages, or SSB), whereas others would dictate what specific types of foods could be purchased (for example, proposals to allow SNAP benefits to be used only for products in the WIC basket). However, the majority of SNAP households spend more on food than the value of their SNAP benefits (see Chapter Four). Thus, restrictions on SNAP purchases would be expected to alter the funding source for disallowed foods, more so than altering overall consumption patterns (however, see Basu et al. 2014 for some contrary evidence from a stylized simulation model, which finds small potential reductions in SSB consumption). Moreover, as there is little evidence pointing to SNAP as a cause of either obesity or poor nutrition, both of which are widespread in the non-SNAP population as well, it is questionable as to whether SNAP restrictions are an appropriate vehicle to address these concerns. Our consensus is that the most likely and far-reaching impact of purchase restrictions, in light of the resulting transaction costs, would be declines in SNAP participation. (The details of these proposals and the anticipated consequences are discussed in Chapter Six.) So, akin to changing SNAP funding to block grants, placing restrictions on SNAP would fundamentally change the role of SNAP in the social safety net.

Labor Supply

Other proposals are intended to limit potential work disincentives associated with SNAP. Such proposals have variously involved "carrots," such as reducing benefits more slowly as earnings rise, or "sticks," such as requiring work as a condition of SNAP receipt. An oft-stated critique of SNAP and other assistance programs is that their existence leads individuals to work less than they otherwise would. In the process, these programs are said, in the long run, to make recipients worse off over at least some dimensions insofar as they do not earn as much and they do not gain as much workforce experience as they would in the absence of SNAP.

In theory and practice, assistance programs can lead individuals to curtail the hours they work in the paid labor force. This could occur if, for each additional dollar earned in the labor market, there was a substantial reduction in benefits. A high benefit-reduction rate keeps program costs lower because fewer people are eligible for assistance, and it directs more of the benefits toward recipients with the lowest incomes. However, it also poses a disincentive for recipients to work. One of the criticisms of the AFDC program was that, in some instances, the benefit-reduction rate due to labor income was so high that program participants were discouraged from working. Similarly, work could be discouraged in a lump-sum benefits program (that is, a household either receives the full amount of a benefit or nothing) whereby earning just a few more dollars may render someone ineligible for a benefit. This can often occur for health insurance for low-income households (that is, Medicaid), where work is discouraged for those near the eligibility cutoff.

Although the benefit structure of SNAP contains these implicit work disincentives, in practice they are not as extreme as in other programs such as the former AFDC program. The official reduction in SNAP benefits is 30 cents for each dollar earned, but, because 20 percent of earnings can be deducted in computing net income, the "effective tax rate" for most recipients is around 24 percent; the practical implications depend on how SNAP is used in conjunction with other programs in the safety net, as such programs have their own benefit structures that variously increase or decline with earnings in ways that either offset or compound the reduction in SNAP (see Chapter Eight). The empirical evidence on the work disincentive effects of SNAP suggests it is small (Fraker and Moffitt 1988; Hagstrom 1996; Hoynes and Schanzenbach 2012). This may be amplified when the program is used in conjunction with other programs in the safety net in certain income ranges, but it is much more common in practice for SNAP recipients to face negative cumulative tax rates on earnings (stemming from the structure of the EITC at low earnings levels) than high cumulative tax rates due to simultaneous phasing out of multiple benefits (see Chapter Eight). For instance, very-low-income families with two children may receive a wage subsidy of 40 percent from the EITC, which more than compensates in magnitude for SNAP's benefit-reduction rate.

A natural response if there is concern over work disincentives would be to lower the benefit-reduction rate facing SNAP recipients due to labor market earnings. This could be achieved either by lowering the official 30 percent rate or by raising the percentage of earnings that may be disregarded from net income. If the goal is to increase SNAP recipients' labor supply without jeopardizing the beneficial impacts of the program, we believe this would be more effective than requiring work for all or some SNAP recipients without regard to labor market constraints, as some have proposed.

Fraud

A common complaint about SNAP is that there is a high level of fraud within the program. As usually discussed, this fraud takes two main forms that policy is used to address. The first form is trafficking, whereby individuals and stores collaborate to turn SNAP benefits into cash. This type of fraud is more common at privately owned small and medium-size stores and at stores in neighborhoods with higher concentrations of poverty (Mantovani, Williams, and Pflieger 2013). During the 2009 to 2011 time period, this type of fraud was quite small—1.3 percent of total SNAP benefits (Mantovani, Williams, and Pflieger 2013, Exhibit E-2). This is substantially lower than in

1993, when it was 3.8 percent. This decline is likely due primarily to the shift from paper coupons in food stamps to Electronic Benefit Transfers (EBT), which allow for improved tracking of SNAP purchases.

The second form of fraud is overpayments to recipients. This can occur when truly eligible households get more benefits than they are entitled to or when ineligible households are enrolled in the program. In both cases, total expenditures on SNAP are higher than they otherwise would be. (In contrast, store-based types of fraud described in the preceding paragraph do not result in higher expenditures on SNAP.) In 2013, 3.4 percent of total SNAP payments were found to be improperly distributed. To put this a different way, 96.6 percent of total SNAP payments were correctly distributed. In addition, the proportion of inaccurate payments was substantially higher in 2000, 8.9 percent.

Overall, the level of fraud and/or overpayments in SNAP is substantially less than in other assistance programs or, for that matter, among federal taxpayers. This is due to many factors including the money spent by the USDA to enforce rules against trafficking and reducing overpayment rates through annual quality control audits. Insofar as additional reductions would be proportionally more expensive (that is, the current efforts are likely to be stopping the most egregious cases), the USDA must ascertain whether these additional funds would be best spent on enforcement or on other activities of the USDA.

RESEARCH TO INFORM POLICY MAKERS ABOUT SNAP

In the current fiscal environment of budget sequestration there is an increasing need for evidence-based policy making guided by research as to what programs work, what programs don't, and how they can be improved (Haskins and Margolis 2014). But even though it is our assessment that SNAP is (and was from the start; see Almond, Hoynes, and Schanzenbach 2011) one of the most successful programs in the social safety net, we also believe that there are many ways research could further strengthen the program. Here, we briefly discuss potential research directions for SNAP, highlighting research gaps with regard to program impacts that have emerged in this volume as well as additional ideas for research into how SNAP could become even more effective, particularly in achieving its primary goal of reducing food insecurity.

Impacts on Health and Nutrition

Whereas SNAP has the potential to affect nutrition and health in the short and long term by strengthening access to food, the research into these impacts lags far behind that into other program impacts (see Chapter Five). The pervasive challenges of differential selection are compounded, in this case, by lack of consensus over what health and nutrition outcomes to measure, the longer time needed for SNAP to generate impacts on health, and the relative scarcity of accessible data that combines health and nutrition outcome measures with appropriate geographic and administrative program data to support use of policy-based instrumental variable strategies such as are prevalent in the food security research domain (see Almond, Hoynes, and Schanzenbach 2011 for an example of where these data were available and convincingly deployed). One way to make progress on evaluations of SNAP is to enhance access to linked administrative and survey data to address the substantial underreporting of benefits in household surveys. The new National Household Food Acquisition and Purchase Survey (FoodAPS) offers an opportunity to use survey data linked to SNAP benefits as well as food prices in the respondents' community. Capitalizing on geographic identifiers, especially state of residence, in key surveys including the NHIS and NHANES (not available in public use versions) would also allow more sophisticated statistical approaches to help address pervasive selection concerns. Greater attention to measures of intensity and duration of exposure to SNAP, as compared to binary measures of participation, would also be of value. And finally, research into the role of SNAP in the management of chronic diseases is warranted; for instance, recent work finding higher rates of hospital admissions for diabetes complications at the end of the month among the low-income population suggests that access to food in resource-constrained households may play an important role in this domain (Seligman et al. 2014).

Benefit Formula

In 1979, the current method of determining SNAP benefit levels was implemented. The benefit level is roughly equal to the maximum benefit level minus 30 percent of one's net income. Over time, there have been changes to the methods used to calculate net income and the maximum benefit level has been adjusted by inflation, but the benefit formula has remained the same. The maximum benefit was temporarily increased by an average of 13.6 percent in 2009 in response to the Great Recession, with the intent that the increase gradually phase out over time; the increase ended ahead of schedule in 2013. The benefit amount is a critical program dimension, as evidenced by research linking increases and decreases in benefits to reductions and growth, respectively, in food insecurity (Nord and Prell 2011; Nord 2013). To enhance program effectiveness, researchers may wish to explore whether the benefit formula could be reconfigured such that (a) the amount received allows more SNAP recipients to cross the threshold from food insecurity to food security, and (b) more eligible people in need of assistance enter the program, especially the elderly who have low take-up rates and those attempting to combine SNAP with work. Various scenarios could be explored including, in recognition of budgetary constraints, ones that do not lead to an overall increase in SNAP expenditures. Examples of changes might entail geographic adjustment of benefits within the continental United States, adjustments to the relative benefits for larger versus smaller households, lowered benefit-reduction rates, enhanced earned-income disregards, and changes to the calculation of net income in terms of components such as the shelter deduction and out-of-pocket medical spending.

Intersection with Other Programs

As articulated in Chapters Seven and Eight, SNAP intersects with many other food assistance programs and the wider social safety net in efforts to improve the well-being of children and other household members. However, research on multiple program participation is limited, and thus building a more enhanced understanding of how SNAP combined with these other programs can reduce food insecurity and improve other health outcomes would be a relevant research path. Food assistance programs are almost always studied in isolation; learning more about both the determinants and impacts of sequencing and packaging of programs would be especially useful to policy makers and program administrators.

Unintended Consequences

Understanding the positive and negative unintended consequences associated with a policy intervention are part of any comprehensive examination of those interventions. With SNAP, there have been some examinations of these unintended consequences (see, for example, the literature on SNAP and labor force participation covered in Chapter Eight) but there are others that have not been investigated. Some potential questions include: How are savings levels and composition influenced by the SNAP liquid asset test? Does the definition of "net income" influence the composition of consumption choices?

Persons with Disabilities

A relatively extensive social safety net for persons with disabilities has emerged in the United States, especially in comparison to the safety net available to those without disabilities. In addition, the SNAP eligibility criteria are less stringent for households containing someone with a disability—the gross income test is waived for these households, and the asset test is set at a higher level. Despite all these efforts, food insecurity rates are substantially higher among households with at least one person with a disability (Balistreri 2012). Alongside research to better identify the determinants of food insecurity among disabled persons (for a discussion, see Gundersen and Ziliak 2014), research can help to identify ways that SNAP can better serve this vulnerable population.

Demonstration Projects

Improving SNAP is an area that is ripe for demonstration projects. One recent random-assignment initiative by the USDA Food and Nutrition Service (FNS) called the Healthy Incentives Pilot (HIP) provided the treatment group with a bonus of $0.30 credited to their EBT card for each SNAP dollar spent on targeted fruits and vegetables. Early estimates suggest that consumption of these foods increased 25 percent relative to the control group, with about 60 percent in the form of vegetables and 40 percent in fruits.[1] Another recent demonstration project sponsored by FNS was designed to address spikes in child food insecurity during summer months when children generally do not have access to school meal programs. Families were provided either $30 or $60 per child per summer month, where preliminary estimates suggest child food insecurity declined by upwards of one-third.[2] Pursuing similar studies with variations in implementation, size of subsidies, timing of benefits, construction of eligibilities, and so on may be useful.

SNAP matters in the U.S. social safety net, and increasingly so over the past decade. The program is the only means-tested transfer with universal entitlement, providing food assistance for millions of low-income households across the age spectrum. The chapters in this book were presented with the aim of informing the policy and research communities of the effects of SNAP, as well as to guide policy on areas of programmatic design and research where further efforts are needed. Future research endeavors on this program will help ensure that SNAP continues to improve the health and well-being of Americans.

NOTES

1. See the "Healthy Incentives Pilot (HIP) Interim Report—Summary," July 2013, on the USDA Food and Nutrition Service website. Available at www.fns.usda.gov/sites/default/files/HIP_Interim_Summary.pdf.

2. See the "Summary of Summer Electronic Benefits Transfer for Children: Evaluation Findings for the Full Implementation Year 2012," August 2013. Available at www.fns.usda.gov/sites/default/files/SEBTC2012Sum.pdf.

REFERENCES

Almond, D., H. Hoynes, and D. Schanzenbach. 2011. "Inside the War on Poverty: The Impact of Food Stamps on Birth Outcomes." *The Review of Economics and Statistics* 93(2): 387–403.

Balistreri, K. 2012. "Family Structure, Work Patterns, and Time Allocations: Potential Mechanisms of Food Insecurity among Children." *University of Kentucky Center for Poverty Research Discussion Paper Series*. Available at www.ukcpr.org/Publications/DP2012-07.pdf.

Basu, S., H. K. Seligman, C. Gardner, and J. Bhattacharya. 2014. "Ending SNAP Subsidies for Sugar-Sweetened Beverages Could Reduce Obesity and Type 2 Diabetes." *Health Affairs* 33(6): 1032–1039.

Bolen, E., D. Rosenbaum, and S. Dean. 2014. *Summary of the 2014 Farm Bill Nutrition Title*. Washington, DC: Center on Budget and Policy Priorities. Available at www.cbpp.org/files/1-28-14fa.pdf.

Coleman-Jensen, A., C. Gregory, and A. Singh. 2014. *Household Food Security in the United States in 2013*. ERS Research Report No. 173. Washington, DC: USDA. Available at www.ers.usda.gov/media/1565415/err173.pdf.

Congressional Budget Office (CBO). 2014 (February). *The Budget and Economic Outlook: 2014 to 2024*, p. 54, Table 3-2. Available at www.cbo.gov/publication/45010.

Fraker, T., and R. Moffitt. 1988. "The Effect of Food Stamps on Labor Supply: A Bivariate Selection Model." *Journal of Public Economics* 35(1): 25–56.

Gundersen, C., and J. Ziliak. 2014. "Childhood Food Insecurity in the U.S.: Trends, Causes, and Policy Options." *Future of Children* Fall.

Hagstrom, P. A. 1996. "The Food Stamp Participation and Labor Supply of Married Couples: An Empirical Analysis of Joint Decisions." *Journal of Human Resources* 31(2): 383–403.

Haskins, R., and G. Margolis. 2014 (December). *Show Me the Evidence: Obama's Fight for Rigor and Results in Social Policy*. Washington, DC: Brookings Institution.

Hoynes, H. W., and D. W. Schanzenbach. 2012. "Work Incentives and the Food Stamp Program." *Journal of Public Economics* 96(1–2): 151–162.

Mantovani R, E. Williams, and J. Pflieger. 2013. *The Extent of Trafficking in the Supplemental Nutrition Assistance Program: 2009–2011*. Washington, DC: Prepared by ICF International for the U.S. Department of Agriculture, Food and Nutrition Service.

Nord, M. 2013. *Effects of the Decline in the Real Value of SNAP Benefits from 2009 to 2011*. Economic Research Report ERR-151. Washington, DC: USDA.

Nord, M., and M. Prell. 2011. *Food Security Improved Following the 2009 ARRA Increase in SNAP Benefits*. Economic Research Report ERR-116. Washington, DC: USDA.

Seligman, H. K., A. F. Bolger, D. Guzman, A. Lopez, and K. Bibbins-Domingo. 2014. "Exhaustion of Food Budgets at Month's End and Hospital Admissions for Hypoglycemia." *Health Affairs* 33(1): 116–123.

as noncitizens, 23, 24; number in household, 31, 35–36, 38, 42, 141, 200, 201, 231; obesity in, 12, 166, 167–68, 170–71, 173, 179nn13,14; participants in NSLP, 2, 13–14, 79, 187, 192, 194–203, 208n5; participants in SBP, 2, 13–14, 79, 187, 190–91, 192, 194–203, 208n5; poverty among, 8, 49, 52, 56, 61–62, 68, 138, 187, 191, 205; role of food assistance programs in household resources, 204–6, 207; SNAP participants vs. nonparticipants, 143, 144, 146, 149, 150–51, 155, 173; in SNAP-participating households, 2, 25, 26, 38, 44n8, 50, 52, 79, 139, 140, 142, 187–88, 194, 195, 196–203, 208n5, 209n9, 218; transitions into food assistance programs, 201–4, 207. *See also* Child Tax Credit (CTC); National School Lunch Program (NSLP); School Breakfast Program (SBP)

child support, 141, 142

Child Tax Credit (CTC), 54, 57–58, 239n13; program changes, 228, 230; and SNAP participation, 15, 16, 215, 216, 217–18, 219, 220, 221, 222–23, 224, 225–26, 227, 229, 230, 232–33, 234, 237, 240n7

Chung, Y., 66, 68

citizenship status: children as noncitizens, 23, 24; citizens vs. noncitizens, 56, 57, 84, 91, 141, 142, 190, 198, 199, 200, 201, 205, 206; noncitizens, 6, 21, 22, 23, 24, 32, 34, 42, 50, 56, 57, 84, 91, 92, 93, 101, 190, 198, 199, 200, 201, 205, 206; school meals and noncitizens, 201, 205, 206; SNAP eligibility and noncitizens, 6, 23, 24, 32, 34, 42, 50

Citro, C. F., 53, 57

Clark, F., 174

Coburn, Tom, 175

Cody, S., 52

Coe, N., 240n23

Cohen, B., 80

Cole, N., 137, 148

Coleman-Jensen, A., 63, 76, 80, 102nn1,10; on food insecurity, 74, 83, 86, 186, 188, 189, 244; on food security scale, 74

Community Eligibility Option (CEO), 14, 191–92, 193

Congressional Budget Office (CBO), 19, 38, 215, 216, 233, 235, 240n23, 243–44

Connor Gorber, S., 165

Consumer Expenditure Survey (CEX), 10, 114–16, 117, 119, 120, 121, 122, 123, 124, 125, 128, 130, 131nn4,5, 132nn7–9,11, 154

Consumer Price Index (CPI), 5

continuous regression model, 80

Cook, J., 178n3

Corcoran, M., 178n3

Cowan, B., 58

Cubbin, C., 179n14

Cunnyngham, K., 22, 189

Current Population Survey (CPS), 7, 61, 63, 66, 67, 68, 84, 123, 157n5, 240n18; Annual Social and Economic Supplement (ASEC), 25, 26, 27, 28, 29, 32, 35, 39–40, 43, 44nn4, 8–10,13, 54, 60, 139, 140, 157; Food Security Supplement (FSS), 8, 74, 75–77, 80, 81, 85, 86–90, 93, 95, 96, 100, 101

Currie, J., 76, 80, 112, 131n1, 136, 147, 152, 153, 155, 178n5, 236

Dahl, M., 192, 195, 196, 209n10

Danielson, C., 19, 29, 30, 31, 189

Dasgupta, I., 65, 175

David, M., 47n4, 152, 154

Dean, S., 5, 244

demographics: African Americans, 31, 35, 49, 56–57, 100, 139, 140, 142, 148, 165, 198, 199, 200, 201, 206;

STUDIES IN SOCIAL INEQUALITY